William James and the Affirmation of God

American University Studies

Series VII
Theology and Religion
Vol. 110

PETER LANG
New York • San Francisco • Bern
Frankfurt am Main • Berlin • Wien • Paris

George P. Graham

William James and the Affirmation of God

PETER LANG
New York • San Francisco • Bern
Frankfurt am Main • Berlin • Wien • Paris

Library of Congress Cataloging-in-Publication Data

Graham, George P.
 William James and the affirmation of God /
George P. Graham.
  p. cm. — (American university studies. Series VII,
Theology and religion ; vol. 110)
  Includes bibliographical references.
  1. James, William, 1842-1910. 2. God—History of
doctrines—20th century.   I. Title. II. Series.
B945.J24G72   1992   212'.1'092—dc20   91-4082
ISBN 0-8204-1609-6   CIP
ISSN 0740-0446

Die Deutsche Bibliothek-CIP-Einheitsaufnahme

Graham, George P.:
William James and the affirmation of God / George P.
Graham.—New York; Berlin; Bern; Frankfurt/M.; Paris;
Wien: Lang, 1992
  (American university studies : Ser. 7, Theology and
religion ; Vol. 110)
  ISBN 0-8204-1609-6
NE: American university studies / 07

From *Pensées* by Blaise Pascal, translated by
A.J. Krailsheimer, London: Penguin Classics,
1966. Copyright by A.J. Krailsheimer, 1966.

The paper in this book meets the guidelines for permanence and durability
of the Committee on Production Guidelines for Book Longevity of the
Council on Library Resources.

© Peter Lang Publishing, Inc., New York 1992

All rights reserved.
Reprint or reproduction, even partially, in all forms such as microfilm,
xerography, microfiche, microcard, offset strictly prohibited.

Printed in the United States of America.

Table of Contents

Introduction 1
Plan of the Study 1
A Brief Survey of James' Life 3
Review of Literature 14

PART ONE: INFLUENCES ON THE DEVELOPMENT OF JAMES' RELIGIOUS PHILOSOPHY 33

I. Henry James the Elder 35
    The James Family 35
        William James (1771-1832) 35
        Henry James (1811-1882) 35
            Relationship with his father 35
            Henry James' leg injury 36
            Henry James — his alcoholism 36
            Henry James — Calvinistic beliefs 37
            Henry James at Princeton Theological Seminary 37
            Henry James — career as a writer 38
            Henry James — his "vastation" 38
            Henry James' discovery of the works of
                Swedenborg 39
            Henry James' idiosyncratic reading of
                Swedenborg 40
            William James' reading of his father's thought
                (*Literary Remains*) 40
    Influence of Henry James on William James'
    Affirmation of God 43
        Profound Psychological Similarity Between Father
        and Son 43
        Concern for Expressing Convictions (Not Just What
        Is Subjectively Desirable) 44
        William James' Experience of a Form of Panic Fear ... 44

  Central Place for Religion in the Lives of Henry
    James and William James.. 45
  Choice Between Monism and Pluralism........................ 45
  Skepticism of William James (1867)................................ 46
  William James' Criticism of His Father's Position
    on Creation/Pantheism.. 47
  R. B. Perry's Comment on the Exchange of
    Letters Between William James and Henry James..... 47
  William James' Last Letter to His Father (1882).......... 48
  William James' Letter to His Wife on the Influence of
    His Father 48
 Summary of the Influence of Henry James on William
   James' Affirmation of God 49

II. Charles Renouvier.. 55
 Renouvier's Life and Work 55
 William James' First Contact with Renouvier 55
 William James' Review of *Essais de Critique* 56
 William James Helped Out of Despondence by
  Renouvier's Book 58
 William James' Later Philosophic Interest in Renouvier 59
 Personal Relationship of William James and Renouvier 60

III. Chauncey Wright... 65
 Wright's Life.. 65
  Four Periods in Wright's Intellectual Life...................... 66
  Thayer's Criticism of Wright 68
 Wright's *Philosophical Discussions*....................................... 69
 Wright's Influence on William James..................................... 71
  Wright as a Model of the Scientific Thinker.................. 71
  Wright's criticism of Herbert Spencer's
   Evolutionary Philosophy.. 72
  Wright's Experimental Approach to Philosophy........... 73
  Wright as Debating Opponent... 73
  William James' Final Estimate of Wright 74

IV. Charles Sanders Peirce 77
 Peirce's Life 77
  The Metaphysical Club 78

Peirce at Johns Hopkins 79
Murray Murphey's Theory of Peirce's
Philosophical Development... 80
Peirce's Influence on William James............................. 81
   Peirce Helped to Free William James from
     Herbert Spencer.. 81
   Peirce's Idea of Pragmatism as a Key to
     Philosophical Method 83
   Affinity Between Peirce's Philosophy and William
     James' "Will to Believe" 85
   Peirce's "Neglected Argument" for the Reality
     of God.. 87
William James' Appreciation of Peirce............................ 90

V. **Josiah Royce**... 95
   Life.. 95
     Royce's First Meeting with William James................. 96
     Royce's Call for Help from California 96
     William James Arranges for Royce to Come
       to Harvard.. 96
     Royce's Poor Health and Death................................. 98
   Royce's Intellectual Development 98
   Royce's *The Religious Aspect of Philosophy*..................... 100
     William James' Review of the Work on Its
       Publication (1885).. 100
     Later Praise from William James................................ 101
     The Argument of *The Religious Aspect of Philosophy* . 102
     Effect of *The Religious Aspect of Philosophy* on
       William James... 110
   The Later Influence of Royce on William James and
     James' Eventual Emancipation................................. 111

**PART TWO: THE REALITY OF GOD FOR
                  WILLIAM JAMES** 121

VI. **Statement of the Problem**....................................... 123

VII. **The Philosopher's "Centre of Vision"**..................... 125

Table of Contents

VIII. Levinson's Reconstruction of James' "Centre of Vision" 129

IX. A Reconstruction of William James' "Centre of Vision" 133

X. William James' Theory of Truth 137
    A Global View of James' Theory of Truth 137
    Pragmatic Realism 138
    The Influence of the "Passional Nature" on Knowing 139

XI. The Meaning of "Faith" as Working Hypothesis 145

XII. Outcome Cases 149

XIII. Pascal and the Wager Argument 155
    Blaise Pascal 155
    The Wager Argument of Pascal 156
    The Meaning of the Wager Argument for Pascal 156
    Reasons of the Heart 158
    Practical Certitude: Pascal and Kant 160
    The Place of the Wager Argument in James' "The Will to Believe" 162

XIV. Newman and James 167
    Newman on Probability as the Guide of Life 167
    Newman and James Compared 172

XV. An Analysis of "The Will to Believe" 177
    The State of the Question 177
    The Wager Argument 179
    An Indirect Argument from Science 179
    The Passional Nature at the Root of All Our Convictions 179

XVI. The Argument of the Varieties of Religious Experience 191
    The Description of the Human Religious Constitution .. 191
    Ontologism Excluded 203
    What Can Philosophy Do for Religion? 204

William James' Science of Religions 205
James' Reconciling Hypothesis 208
A Philosophical Postscript 212

XVII. Conclusion **221**

Bibliography **227**

Acknowledgments

Quotations from *The Works of William James* are in most cases taken from *The Works of William James*, Frederick H. Burkhardt, General Editor, Fredson Bowers, Textual Editor, and Ignas K. Skrupskelis, Associate Editor, and are reprinted by permission of the publishers, Harvard University Press.

The individual volumes are as follows:

The Principles of Psychology, copyright ©. 1981 by the President and Fellows of Harvard College.

A Pluralistic Universe, copyright ©. 1977 by the President and Fellows of Harvard College.

Pragmatism, copyright ©. 1975 by the President and Fellows of Harvard College.

The Meaning of Truth, copyright ©. 1975 by the President and Fellows of Harvard College.

The Will to Believe, copyright ©. 1979 by the President and Fellows of Harvard College.

The Varieties of Religious Experience, copyright ©. 1985 by the President and Fellows of Harvard College.

Essays in Religion and Morality, copyright ©. 1982 by the President and Fellows of Harvard College.

Some Problems of Philosophy, copyright ©. 1979 by the President and Fellows of Harvard College.

Quotations from Charles Sanders Pierce are reprinted by permission of the publishers from *Collected Papers of Charles Sanders Pierce*, edited by Charles Hartshorne and Paul Weiss, Cambridge, Mass: Harvard University Press, copyright ©. 1931, 1932, 1959, 1960, by the President and Fellows of Harvard College.

Introduction

Plan of the Study

The question of the existence of God is one of the great philosophical questions that have to be raised again and again in each generation. At the present time, when many philosophers of religion are giving their attention to religious experience as a source of philosophical insight,[1] it is relevant to inquire into the possibility of affirming the existence of God on the basis of religious experience. Among the many studies of religious experience, that of William James, *The Varieties of Religious Experience*,[2] is commonly acknowledged as of great importance.

This study will attempt to explore William James' approach to the affirmation of God, as developed in *Varieties* and in other works of James, especially *The Will to Believe*.[3]

The Varieties of Religious Experience, which was published more than three quarters of a century ago, is still in print in the new Harvard edition of the works of William James, and is also still available in several paperback editions. Philosophers of religion and psychologists still turn to the *Varieties* for its rich description of religious experience.[4]

Nevertheless, few philosophers have followed James in his attempt to ground the affirmation of God in religious experience. Naturalists, who do not accept the reality of God, have not followed his lead, nor have the Thomists, who are unhappy with James' rejection of the metaphysical proofs for the existence of God. One might think that such rejection by both naturalists and Thomists is an indication that James' approach to God has no philosophical value. On the other hand, it may be that James' approach to God was misinterpreted by critics. It may also be true that later philosophers thought that James' approach to God had been made obsolete by the work of Freud and Wittgenstein. The works of the psychoanalysts have led some philosophers to be skeptical of the value of religious experience. The work of language analysis thinkers has led some philosophers to reject anything that smacks of metaphysics.

Despite this widespread rejection of William James' approach to God, it seems clear that there is need of a careful study of James' position which will set out clearly the meaning of his position, the inadequacy of several critiques of his work, and the relevance of James' approach for philosophy and religion today.

This work therefore is a study of William James' approach to the affirmation of God by reflection on religious experience. The work has an introduction and two parts. After an outline of the dissertation, the introduction will contain a survey of the religious life and thought of William James with some indication of its historical context. In a third section of the introduction a review of some of the literature on James will provide the opportunity to survey some of the interpretations of his philosophy in general and of his religious thought. After the introduction, the first part will attempt to show how several religious thinkers influenced the development of James' position on the affirmation of God. Here the concept of influence will be taken in a very broad sense. By stating that James was influenced by these thinkers I mean to indicate that William James' approach to God assumed its form as the result of James' contact with some idea or problem addressed by these thinkers or through his personal encounters and sometimes vigorous dialogue with them. This type of influence can only be shown through the historical description of the impact of one personality on another.

One might object that such an understanding of influence is exclusively psychological. In fact, however, the influence of each of the five writers chosen was a mixture of personal and psychological and doctrinal elements. In dealing with James' approach to God through the interpretation of religious experience, the biography and psycho-history of James has to be considered significant as a hermeneutic method. It should be noted that even the language analysis philosophers, whose basic insights would, one might expect, make biographical and psychological inquiries useless, nevertheless have produced biographical[5] and historical[6] studies of Wittgenstein.

The study of the five writers in PART ONE fits into the plan of the dissertation by showing the intellectual atmosphere in which William James' thought developed. It also provides insights into the personality of James by showing him in interaction with several significant persons in his life. The neglect of such biographical material may well have weakened some of the works on William James' religious thought.

In PART TWO of this work, James' approach to the existence of God will be studied directly. First of all his "centre of vision" will be established; then his theory of truth will be considered, along with the criticisms of it. After this, James' description of religious experience will be surveyed briefly. James' philosophical evaluation of religious experience in *The Will to Believe* and *The Varieties of Religious Experience* will then be examined, and attention will be given to recent critical studies of James' position. The second part will be concluded then with a brief summary of the conclusions.

William James' approach to God has much to offer traditional Catholic philosophers. Since James was not a Catholic, however, and since his religious position was individualistic, he saw no need for church structure and the shared affirmations which form the basis for dogmatic theologies. From the viewpoint of Catholic theology, it is easy to write off William James by labeling him a "modernist."

Despite James' anti-metaphysical positions, however, his approach to the reality of God can be integrated into traditional Catholic thought, and might well serve as a bridge between modern Catholic thought and the pragmatic culture of America.

It would be a loss to traditional Catholic philosophy and theology if James' approach to the existence of God were to be neglected. As a way of calling attention to James' work, therefore, this study will try to show striking similarities between the approach of William James and that of Cardinal John Henry Newman. A comparison of these two great religious thinkers should have significant value in commending William James' approach to God to Catholic philosophers.

A Brief Survey of James' Life

In order to understand William James' approach to God, it is helpful to be familiar with his philosophical and religious development. In this section of the introduction, an attempt will be made to provide an outline of James' life, his religious development, and his religious thought.

William James was the oldest son of Henry James and Mary Robertson Walsh James. Henry had graduated from Union College in 1830. After spending about two years at the Princeton Theological Seminary preparing for the Presbyterian ministry, he abandoned his studies at Princeton in 1837. By the time Henry James and Mary Walsh had decided to marry, both of them had resigned from the Presbyterian church. The marriage was a civil ceremony, before the Mayor of New York, on July 28, 1840. William was born on January 11, 1842.[7]

Henry James, Sr., whose leg had been amputated, and who received an income from property inherited from his father, was free to devote his life to writing and speaking about religion. He became a close friend of Ralph Waldo Emerson[8] shortly after the birth of William. Through Emerson, and through his own efforts, he became acquainted with most of the leading religious thinkers on both sides of the Atlantic.

Since Emerson was one of the most important thinkers in the mid-nineteenth century as William James was growing up, the visit to the James home in New York by the Seer of Concord put young William into direct contact with a man whom John Dewey once said was the only American thinker worthy of being ranked with Plato. The controversy over his ideas and the fame of the Transcendentalist movement formed a centerpiece in the religious milieu in which William James grew up.[9]

From his earliest days, therefore, William James was face to face with a view of religion in which the preacher who spoke of divine revelation and ecclesiastical doctrine was scorned. Emerson said: "But the man who aims to speak as books enable, as synods use, as the fashion guides, and as interest commands, babbles. Let him hush."[10] Religion, rather, was a matter of the heart, of religious experience.[11]

This emphasis on religious experience was not a new element in the American religious culture. Perry Miller has argued that there are certain basic continuities from the Calvinism of Jonathan Edwards (1703-1758) to Emerson.[12]

Henry James the elder, William's father, was Emerson's close friend. The theology of Henry James was in the same stream of religious experience. Henry James held that science "teaches man in his researches after deity, to look no longer outward but inward ..."[13]

In view of his father's philosophy, it is not surprising that William James was brought up with little contact with organized religion. His brother, Henry James the younger, expressed it very clearly.

> ... We flocked to the sound of the fiddle more freely, it need scarce be said, than to that of the psalm. "Freely," indeed, in our particular case, scarce expresses the latter relation; since our young liberty in respect to churchgoing was absolute and we might range at will through the great city, from one place of worship and one form of faith to another, or might on occasion ignore them all equally, which was what we mainly did. ...[14]

Henry James the younger described their discomfort at being asked "What church do you go to?" When the children asked their father where they "went," he would reply that they could "plead nothing less than the whole privilege of Christendom and that there was no communion, even that of the Catholics, even that of the Jews, even that of the Swedenborgians," from which they need find themselves excluded.[15]

This eclectic type of religion apparently did not present any problem for William James as he was growing up. In the 1860s, however, when William entered into a deep period of depression, his father's theology and his chance contacts with the churches were not sufficient to provide him with an acceptable basis for his own life. It was in this period of despair that James discovered the works of Charles Renouvier. In PART ONE, CHAPTER II of this work, the key ideas of Renouvier, and their success in rescuing William James, will be described.

William James began to read philosophy in the 1860s and he found the writings of Herbert Spencer of special interest. James at first accepted Spencer's evolutionary philosophy. Through the influence of Chauncey Wright and Charles Sanders Peirce, however, James concluded that Spencer's work was fundamentally unscientific in character.[16]

During the early 1870s James was in regular contact with Chauncey Wright, who was philosophically an agnostic but who, nevertheless, accepted a Christian view of the world on religious grounds. After James' discovery of Renouvier, his need for a defensible religious position seemed to develop, and his dialogue with Wright helped James to forge a personal position.

After Wright's death, James formed a friendship with Josiah Royce, and this friendship provided further evidence of James' growing religious convictions. Religion was a continuing subject for reflection and dialogue between James and Royce.[17]

In 1882, both William James' parents died. In late January of that year, his mother suffered an acute attack of pneumonia. Both William and his wife visited his mother frequently during the illness. On Sunday night, January 29, Mrs. James took a turn for the worse, and she died shortly afterward.

Gay Wilson Allen, one of William James' biographers, was unable to find any record of the effect of his mother's death on William James. There is no record of his thoughts either in his letters that survived or in his private journal. In William's last letter to his father, however, dated December 14, 1882, William spoke very frankly. After referring to his father's illness following the death of his mother, William admitted that the thought that this might be his father's last illness conveyed no sudden shock. He said: "You are here left alone, and on the other side, let us hope and pray dear, dear old Mother is waiting for you to join her. If you go, it will not be an inharmonious thing."[18]

The elder Henry James died on the 19th of December 1882. William James expressed his feelings on the death in a letter from London to his wife shortly after receiving the news. Two months later, in a letter to Mrs. Gibbens, William acknowledged his continuing sense of loss. He wrote:

> It is singular how I'm learning every day now how the thought of his comment on my experiences has hitherto formed an integral part of my daily consciousness, without my having realized it at all. I interrupt myself incessantly now in the old habit of imagining what he will say when I tell him this or that thing I have seen or heard.[19]

During the 1880s, William James was at the height of his powers, and his great project for the decade was the large two-volume work, *The Principles of Psychology*.[20]

During this period, James' religious thought was strongly influenced by the writings and conversation of Josiah Royce. In particular, he was unable for a long time to refute Royce's proof for the existence of God.[21]

During the 1880s and 1890s, William James continued to produce periodical articles which established the basic ideas of his philosophy of religion. The articles originated in lectures to students and to university philosophical clubs and other non-professional audiences. With the exception of his edition of his father's *Literary Remains*, the first books that William James published were *The Principles of Psychology*, in 1890, and the one volume *Psychology, Briefer Course*, in 1892.[22]

Most students of James consider that the *Principles of Psychology* is his most important work. Even those who are not impressed by the value of James' philosophy are willing to acknowledge the greatness of the *Principles*, and a number of commentators have pointed out its continued relevance for psychology.[23]

The Principles is also important from the viewpoint of philosophy,[24] insofar as in it James deals with our knowledge of the world and our reasoning powers. With regard to the philosophy of religion, the *Principles* contains important sections on doubt,[25] and on the relations of belief and will.[26] There is also an important long chapter on the will.[27]

James' first book in philosophy appeared in 1897. For this book he put together ten of his "Essays in Popular Philosophy" and published them under the title *The Will to Believe*.[28]

Edward H. Madden in his introduction to the Harvard edition of *The Will to Believe* expressed the general theme of all the essays in the book as the conviction that "intellectual decisions unaffected by the volitional and passional natures of man are pure fictions. All philosophies carry the badge of their professors' preferences. . . . The intellect is *subordinate* to the affections."[29]

Since *The Will to Believe* is one of the two most important writings of William James on the affirmation of God, a discussion of its central ideas will be postponed until later in this study. At this point it is adduced as evidence of James' developing interest in the problem of God.

In 1896, it was proposed that James be appointed to deliver the prestigious Gifford Lectures. The formal appointment was made in 1898. The lectures were originally scheduled to begin in 1900, but they had to be postponed for a year because of James' severe illness in the summer of 1899. The first series of lectures began in Edinburgh on May 16, 1901. The second series was delivered in the spring of 1902. Both series were published in book form with the title *The Varieties of Religious Experience*.

The aim of the *Varieties* is best summed up by James in a letter to Miss Frances R. Morse of April 12, 1900.

> The problem I have set myself is a hard one: *first*, to defend (against all the prejudices of my "class") "experience" against "philosophy" as being the real backbone of the world's religious life — I mean prayer, guidance, and all that sort of thing immediately and privately felt, as against high and noble general views of our destiny and the world's meaning; and *second*, to make the hearer or reader believe what I myself invincibly do believe, that, although all the special manifestations of religion may have been obscured (I mean its creeds and theories), yet the life of it as a whole is mankind's most important function. A task well nigh impossible, I fear, and in which I shall fail; but to attempt it is *my* religious act.[30]

The Gifford Lectures were to consist of two courses of ten lectures each. James initially thought that: "The first course might well be a descriptive one on 'Man's Religious Appetites,' and the second a metaphysical one on 'their satisfaction through Philosophy.'"[31]

The unexpected growth of the psychological matter, however, led James to postpone the second subject almost entirely. The description of man's religious constitution now fills the nineteen lectures. In Lecture XX, James suggests his own philosophic conclusions, and this summary statement is amplified in a brief "postscript" to the book.[32]

As in the case of *The Will to Believe*, *The Varieties of Religious Experience* will be studied in PART TWO of this dissertation. For now, it is sufficient to note that his work on this book is an indication of James' continued engagement with the problems of religious philosophy through the last years of the nineteenth century and into the beginnings of the twentieth century.

During the remaining years of his life, from 1902 to 1910, James continued to be interested in the problem of religion and religious philosophy. One evidence of this is his interest in psychical research.[33]

During this period, a number of philosophical lectures and lecture series were prepared by James, and they formed the basis of important philosophical books. In 1904, James began publishing a group of essays on humanism and radical empiricism. Many of these lectures were edited by Ralph Barton Perry under the title *Essays in Radical Empiricism*.[34]

These essays do not deal specifically with the problem of religion, but they offered James an opportunity to describe his philosophical position as a humanism. James understood humanism as holding that: *"Tho one part of our experience may lean upon another part to make it what it is in any one of several aspects in which it may be considered, experience as a whole is self-containing and leans on nothing."*[35]

James notes that this formula also expresses the main contention of transcendental idealism. It seems at first sight to deny both theism and pantheism, but need not deny either. James prefers to keep the ambiguity of the formula, but he states: "I myself read humanism theistically and pluralistically. . . . Humanism is for me a religion susceptible of reasoned defense."[36] This is the only reference to God in the *Essays in Radical Empiricism*.

William James' most popular philosophical work was *Pragmatism*.[37] This volume originated with a lecture delivered in 1898 before the Philosophical Union of the University of California at Berkeley. The lecture was revised and published in 1904 under the title "The Pragmatic Method." The material was used as the basis for several other lecture series at Wellesley College, at the University of Chicago, and in Keane, N.H., and finally was given as the Lowell Lectures in Boston and at Columbia University in New York. The Columbia lectures were a great triumph, with an audience of over a thousand people. James wrote to his brother Henry and to his son, William Junior, who were in Europe at the time: "It was certainly the high tide of my existence, so far as *energizing* and being 'recognized' were concerned. . . ."[38]

Pragmatism appeared in book form in May 1907, and was very successful. James expected that it would later be considered as epoch-making for the triumph of a way of thinking.[39]

The book was an attempt to establish pragmatism as a philosophical method. James wrote:

> The pragmatic method is primarily a method of settling metaphysical disputes that otherwise might be interminable. . . . The pragmatic method in

such cases is to try to interpret each notion by tracing its respective practical consequences. What difference would it practically make to anyone if this notion rather than that notion were true? If no practical difference whatever can be traced, then the alternatives mean practically the same thing, and all dispute is idle. Whenever a dispute is serious, we ought to be able to show some practical difference that must follow from one side or the other's being right.[40]

This philosophical method called pragmatism is not a religious doctrine. It is compatible, however, with religion, provided that one accepts a religious philosophy that is pluralistic or melioristic in type. James offered his religious synthesis as a mean between crude naturalism on the one hand and transcendental absolutism on the other. He noted, however, that his pragmatistic or melioristic type of religion deserves to be called theism.[41]

"The pivotal part" of *Pragmatism* is its account of truth. The work however was developed on a broad front as a new and comprehensive philosophy. The book was "The most important thing I have written yet, and bound I am sure to stir up a lot of attention."[42]

The success of *Pragmatism* can be seen not only from the amount of praise the book received but also from the passionate opposition it evoked. James felt called upon to defend his account of truth, especially against the criticism of Bertrand Russell and others. He responded with a series of journal articles in defense of his position. He then joined these articles with others he had written earlier to form the book published under the title *The Meaning of Truth*.[43] This work is of great importance in bringing out James' realistic understanding of truth as "agreement with reality." It also provides an effective refutation of the subjectivist interpretation of James' position.[44]

In 1904, William James wrote several short statements which brought out aspects of his religious life. On August 24, 1904, he wrote to Edwin D. Starbuck (1866-1947),[45] the American psychologist. Responding to a criticism by Starbuck in a review of the *Varieties* that James had exaggerated the role of a "higher power" in religion, James replied:

> I think that the fixed point with me is the conviction that our "rational" consciousness touches but a portion of the real universe and that our life is fed by the "mystical" region as well. I have no mystical experience of my own,

> but just enough of the germ of mysticism in me to recognize the region from which their voice comes when I hear it.[46]

This letter provides evidence that James did not consider himself to be a mystic. It is often joined with two other bits of evidence of the same year, a letter to Professor Leuba, and a response to a questionnaire from Professor Pratt.

James Henry Leuba (1868-1946), an American psychologist, had written an article on "Professor James' Interpretation of Religious Experience."[47] Leuba claimed to take a scientific viewpoint on religious experience so that such experiences were explained by purely psychological causes. After pointing out the difficulty of dialogue with Leuba, since the latter did not indicate his own religious standpoint as an atheist or a theist, James indicated that mystical states should be seen to have a common nucleus, the non-rational sense of a higher power. He then said:

> I find it preposterous to suppose that if there be a feeling of unseen reality shared by best men in their best moments, responded to by other men in their "deep" moments, good to live by, strength-giving, — I find it preposterous, I say, to suppose that the goodness of that feeling for living purposes should be held to carry no objective significance, and especially preposterous if it combines harmoniously with our otherwise grounded philosophy of objective truth.
>
> My personal position is simple. I have no living sense of commerce with a God . . . yet there is *something in me which makes response* when I hear utterances from that quarter made by others. I recognize the deeper voice. Something tells me: — *"thither lies truth"* — and I am sure it is not old theistic prejudices of infancy.... Call this, if you like, my mystical *germ*. It is a very common germ. It creates the rank and file of believers....[48]

This letter is a significant text for determining James' personal belief. It is important to note that James' denial of a "living sense of commerce with a God" should not be given too much emphasis, but should be related to his sense of "something in me which makes response." The latter is also important for the understanding of James' affirmation of God. That affirmation is not the conclusion of a compelling syllogism but the response to a "deeper voice." Even though mystical and religious experiences are not infallible revelations of God, they are not *nothing*. James says: "Why may they not be *something* although not everything?"[49]

In other words, one should look to religious experience for probability, not certitude.

In 1904, Professor James B. Pratt of Williams College sent out a questionnaire about personal religious experiences. James answered the questionnaire, and his answers throw light on his own religious experience.[50]

James agrees that religion means a belief that something exists. It is also an emotional experience for him, but not powerfully so. It is a social reality. It involves a general attitude of the will toward God, and a moral element of tending toward righteousness. When asked if God is a person, James said that "*He* must be cognizant and responsive in some way." James answered "emphatically no" when asked whether he believed in God from some argument. He also denied that he experienced God's presence, although he did express a need for God. His belief rather was based on "the whole tradition of religious people, to which something in me makes admiring response." James did not think he could "use" God, but he did believe in Him as a "more powerful ally of my own ideals. . . ." James did not see that God was "as real as an earthly friend," but he did see God as dimly real.

When James was asked whether he had ever experienced the presence of God, his reply was brief: "Never." At the same time, however, he felt the impact of the whole line of testimony of those who claimed to have felt God's presence directly, and he added, "no doubt there is a germ in me of something similar that makes response."

When asked whether he believed in personal immortality, James replied, "Never keenly, but more strongly as I grow older. Why? Because I am just getting fit to live."

The final question on the form was "What do you mean by a religious experience?" James replied: "Any moment of life that brings the reality of spiritual things more 'home' to one."

The Pratt questionnaire has a number of interesting replies. One should not, however, isolate the individual answers but keep them in their context of the total questionnaire. Within that context, it is clear that James does believe in God as a personal being who has some power to act in support of ideals. That belief is not based on philosophical argument but on the long tradition of testimony about religious experience and his own response to it. That response, which brought home to him the reality of spiritual things, is itself a form of religious experience.

In November 1907, William James was invited to deliver the Hibbert Lectures at Manchester College, Oxford, on "The Present Situation on Philosophy." James began working on the lectures in December and, despite poor health, he sailed for England on April 24, 1908. He delivered the eight lectures between May 4 and May 28. The following year the lectures were published as *A Pluralistic Universe*.[51]

Despite the lecture format, *A Pluralistic Universe* is a mature statement of James' distinctive position in metaphysics. In the first lecture he criticizes that kind of philosophical professionalism which turns philosophy into a labored technicality in which metaphysical questions are not discussed directly and on their own merits.

> Almost always they are handled as if through a heavy woolen curtain, the veil of previous philosophers' opinions. Alternatives are wrapped in proper names as if it were indecent for a truth to be naked.... You must tie your opinion to Aristotle's or Spinosa's [sic]; you must define it by its distance from Kant's; you must refute your rival's view by identifying it with Protagoras's.[52]

James agrees with Professor Paulsen in criticizing the over-professionalism of philosophy whereby philosophy becomes an esoteric and occult science. "There is a genuine fear of popularity. Simplicity of statement is deemed synonymous with hollowness and shallowness."[53]

In that same chapter, James states one of the central points in his philosophical position:

> Let me repeat once more that a man's vision is the great fact about him. Who cares for Carlyle's reasons, or Schopenhauer's or Spencer's? A philosophy is the expression of a man's intimate character, and all definitions of the universe are but the deliberately adopted reactions of human characters upon it.[54]

A Pluralistic Universe has several sections which bring out William James' religious development. One point which is helpful in understanding James' approach to the affirmation of God is found in Lecture VII, "The Continuity of Experience." At the close of that lecture James said:

> I think it may be asserted that there *are* religious experiences of a specific nature, not deductible by analogy or psychological reasoning from our other sorts of experience. I think that they point with reasonable probability to the continuity of our consciousness with a wider spiritual environment from which the ordinary prudential man (who is the only man that scientific psychology, so called, takes cognizance of) is shut off.[55]

This statement is of the highest importance in bringing out the nature of the affirmation of God for William James. That affirmation is not the conclusion of a reasoning process (as in the case of Thomas Aquinas' "Five Ways") but a judgment based on religious experience. The conclusion is not held with metaphysical certitude, but is accepted as a "reasonable probability."

In 1909, William James began writing his textbook of philosophy, which was published after his death as *Some Problems of Philosophy*.[56] He said: "I propose in this book to take philosophy in the narrow sense of metaphysics, and to let both religion and the results of the sciences alone."[57] In fact, however, he did deal with religion in Chapter Five, "The One and the Many," and he asked that a part of the printed syllabus from his Stanford University course for the spring semester of 1906 be included in the book as an appendix.[58]

In that appendix, James distinguishes between the householder who tries to protect himself by taking out insurance and the person faced with metaphysical or religious alternatives. There is no insurance company to cover us and, if we are wrong, our error may be momentous. As a result, we must go in for the more probable alternative as if the other one did not exist, and suffer the full penalty if the event belies our faith.[59]

From this brief survey it is clear that during the final period of his life, James' interest in religion continued. During this period, however, he did not advance any further his position on the affirmation of God. It is that position which will be considered in PART TWO.

Review of Literature

William James' approach to the existence of God is developed especially in two works, *The Will to Believe* and *The Varieties of Religious Experience*. In order to understand James' positions it is helpful to review the literature about James' philosophical work in general and his religious thought in particular.

A general survey of his thought was written by Ralph Barton Perry in 1910, at the time of James' death, for the *Harvard Graduates Magazine*. The survey was later published as an appendix to Perry's work, *Present Philosophical Tendencies*.[60]

Perry's book was dedicated to "The dear and revered memory of William James": and it is the work of an admirer. Nevertheless, Perry was so familiar with James' work that his survey possesses a unique value. Perry pointed out that James' philosophy was complete in that it touched every traditional problem, but James never completed a systematic statement of his thought. Perry, therefore, attempted to compensate for this. He said: "But I should like to make a first rude sketch, which may, I hope, despite its flatness and its bad drawing, at least suggest the form of the whole and the proper emphasis of the parts."[61]

Perry held that James' philosophical work "treated of three great topics: the nature of the human mind, the structure and criteria of knowledge, and the grounds of religious belief."[62] With regard to the human mind, James adopted a standpoint which emphasized the teleological factor; that is, that the human mind attempts to preserve itself and to assert its interests within its environment. "The mind is not a 'mirror' which passively reflects what it chances to come upon. It initiates and tries; . . . The mind, like an antenna, feels the way for the organism."[63] Perry points out, however, that the action of the mind for James is not creative. "Its ideas are not of its own making, but rather of its own *choosing*. . . . The mind is essentially a selective agency."[64]

James was confronted with a problem concerning knowledge which Perry formulated as follows: "How can idea and object be *two*, and yet one be knowledge *of* the other, and both fall within the same individual conscious field?"[65]

According to Perry, James did not attempt to solve this problem by abstract logic but through an examination of cognition in the concrete, that is, "knowledge about the thing *b* which I have by virtue of the idea *a*." Such knowledge is "knowledge about" rather than "direct knowledge," and is a provisional substitute for direct knowledge. The most notable case of such knowledge is sense perception. The function of such knowledge is to make it possible to act upon things. For James, "an experience that knows another can figure as its *representative*, not in any quasi-miraculous 'epistemological' sense, but in the definite practical sense of being its *substitute* in various operations."[66] This gives rise to a more limited problem: "When may one item be, for cognitive purposes, substituted for another? . . . So that our question is equivalent to the traditional question, 'what is the relation between an idea and its object?'"[67]

In order to answer that question, Perry notes that James analyzed the relation of the idea and its object into two factors, *intention* and *agreement*. Intention is essentially a practical matter, a kind of goal or destination. An object is *intended* insofar as there is a train of action which, if completed, would terminate in that thing.[68]

An idea, however, must not only intend its object; it must also agree with it. The agreement in question is not just a resemblance. A word agrees with its intended object; it leads to that object. The possibility of agreement also implies the possibility of disagreement, and therefore the question of truth and error arises. Perry holds that for James, agreement is the same thing as truth and disagreement the same thing as error.[69]

The pragmatic theory of truth is closely connected with the pragmatic method which is a form of empiricism. James was an empiricist in that he insisted on the testing of an idea by resorting to the particular experience which it means. James offered the postulate that the only things "that shall be debatable among philosophers shall be things definable in terms drawn from experience."[70]

The third great topic which Perry has investigated in James' philosophy is his philosophy of religion. Religion is here defined in practical terms as a person's "total reaction upon life." The positive or hopeful religion says that "the best things are the more eternal things" and "that we are all better off even now" if we believe so. No idea of the ultimate nature of things can be verified, according to Perry. Nevertheless, it is necessary in practice to adopt some such an idea. To accept an idea is an act of faith. What then is the justification of faith? The test of belief is willingness to act. Even if the outcome cannot be guaranteed in advance, it may still be proper to act with confidence. That religious belief which is most probable is theism. Such an interpretation of the world most completely answers our needs. But what evidence may be adduced in its support?[71]

The answer to this question is complex. It consists in the removal of difficulties, especially the dogmatism of science and the acceptance of "transmarginal consciousness." Finally, Perry holds that "the evidence afforded by mystical experiences . . . 'creates a decidedly formidable probability' in favor of the theistic hypothesis."[72]

Perry's survey of James' philosophy of religion next deals with the belief in freedom. There is an option between a rigidly determined world and a world with alternative possibilities in it. Indeterminism, which is hospitable to freedom, implies that several futures are really possible as compatible with the same past. Neither determinism nor indeterminism can be established after the fact, since one cannot discover whether another thing might or might not have happened. Freedom is always a hypothesis, but, if one fails to accept that hypothesis, one is in effect choosing the alternative which is worse without being any more probable. In a world of determinism, evil is not only a fact but a necessity. Indeterminism, on the other hand, is a doctrine of promise; it offers a world with a chance, with the possibility of an escape from evil.[73]

Perry presents James' philosophy as a pluralism. Absolute unity brooks no degrees, whereas pluralism demands no more than *some separation* among things, some real novelty. With a pluralistic philosophy, since evil is not necessarily implied by the universe, the universe as a whole is not compromised by it. While the supremacy of the good is not guaranteed, it is set up as a goal for one's endeavor. Pluralism is no philosophy for the "tenderminded"; it does however make life worth living for those in whom the fighting spirit is alive.[74]

Perry was not a member of a school of philosophy founded by James. He said:

> James did not found a school . . . the number of those who borrowed his ideas is small and insignificant beside the number of those who, through him, were brought to have ideas of their own. His greatness as a teacher lay in his implanting and fostering of intellectual independence.[75]

Perry's interpretation of James has been attacked by Henry Samuel Levinson as a hagiography which "makes the line between historical narrative and mythical construction somewhat hard to judge."[76] This negative judgment, however, may well reflect Levinson's own distance from the religious concerns which animated James. A more serious charge is that of Bruce Kuklick, that Perry's interpretation of James was "persuasive but wrongheaded,"[77] because Perry had urged that James was a "metaphysical realist."[78]

Comparison of the texts alleged by Kuklick, however, supports Perry's interpretation rather than Kuklick's. Kuklick agrees that James was an epistemological realist.[79] He claims that this epistemological realism did not entail "metaphysical realism," and he defined the latter as the belief "that objects existed independently of all consciousness."[80] This definition, however, seems hard to defend historically, since it would imply that no theistic philosophy could be called realistic. The *"reductio ad absurdum"* would be that St. Thomas Aquinas would have to be labeled an idealist. Despite Kuklick, therefore, it seems clear that the criticism of Perry for describing James as a realist is unfounded, and that there is no room for a distinction between an epistemological and metaphysical realism.

After Perry's survey of James' philosophy, many others have tried their hand at providing a brief summary of James' work. It is not necessary to provide a survey of this literature here, since Henry Samuel Levinson has done it well recently.[81]

In addition, John J. McDermott, in his thirty-page introduction to *The Writings of William James*, has provided a much praised synthesis of James' thought, with ample reference to the secondary literature. McDermott's book also contains an annotated bibliography of the writings of William James arranged by years.[82]

After considering William James' philosophical position in a general way, it will be helpful now to look at an outline of his thought on religion. This will provide the context within which his approach to God can be understood.

The first book-length treatment of the religious philosophy of William James was published in 1926 by Julius Seelye Bixler.[83] Bixler's work was a revision of a dissertation presented to Yale University. Bixler attempted to bring together the various strands of James' religious thought and to coordinate them with the larger outlines and main emphasis of his world view. Bixler's work was done shortly after the publication of James' letters, and Bixler was moved by these letters to unify his presentation of James' religious thought in an understanding of James' personality rather than in some abstract concept. Bixler noted James' belief that philosophy is

> . . . a personal concern, "more a matter of passionate vision than of logic," and especially susceptible to the personal touch when it enters the field of religion. The better we know James' personality, therefore, the more clearly can we understand the significance of his religious ideas.[84]

Bixler characterized James' religious philosophy as realistic and romantic. By realistic he means being willing to look the facts of life in the face with an unflinching gaze. While the phrase "problem of evil" rarely appears on James' pages, still his religious view of the world includes an awareness of the tragic element in life.[85]

In describing James' religious thinking as "romantic," Bixler means that James held implicitly "that the most satisfactory statements of man's place in the cosmos will be found in the most inclusive view of what human life truly is."[86]

Bixler begins his study of James by considering texts which bring out James' alternating moods, which influenced his philosophical and religious views. Bixler saw a conflict in James' thought.

> On the one hand he felt the press of the active impulses, their aggressive demands for power, their challenge to the environment and their eager desire to remake it. . . . But on the other hand he was not insensitive to the more passive desire for assurance, stability and comfort.[87]

Bixler sees this religious conflict with James as a real dilemma and a live issue when the values at stake are religious values. As early as his introduction to *The Literary Remains of the Late Henry James*, William James saw the conflict of moods as having metaphysical significance, especially in the choice between pluralism and monism. Pluralism is the view to which one is drawn "when in the full and successful exercise of our moral energy." It is a philosophy of healthy-mindedness. Monism on the other hand is a philosophy for the morbid mood, for one "all sicklied o'er with the sense of weakness, of helpless failure, and of fear." In such a mood one craves to be consoled in his very impotence.[88] In such a morbid mood there grows a demand for assurance, and William James sees this as a demand for a monistic philosophy.[89]

Bixler points out that, for James, the distinction between monism and pluralism is "the deepest of all philosophic differences." By 1884, William James had already decided for pluralism. The choice was made not on epistemological grounds but on moral grounds. The moralistic basis of James' pluralism was discovered by Bixler in James' essay, "The Moral Philosopher and the Moral Life." The essay was first published in 1881 and was later reprinted in *The Will to Believe*. Bixler drew from this essay James' contention that, in a world without God, the appeal to our moral energy falls short of its maximal stimulatory power. So true is this that, even if there were no metaphysical or traditional grounds for believing in a God, a God would have to be invented as a pretext for living hard and for getting the most zest out of the game of existence. Bixler describes such a God as a God of battles rather than a comforter, and he interprets the essay in *The Will to Believe* as representing this view consistently. Bixler sees the *Varieties* however as giving the contrasting attitude more attention.[90]

After chapters dealing with the absolute, pluralism, and free will, Bixler devotes his fifth chapter to "The Believing Will." Bixler begins by recalling that, on moral grounds, James established our freedom to choose between alternative courses of action. He deliberately chose to be free, following the suggestion of the French philosopher Charles Renouvier.[91]

James was also interested in the Wager Argument of Blaise Pascal, who had depicted religious faith by saying that "the heart has its reasons which reason does not understand." James used Pascal's Wager Argument in *The Will to Believe*.[92] James expressed the argument as follows:

> Translated freely his words are these: You must either believe or not believe that God is — which will you do? Your human reason cannot say. A game is going on between you and the nature of things which at the day of judgment will bring out either heads or tails. Weight what your gains and your losses would be if you should stake all you have on heads, or on God's existence: if you win in such a case, you gain eternal beatitude; if you lose, you lose nothing at all. If there were infinity of chances, and only one for God in this

wager, still you ought to stake your all on God; for though you surely risk a finite loss by this procedure, any finite loss is reasonable, even a certain one is reasonable, if there is but the possibility of infinite gain. . . . At bottom, what have you got to lose?[93]

Bixler holds that James' position in *The Will to Believe* had three emphases: the stress on the importance of the subjective factor in beliefs and in the truth itself, the stress on their practical nature, and the underlining of the creative part which man himself plays in the making of truth.[94]

Bixler closes his chapter with a defense of James' point of view against several criticisms by unnamed writers, and he concludes by praising *The Will to Believe* as the point of clarification and crystallization of James' entire pragmatic theory.[95]

In his sixth chapter, on "The Purposive Will," Bixler deals with values and theology in James' thought. Referring to James' essay, "The Moral Philosopher and the Moral Life,"[96] Bixler notes that, on the final page of the essay, James gave us his conclusion that "The stable and systematic moral universe for which the ethical philosopher asks is fully possible only in a world where there is a divine thinker with all-enveloping demands."[97] This insight into the moral dimension of the universe is significant in showing that ethical experience has to be taken into account as a variety of religious experience. Bixler points out that moral values reach their consummation in a religious environment. "From whatever angle we view it, morality points to religion."[98]

In Chapter Seven, Bixler deals with William James' conception of God. Bixler considered that James' understanding of God underwent a development marked by three stages. The first position is that of *The Will to Believe*, which included articles published between 1880 and 1895. The second position is set forth in *The Varieties of Religious Experience*, published in 1902. The final position is found in *A Pluralistic Universe*, published in 1909.

In the first stage, Bixler held that James conceived of God "primarily as a postulate necessary for the letting loose of the strenuous mood, an essential stimulus to the most vigorous and most highly moral life."[99] In the second stage of James' developing conception of God, Bixler held that James' interest shifted from "man's active energies to God's saving power."[100]

In the *Varieties*, James is impressed by the power of God who

> . . . comforts the sick soul, encourages the healthy-minded, knits up the divided self, accomplishes conversion, leads on to saintliness, communicates with mystics, and is the author of saving experiences. . . . saving experiences in which work is undeniably accomplished. These experiences are so real that their cause must be real. So much work must require a worker.[101]

In this second stage, the emphasis is on our passive reception of gifts from on high, our capacity to receive help from God.

The third stage in the development of William James' conception of God, according to Bixler, combines the chief characteristics of the other two. In *A Pluralistic Universe*, James continues to speak of the working of God's power. There is also, however, an emphasis on the fact that God calls forth our most active response. In this third period, James also emphasized the idea that God's consciousness is not all-embracing, that God is "finite, either in power or knowledge, or in both at once."[102]

In the eighth chapter of his book, Bixler developed very well William James' belief in immortality. Bixler was aware of the passages in *Human Immortality* and *The Varieties of Religious Experience* in which James played down his interest in personal immortality. For example, James wrote:

> I have to confess that my own personal feeling about immortality has never been of the keenest order, and that, among the problems that give my mind solicitude, this one does not take the very foremost place.[103]

In *The Varieties of Religious Experience* James wrote: "I have said nothing in my lectures about immortality or the belief therein, for to me it seems a secondary point."[104]

Bixler rightly noted, however, that these isolated texts seemed to be misleading, and he filled the chapter with evidence from James' correspondence which leads to the conclusion that James not only had an interest in immortality but a fair share of belief in immortality. Death does not mark the end of one's personal experience but an entrance into "some still better chance" where "no clouds will veil the essence of her soul."[105]

In Chapter Nine, Bixler deals with the role of mysticism in William James' philosophy. Bixler notes that, in *The Will to Believe*, James had emphasized our power of moral and volitional response as the vehicle of insight into the nature of things. In *The Varieties*, however, it is the passive experience where one feels the touch of a power greater than one's self that helps one to find a new source of strength. Mysticism is a passive experience in which the cognitive element is strong. For religion, the mystical experience is one of revelation, but mysticism has a philosophical value also as a way of finding a new source of strength.

Bixler points out that, for James, the mystical experience may be described as an extension of the ordinary state of consciousness. Consciousness is the succession of psychic states, and it is surrounded by a margin of subliminal states which can be brought into consciousness by a kind of lowering of the threshold. The material which is ordinarily below the threshold is a part of the subliminal self. When the threshold falls, this material becomes conscious, or in other words, the conscious state is widened to include it. For William James, the area of mysticism is a psychical state in which the matters usually subliminal have come into view.

Mystical states have a noetic quality, and they bring an insight into a kind of truth. Thus mysticism fits naturally into an empirical philosophy. Its approach to truth is thoroughly experiential. Bixler holds that mysticism, in James' theory, is also *radically* empirical. "For radical empiricism is a demand that the relations between terms, just as truly as the terms themselves, shall be matters of direct particular experience."[106]

What of mysticism's cognitive content? It brings knowledge of acquaintance, not knowledge about its object. It brings insight and appreciation. Nevertheless, it is individual and incommunicable. The mystic has the right to consider the experience as authoritative. Other persons should not accept that authority uncritically. All have to recognize that mystical experiences open out the possibility of other orders of truth.[107]

In his tenth chapter Bixler deals with broader considerations concerning the definition of religion for William James. He also deals with James' intellectual relationship with his father. In Chapter Eleven Bixler tries to relate James' religious thought to the thought of Bixler's day, that is, 1926.

It is interesting to note that one recent book-length study on the religious philosophy of William James by Robert J. Vanden Burgt mentions Bixler's work only as a book "published in 1926 and now out of print."[108]

Vanden Burgt provides a summary of James' religious thought which is less ambitious than that of Bixler, and without the extensive documentation which makes Bixler's work still valuable. The work might be helpful in creating a desire to read James' own works.

A more important recent work on James' religious philosophy is that of Henry Samuel Levinson.[109] Levinson considers that his view of James coincides to a great extent with that of Bixler. Levinson's criticism of Bixler, however, indicates that Bixler's positions on the meaning of God and the realism of James' metaphysics are closer to James than are Levinson's own. As a result, Levinson's work, with all its superb scholarship, seems to dwell in a different spiritual atmosphere than William James. Levinson's center of vision has moved away from that of James.

It is not necessary to provide a complete survey here of all the literature concerning William James' thought and his philosophy of religion. This has already been done by Levinson.[110] The most authoritative works have been reported in this brief section. In PART ONE of the dissertation additional background material will be presented through a description of James' personal relationships with five writers who have helped to shape his approach to the affirmation of God.

Notes

1 See, for example, William J. Wainwright, *Philosophy of Religion: An Annotated Bibliography of Twentieth Century Writings in English* (New York and London: Garland Publishing, Inc., 1976).

2 William James, *The Varieties of Religious Experience: A Study in Human Nature* (New York and London: Longmans, Green & Co., 1902; reprint ed., Cambridge, Mass. and London: Harvard University Press, 1985). (Henceforth referred to as *Varieties*.)

3 William James, *The Will to Believe, and Other Essays in Popular Philosophy* (New York and London: Longmans, Green & Co., 1897; reprint ed., Cambridge, Mass., and London: Harvard University Press, 1979) (referred to as *TWTB*).

4 For example, see Sir Alister Hardy, *The Spiritual Nature of Man: A Study of Contemporary Religious Experience* (Oxford: The Clarendon Press, 1979), p. 141; and Edwin Robinson, *The Original Vision: A Study of the Religious Experience of Childhood*, introduction by John H. Westerhoff, III (New York: The Seabury Press, 1983), p. 14.

5 Norman Malcolm, *Ludwig Wittgenstein: A Memoir*, with a biographical sketch by George Henrik von Wright (London: Oxford University Press, 1958; reprint ed., New York: Oxford University Press, 1975).

6 Allen Jenik and Stephen Toulmin, *Wittgenstein's Vienna* (New York: Simon and Schuster, 1973).

7 For a more detailed study of the life and thought of Henry James Senior, see PART ONE, CHAPTER I, below. Except where otherwise noted, biographical materials on William James will be taken from Ralph Barton Perry, *The Thought and Character of William James*, 2 vols. (Boston and Toronto: Little, Brown and Co, 1935); Gay Wilson Allen, *William James* (London: Rupert Hart-Davis, 1967); and Jean Strouse, *Alice James: A Biography* (New York: Bantam Books, 1982), all of which are well indexed.

8 Ralph Waldo Emerson (1803-1883) was the most important religious thinker in America for the central portion of the nineteenth century. For a recent excellent biography of Emerson, see Gay Wilson Allen, *Waldo Emerson* (New York: The Viking Press, 1981; reprint ed., New York: Penguin Books, 1982). For important works of the Transcendentalist movement, of which Emerson was the principal leader, see Perry Miller, *The Transcendentalists: An Anthology* (Cambridge, Mass.: Harvard University Press, 1950).

9. For a detailed treatment of nineteenth century American religion, see Sidney E. Ahlstrom, *A Religious History of the American People* (New Haven and London: Yale University Press, 1972), pp. 385-762.

10. Ralph Waldo Emerson, *Selected Writings of Ralph Waldo Emerson*, ed. with a foreword by William H. Gilman (New York: New American Library, 1965).

11. Emerson, *Selected Writings*, p. 250.

12. Perry Miller, "From Edwards to Emerson," in *Errand into the Wilderness* (Cambridge, Mass.: Harvard University Press, 1956), pp. 184-203. For Edwards' description of his conversion, see his "Personal Narrative" in Ola Elizabeth Winslow, ed., *Jonathan Edwards: Basic Writings* (New York: New American Library, 1966), pp. 81-96.

13. William James, ed., *The Literary Remains of the Late Henry James* (Boston: James R. Osgood and Co., 1885), p. 279.

14. Henry James, *Autobiography (A Small Boy and Others; Notes of a Son and Brother; The Middle Years)*, ed. with an introduction by Frederick W. Dupee (Princeton: Princeton University Press, 1983), p. 132.

15. James, *Autobiography (A Small Boy and Others)*, pp. 133f.

16. See PART ONE, CHAPTER III, pp. 99f, and CHAPTER IV, pp. 112f.

17. See PART ONE, pp. 158f.

18. William James, *Letters of William James*, 2 vols., ed. Henry James (Boston: The Atlantic Monthly Press, 1920), 1:219. (Henceforth cited as *Letters*.)

19. *Letters*, 1:222.

20. William James, *The Principles of Psychology*, 2 vols. (New York: Henry Holt & Co., 1890; reprint ed., Cambridge, Mass.: Harvard University Press, 1983).

21. See PART ONE, CHAPTER V, pp. 158-159.

22. William James, *Psychology, Briefer Course* (New York: Henry Holt, 1892; reprint ed. with a new foreword by Gardner Murphey, New York: Collier Books, 1962).

23. For references, see William James, *The Writings of William James: A Comprehensive Edition*, ed. with an introduction by John J. McDermott (Chicago: The University of Chicago Press, 1977), p. xxxiii, especially note 33.

24. See McDermott's "Introduction," p. xxxiii, especially note 34. See also John Wild, *The Radical Empiricism of William James* (Garden City, N.Y.: Doubleday & Co. Inc., 1969; reprint ed., Doubleday Anchor Books, 1970).

25. *The Principles of Psychology*, pp. 946f.

Introduction 27

26 *The Principles of Psychology*, pp. 947f.

27 *The Principles of Psychology*, pp. 1098-1193.

28 *TWTB*.

29 *TWTB*, p. xi.

30 *Letters*, 2:127.

31 *Varieties*, p. 17.

32 *Varieties*, pp. 7-10.

33 For a listing of his essays on psychical research see the annotated bibliography in *The Writings of William James: A Comprehensive Edition*, ed. John J. McDermott, pp. 811-858.

34 William James, *Essays in Radical Empiricism*, ed. Ralph Barton Perry (New York and London: Longmans, Green & Co., 1912; reprint ed., Cambridge, Mass. and London: Harvard University Press, 1976).

35 James, *Essays in Radical Empiricism*, p. 99.

36 James, *Essays in Radical Empiricism*, p. 99.

37 William James, *Pragmatism: A New Name for Some Old Ways of Thinking* (New York and London: Longmans, Green & Co., 1907; reprint ed., Cambridge, Mass. and London: Harvard University Press, 1979).

38 *Letters*, 2:265.

39 *Letters*, 2:279.

40 *Pragmatism*, p. 28.

41 *Pragmatism*, p. 144.

42 *Letters*, 2:276.

43 William James, *The Meaning of Truth: A Sequel to "Pragmatism"* (New York and London: Longmans, Green & Co., 1909; reprint ed., Cambridge, Mass. and London: Harvard University Press, 1975). See pp. 201-225 for publication information on the original articles.

44 This will be considered in PART TWO, especially pp. 187-196.

45 See *Varieties*, p. 428. James had written the preface to Starbuck's *The Psychology of Religion: An Empirical Study of the Growth of Religious Consciousness* (London: Walter Scott, 1899). For the text of James' Preface, see William James, *Essays in Religion and Morality* (Cambridge, Mass. and London: Harvard University Press, 1982), pp. 102-105.

28 *Introduction*

46 *Letters*, 2:210.

47 J. H. Leuba, *International Journal of Ethics*, 45 (1903-1904). I owe this reference to Perry, 2:348.

48 Perry, 2:350f.

49 Perry, 2:348-351.

50 The questionnaire with James' replies is printed in *Letters*, 2:212-215. In the following paragraphs, all of James' comments are taken from that source.

51 William James, *A Pluralistic Universe: Hibbert Lectures at Manchester College on the Present Situation on Philosophy* (New York and London: Longmans, Green & Co., 1909; reprint ed., Cambridge, Mass. and London: Harvard University Press, 1977).

52 *A Pluralistic Universe*, pp. 12f.

53 *A Pluralistic Universe*, p. 13.

54 *A Pluralistic Universe*, p. 13.

55 *A Pluralistic Universe*, p. 135.

56 William James, *Some Problems of Philosophy, A Beginning of an Introduction to Philosophy* (New York and London: Longmans, Green & Co., 1911; reprint ed., Cambridge, Mass. and London: Harvard University Press, 1979).

57 *Some Problems of Philosophy*, p. 20.

58 *Some Problems of Philosophy*, pp. xxxiii, 235. The text of the syllabus, entitled "Faith and the Right to Believe," is found on pp. 111-117.

59 *Some Problems of Philosophy*, pp. 114f.

60 Ralph Barton Perry, *Present Philosophical Tendencies* (New York: Longmans, Green & Co., 1912; reprint ed., New York: Kraus Reprint Co., 1969). The work originally appeared in *The Harvard Graduates Magazine* 19 (1910) and was then reprinted in the *Philosophical Review* 20 (1911).

61 Perry, *Present Philosophical Tendencies*, p. 349.

62 Perry, *Present Philosophical Tendencies*, p. 350.

63 Perry, *Present Philosophical Tendencies*, p. 351.

64 Perry, *Present Philosophical Tendencies*, p. 351.

65 Perry, *Present Philosophical Tendencies*, p. 356.

66 Perry, *Present Philosophical Tendencies*, p. 357, quoting William James, *Essays in Radical Empiricism*, p. 131.

67 Perry, *Present Philosophical Tendencies*, p. 357.

68 Perry, *Present Philosophical Tendencies*, p. 358.

69 Perry, *Present Philosophical Tendencies*, p. 359.

70 Perry, *Present Philosophical Tendencies*, p. 363f. Perry is quoting William James, *The Meaning of Truth*, p. 6.

71 Perry, *Present Philosophical Tendencies*, pp. 369-371.

72 Perry, *Present Philosophical Tendencies*, p. 371, quoting from James' *Varieties of Religious Experience*, p. 513, and from *A Pluralistic Universe*, p. 309 (Harvard edition, p. 140). The quotation given is from the latter.

73 Perry, *Present Philosophical Tendencies*, pp. 371-373.

74 Perry, *Present Philosophical Tendencies*, p. 374.

75 Perry, *Present Philosophical Tendencies*, p. 378.

76 Henry Samuel Levinson, *The Religious Investigations of William James* (Chapel Hill: The University of North Carolina Press, 1981), p. 275.

77 Bruce Kuklick, *The Rise of American Philosophy: Cambridge, Massachusetts, 1860-1930* (New Haven and London: Yale University Press, 1977), p. 567.

78 Kuklick, *The Rise of American Philosophy*, pp. 328f.

79 Kuklick, *The Rise of American Philosophy*, p. 329.

80 Kuklick, *The Rise of American Philosophy*, p. 329.

81 Levinson, *The Religious Investigations of William James*, pp. 270-283 (epilogue) and pp. 291-299 (bibliographical essay).

82 William James, *The Writings of William James: A Comprehensive Edition*, ed. with introduction by John J. McDermott (Chicago: The University of Chicago Press, 1977), pp. xix-1, 810-858.

83 Julius Seelye Bixler, *Religion in the Philosophy of William James* (Boston: Marshall Jones Co., 1926).

84 Bixler, *Religion in the Philosophy of William James*, p. vii.

85 Bixler, *Religion in the Philosophy of William James*, pp. viiif.

86 Bixler, *Religion in the Philosophy of William James*, p. ix.

87 Bixler, *Religion in the Philosophy of William James*, p. 3.

88 Bixler, *Religion in the Philosophy of William James*, p. 5.

89 Bixler, *Religion in the Philosophy of William James*, p. 5.

90 Bixler, *Religion in the Philosophy of William James*, p. 12f.

91 On James and Renouvier, see below, PART ONE, pp. 76-86.

92 Bixler, *Religion in the Philosophy of William James*, p. 83f. See William James, *The Will to Believe*, pp. 16-20. Blaise Pascal (1623-1662) was the French mathematician, physicist, inventor, philosopher, and theologian. For his famous Wager Argument, see Blaise Pascal, *Pensees*. *Texte de L'edition Brunschvicq*, ed. Ch.-M. Des Granges (Paris: Librairie Garnier Freres, n.d.), No. 233; or Pascal, *Oeuvres Completes*, Preface d'Henri Gouhier, Presentation et Notes de Louis Lafuma (Paris: Editions du Seuil, 1963), n. 418. For James' use of the wager argument, see Robert J. O'Connell, *William James on the Courage to Believe* (New York: Fordham University Press, 1984), pp. 33-52. This use will be considered in PART TWO of this dissertation.

93 William James, *The Will to Believe*, p. 16.

94 Bixler, *Religion in the Philosophy of William James*, p. 92f.

95 Bixler, *Religion in the Philosophy of William James*, p. 103.

96 This address was delivered in 1891, and later incorporated in *The Will to Believe*, pp. 141-162.

97 Bixler, *Religion in the Philosophy of William James*, p. 114, quoting William James, *The Will to Believe*, p. 161.

98 Bixler, *Religion in the Philosophy of William James*, p. 115.

99 Bixler, *Religion in the Philosophy of William James*, p. 123.

100 Bixler, *Religion in the Philosophy of William James*, p. 128.

101 Bixler, *Religion in the Philosophy of William James*, p. 129.

102 Bixler, *Religion in the Philosophy of William James*, p. 138. See also William James' *A Pluralistic Universe*, p. 141.

103 William James, *Human Immortality: Two Supposed Objections to the Doctrine*, 2nd ed. (Boston and New York: Houghton Mifflin, 1899; reprinted with *The Will to Believe*, New York: Dover Publications, Inc., 1956), p. 3.

104 Bixler, *Religion in the Philosophy of William James*, p. 145. The complete passage may be found in *The Varieties of Religious Experience*, p. 412.

105 Bixler, *Religion in the Philosophy of William James*, pp. 145, 161, 162.

106 Bixler, *Religion in the Philosophy of William James*, pp. 167-169.

107 Bixler, *Religion in the Philosophy of William James*, pp. 170f.

108 Robert J. Vanden Burgt, *The Religious Philosophy of William James* (Chicago: Nelson-Hall, 1981), p. 2.

109 Henry Samuel Levinson, *The Religious Investigations of William James* (Chapel Hill: University of North Carolina Press, 1981).

110 Levinson, *The Religious Investigations of William James*, pp. 270-283, 291-299.

PART ONE

INFLUENCES ON THE DEVELOPMENT OF JAMES' RELIGIOUS PHILOSOPHY

William James was a cosmopolitan figure. His relationship with his own father brought him into contact with many of the leading American thinkers. In addition, James was educated in Europe, and he became familiar with the leading English, French, German, and Italian philosophers. The extent of these influences on both sides of the Atlantic is brought out vividly by the table of contents and the index of Ralph Barton Perry's monumental work, *The Thought and Character of William James.*[1] Perry's work, which was based on William James' published writings and his unpublished correspondence and notes, documents the broad circle of acquaintances which formed the background for James' development.

In this study it will not be possible to deal with all of the thinkers mentioned in Perry's great work. A survey of the persons mentioned in that work has brought out the special interest and importance of five writers for this study of James' approach to God. The choice is not based on any single criterion. In the case of the elder Henry James, for example, the choice was based on both biographical importance and doctrinal similarities. In the case of Charles Renouvier, the choice was made because his work led James to a significant decision which was later seen to have doctrinal significance. Chauncey Wright was a partner in a dialogue which helped to shape James' thought. Charles Sanders Peirce was another partner in dialogue who gave a name to tendencies which James found in his own thought and steered him away from blind alleys. Finally, Josiah Royce was the friend and neighbor whose thoughts about God's existence spurred James on to a more experiential approach to God. The first part of this dissertation, will, therefore, be directed to the study of these writers and their interaction with William James, encounters which helped to shape James' approach to God.

Chapter I

Henry James the Elder

The first and perhaps the greatest influence on the development of William James' philosophy of religion was his father, the elder Henry James. Perry recognized the importance of this influence when he entitled Part One of his work "His Father's Son."[2] What kind of family did William and Henry come from?

The James Family

William James (1771-1832)
 The founder of the James family in America, William James, was an Irish immigrant who came to the United States in 1789, at the age of eighteen, "with a little money, a Latin grammar and a desire to see a revolutionary battlefield."[3]
 William settled in Albany and began as a store clerk. He became involved in merchandising, commerce, banking, real estate, and public utilities, and he eventually became one of the richest men in New York State. When he died in 1832, he left an estate worth 3 million dollars. William James became one of the leading citizens of New York State, and he was chosen as a trustee of Union College in Schenectady. He was an active parishioner in the Presbyterian Church and accepted a Calvinist theology with its doctrine of election and the Puritanical idea of a punishing God.[4] William James had three wives and fourteen children. His son Henry was born in Albany on June 2, 1811. Catherine Barber James was his mother.

Henry James (1811-1882)
 Relationship with his father. In his "Autobiographic Sketch," Henry James reflected on his relationship with his father:

> When I was very young I do not remember to have very much intellectual contact with my father save at family prayers and at meals, for he was always occupied during the day with business; and even in the frank domestic intercourse of the evening, when he was fond of hearing his children read to him, and would frequently exercise them in their studies, I cannot recollect that he ever questioned me about my out-of-door occupations, or about my companions, or showed any extreme solicitude about my standing in school.[5]

Henry James' leg injury. When Henry James was seventeen years old he suffered a severe leg injury. He was playing fireball with some of his friends. In this game, balls of tow soaked in turpentine were used to fly paper balloons. The tow was ignited under the balloon which rose into the air as it was heated. When a balloon caught fire, the ball of tow dropped to the ground and was kicked about like a flaming ball. During the game, Henry's pants were splashed with turpentine. When a ball of flaming tow fell through an open stable window, Henry tried to stamp out the fire. His pants were set aflame, and one of his legs was severely burned. The leg did not heal properly and, on May 6, 1828, his leg was cut off some distance above the knee. The protracted illness of the young man established a new relationship with his father. Through the experience Henry gained his father's affection in a way he might not otherwise have done. The amputation of his leg also brought about a change in Henry's life and character.

> Now the ardent nature that had set him roving before dawn could find expression only in his emotions and mind. His inner life proved to be as intense and turbulent as his brief life of physical activity had been — The characteristic strain in all his adult writing is a roaming passionate energy.[6]

Henry James — his alcoholism. After his recovery from the amputation, Henry developed an additional problem. He was addicted to alcohol. During his long illness his parents, doctors, and nurses had plied him with all manner of stimulants, and, by the time he went off to Union College in 1829, he was hopelessly addicted. At Union, instead of studying law as his father had wished him to do, Henry treated himself to liquor, fine clothes, expensive books, "segars" and oysters, and he paid for them with drafts on his father's account. He finally returned to graduate from Union College in 1830, cured of alcoholism but not of religious doubt, and the peace he re-established with his father on returning to college was an uneasy one.[7]

Henry James — Calvinistic beliefs. The Calvinistic beliefs of his father had established in the mind of Henry James a view of God as harsh and unloving. In his "Autobiographic Sketch," he described his belief in God in these terms:

> I doubt whether any lad had ever just so thorough and pervading a belief in God's existence as an outside and contrarious force to humanity as I had. The conviction of His supernatural being and attributes were burnt into me as with a red-hot iron, and I am sure no childish sinews were ever more strained than mine were in the wrestling with the subtle terror of His name. This insane terror pervaded my consciousness more or less. It turned every hour of unallowed pleasure I enjoyed into an actual boon wrung from His forebearance; made me loath at night to lose myself in sleep, lest His dread hand should clip my thread of life without time for a parting sob of penitence, and grovel at morning dawn with an abject slavish gratitude that the sweet sights and sounds of Nature and of man were still around me.[8]

William James, father of Henry, died in 1832. Leon Edel suggests that the death of his father only exacerbated the deep emotional problems of the young man.[9]

Henry James at Princeton Theological Seminary. The breaking of his father's will left Henry in possession of property yielding an annual income of 10 thousand dollars, making it unnecessary for him to go to work to earn a living. Then, seeking to understand his misgivings over religion and to comprehend his relationship with God. Henry gravitated to Princeton Theological Seminary — "almost as if to do penance to the ghost of his father."[10]

In his brief "Autobiographic Sketch," Henry James described his sense of being out of place as a student at the Princeton Seminary.

> Indeed, he contrasted signally with the entire mass of student life in the Seminary, by the almost total destitution which his religious character exhibited of the dramatic element, — that element of unconscious hypocrisy which Christ stigmatized in the religious zealots of his day, and which indeed seems to be inseparable from the religious profession. The ordinary theological student, especially, has a fatal professional conscience from the start, which vitiates his intellectual integrity. He is personally mortgaged to an *institution* — that of the pulpit — which is reputed sacred.... [11]

By the time that Henry James had completed two years of his seminary course at Princeton Theological Seminary, his discontent with orthodox Calvinism was complete. "He left Princeton, and the truth seems to be that he had already conceived some measure of antipathy to all ecclesiasticisms which he expressed with abounding scorn and irony throughout all his later years."12

Henry James — career as a writer. Henry James' insistence on his own interpretation of Christ and heaven and hell made it impossible for him to consider a career in the ministry. Since the ministry was closed to him, Henry entered upon a career as a writer. His son Henry James, the novelist, noted that he had repeatedly appealed to his father for some presentable account of his work that would prove the family respectable. When a boyhood friend said that *his* father was in the business of a stevedore, Henry had to go to his father with a more constant appeal to name his occupation. "What shall we tell them we *are*, don't you see?" The father was amused and put his son off with strange attributions that if repeated would have made them ridiculous. The father would advise, "Say I'm a philosopher, say I'm a seeker for truth, say I'm a lover of my kind, say I'm an author of books if you like; or, best of all, just say I'm a student."13

Henry James — his "vastation." In 1843, Henry James took his wife and two sons, William and Henry, to England. During the spring of 1844, Henry James was living with his family at Windsor, England. During this period he was absorbed in the study of the Scriptures. He had written a course of lectures giving his new approach to theology, and in England he continued his theological studies. It was then that he suffered the greatest crisis in his life. He described the crisis as follows:

> I remember I felt especially hopeful in the prosecution of my task all the time at Windsor. My health was good, my spirits cheerful, and the pleasant scenery of the Great Park and its neighborhood furnished us a constant temptation to long walks and drives.
>
> One day, however, towards the close of May, having eaten a comfortable dinner, I remained sitting at the table after the family had dispersed, idly gazing at the embers in the grate, thinking of nothing, and feeling only the exhilaration incident to a good digestion, when suddenly — in a lightning-flash as it were — "fear came upon me, and trembling, which made all my bones to shake." To all appearance it was a perfectly insane and abject terror, without ostensible cause, and only to be accounted for, to my perplexed imagination, by some damned shape squatting invisible to me within the precincts of the room, and raying out from his fetid personality influences fatal to life. The thing had not lasted ten seconds before I felt myself a

Virtue as a Recognition of Duty 39

> wreck; that is, reduced from a state of firm, vigorous, joyful manhood to one of almost helpless infancy. The only self-control I was capable of exerting was to keep my seat. I felt the greatest desire to run incontinently to the foot of the stairs and shout for help to my wife, — to run to the roadside even, and appeal to the public to protect me; but by an immense effort I controlled these frenzied impulses, and determined not to budge from my chair till I had recovered my lost self-possession. This purpose I held to for a good long hour, as I reckoned time, beat upon meanwhile by an ever-growing tempest of doubt, anxiety, and despair, with absolutely no relief from any truth I had ever encountered save a most pale and distant glimmer of the divine existence, when I resolved to abandon the vain struggle, and communicate without more ado what seemed my sudden burden of inmost, implacable unrest to my wife.[14]

This condition of mind which began so dramatically lasted for more than two years. Henry James consulted eminent physicians who told him that he had "overworked his brain." They recommended such remedies as a water-cure treatment, life in the open air, and cheerful company, ultimately leaving Henry to his own resources. An important change took place in Henry's intellectual life.

> It struck me as very odd, soon after my breakdown, that I should feel no longing to resume work which had been interrupted by it: and from that day to this (nearly thirty-five years) I have never once cast a retrospective glance even of curiosity, at the immense piles of manuscript which had erewhile so absorbed me.[15]

Henry James' discovery of the works of Swedenborg. The crisis which had begun so suddenly was finally diagnosed and brought to a close in a chance meeting with a woman friend, Mrs. Chichester, who lived in the vicinity of the water-cure. When he told her of his experience, she replied: "You are undergoing what Swedenborg calls a *vastation*; and though, naturally enough, you yourself are despondent or even despairing about the issue, I cannot help taking an altogether hopeful view of your prospects." While professing that she only read Swedenborg as an amateur, she expressed the belief that Henry James was undergoing a kind of new birth, and that the *vastation* was one of the stages of the regenerative processes as described by Swedenborg.[16]

Henry James went to London and purchased several volumes of the works of Emanuel Swedenborg (1688-1772), a Swedish scientist and mystic. Henry describes how he read the treatise on *Divine*

Love and Wisdom and that on *Divine Providence* with growing interest and he became convinced by the truth he found in them.

> Imagine a fever patient, sufficiently restored of his malady to be able to think of something beside himself, suddenly transported where the free airs of heaven blow upon him, and the sound of running waters refreshes his jaded senses; and you have a feeble image of my delight in reading.[17]

Henry James became a follower of Swedenborg. His experiences as a Presbyterian, however, and his dislike of ecclesiasticisms, kept him from becoming involved with the sectarian Swedenborgians. He adopted a universal, humanitarian form of religion, with his own peculiar interpretation of Swedenborg. Resuming his work as a theologian, Henry attempted to apply that interpretation to the criticism and evaluation of contemporary Society.[18]

Henry James' idiosyncratic reading of Swedenborg. In order to determine the influence of Henry James Sr. on William James, it is clear that a study of Swedenborg's philosophy would not be helpful. Swedenborg's writing helped Henry James to recover from his spiritual crisis, but James interpreted the writings in such an idiosyncratic way that it would not help our understanding of Henry James to begin with an objective study of Swedenborg's thoughts.[19]

William James' reading of his father's thought (Literary Remains). The purpose of this section is not to develop an analysis of Swedenborg's philosophy or to study that of Henry James, Sr., but, rather, to examine the influence of Henry James on his son William. It is clear then, that the ideas of Henry James should be explored insofar as they were understood by William. The principal source for William's understanding of his father's thought is the introduction to the *Literary Remains*.

William James began his treatment of his father's thought with the interesting observation that, with all of Henry's richness of style, the ideas are singularly unvaried and few.

> Probably few authors have so devoted their entire lives to the monotonous elaboration of one single bundle of truths. Wherever the eye falls upon one of Mr. James' pages, whether it be a letter to a newspaper or to a friend, whether it be his earliest or his latest book, we seem to find him saying again and again the same thing; telling us what the true relation is between mankind and its creator.[20]

William James described this position of his father as "an intensely positive, radical and fresh conception of God, and an intensely vital view of our connection with him."[21] William held that the center of his father's whole view of things was his intense conception of God as creator. The reality of this creator God is to be accepted without a reasoning process or philosophical criticism. William comments, "He nowhere attempts by metaphysical or empirical arguments to make the existence of God plausible; he simply assumes it as something that must be confessed."[22]

To emphasize his point, William James quoted a study of his father by J. A. Kellogg who wrote, "The usual problem is, given the creation, to find the creator. To Mr. James it is, — given the creator to find the creation. God is: of His being there is no doubt; but who and what are *we*?"[23]

At first this would seem like an appeal to blind faith. William James, however, interprets his father's work as a going back

> ... so far and so deep as to find the religious sentiment in its purest and most unsophisticated form. He lived and breathed as one who knew he had not made himself, but was the work of a power that let him live, from one moment to the next, and could do with him what it pleased. His intellect reacted on his sense of the presence of this power, so as to form a system of the most radical and self-consistent as well as the most simple kind.[24]

William described his father's view of the world as at bottom a very simple and harmonious view. It all flowed from two insights. In the first place, Henry felt that the individual man as such is nothing. He owes all he is and has to the nature which he has inherited and to the society into which he was born. The second insight was that Henry James scorned to admit even as a possibility that the great and loving creator should not bring us "*through* and *out* into the most triumphant harmony."[25]

William James contrasts his father's intensely personal view of creation with that of the ordinary orthodox view in which

> Jehovah explodes the universe absolutely out of what was previously pure blank; his *fiat* whacks it down upon the *tabula rasa* of time and space, and there it remains. Such simple, direct, and "magical" creation is always derided by Mr. James as a childish idea. The *real* nothingness cannot become thus promptly the seat of real being; it must taint with its own "abysmal destitution" whatever first comes to fill it, and reduce it to the status of a sham, or unreal magic-lantern picture projected on the dark inane.[26]

Henry saw creation as made up of two stages, the first of which he called formation or Nature and the second, redemption or Society. William James interpreted his father's thought to mean that "Nature" and "Society" do not differ from each other at all in substance or material. "Their substance is the Creator himself, for his is the sole positive substance in the universe, all else being nothingness."[27]

After giving this definition in the text, William James then added a footnote:

> This is why I said one might call the system pantheistic. Mr. James denounces pantheism, however. . . . One might say that the gist of his differences, both with pantheism and with ordinary theism, is that while the latter represents creation to be essentially the formation of Two out of an original One, to Mr. James it is something more like the union into One of an original Two.[28]

William further describes his father's doctrine of creation as "nothing short of a real *bringing to life* of the essential nothingness which is the eternal antithesis to God, a work, therefore, upon that nothingness actually performed.[29] He adds: "God then must, *in the final instance*, make a being that has the void for its other parent, and *involves* nothingness in itself."[30]

It is clear that both Henry and William James saw a need to choose between a doctrine of creation understood as the production of something out of the being of God, and creation, understood as the production of something out of nothingness, with nothingness conceived as a positive reality. Both positions are different from the traditional doctrine of creation: *PRODUCTIO REI EX NIHILO SUI ET SUBJECTI* (The production by God of a thing independent of the creator and of any pre-existing subject).

In his description of creation, Henry James used language which even his son seems to fear as skirting too close to pantheism. The clear proof, however, that Henry was not a pantheist is in his concept of selfhood. William James quotes an interesting passage in this regard from his father's work, published in 1863, entitled *Substance and Shadow*.

> "In short, the everlasting miracle is that God is able, in giving us himself, to endow us with our own finite selfhood as well; leaving us thereby so unidentified with himself, so utterly free and untrammelled to our own consciousness,

as to be able very often seriously to doubt, and not seldom permanently to deny, his own existence."³¹

This text is solid evidence that despite his inadequate philosophical analysis of the idea of creation, Henry James was convinced that he had a finite selfhood created by God but nevertheless distinct from God.

An important aspect of Henry James' understanding of God which influenced his son, William, was his belief in a limited God. Henry wrote:

> "I am free to confess for my own part that I have no belief in God's absolute or irrelative and unconditional perfection. I have not the least sentiment of worship for his name, the least sentiment of awe or reverence towards him, considered as a perfect person sufficient unto himself. That style of deity exerts no attraction either upon my heart or understanding.... I for my part will cherish the name of him alone whose insufficiency to himself is so abject that he is incapable *of realizing himself except in others*."³²

Influence of Henry James on William James' Affirmation of God

Profound Psychological Similarity Between Father and Son

What influence did Henry James have on the development of his son William's affirmation of God? First of all, there was a profound psychological similarity between father and son. Morris Raphael Cohen has said of William James himself what William in substance said of his father: "His thought ran in vivid pictures, and he could not trust logical demonstration as much as his intuitive suggestions."³³

Ralph Barton Perry also was convinced that William James resembled his father in both personal flavor and genius.

> Like his father he was warm-blooded, effervescent, and tenderly affectionate. Both men were unstable and impatient, though in neither case did this quality prevent long periods of intense and fruitful application.... Beyond a similarity of temperamental physiognomy which is immediately recognizable, any explanation in terms of deeper biological causes must remain entirely speculative. Both were fond of laughter. Both were men of extreme spontaneity, with a tendency to embellishment and immoderate affirmation; both were mobile or even erratic in a degree that made it impossible for them to drive readily in harness or to engage easily in organized, long-range, institutionalized activity.³⁴

Perry also commented on the similarity of temperament which predisposed father and son to the same style of utterance.

William was also a talking writer, with a genius for picturesque epithets, and a tendency to vivid coloring and extreme freedom of manner. William, too, was one who wrote primarily to express convictions, giving the result a peculiar quality of sincerity.[35]

Concern for Expressing Convictions
(Not Just What Is Subjectively Desirable)

This concern for expressing conviction sincerely is an important factor in understanding both Henry and William James. In the case of William, this characteristic is enough to throw doubt on any interpretation of his pragmatism which would caricature it as believing whatever is in some way subjectively desirable. William James like his father really accepted the reality of God. William would not have been satisfied with an acceptance of the existence of God as a merely practical solution to life's problems.

William James' Experience of a Form of Panic Fear

The psychological similarity between William James and his father even extended to an experience of melancholy in the form of panic fear. In the case of Henry James, the experience has already been described as his "vastation." William James, in his *The Varieties of Religious Experience*,[36] described a similar experience, "for permission to print which I have to thank the sufferer." He described the experience as follows:

> Whilst in this state of philosophic pessimism and general depression of spirits about my prospects, I went one evening into a dressing room in the twilight to procure some article that was there; when suddenly there fell upon me without any warning, just as if it came out of the darkness, a horrible fear of my own existence. Simultaneously there arose in my mind the image of an epileptic patient whom I had seen in the asylum, a black haired youth with greenish skin, entirely idiotic, who used to sit all day on one of the benches, or rather shelves against the wall, with his knees drawn up against his chin and the coarse gray undershirt, which was the only garment, drawn over them inclosing his entire figure. He sat there like a sort of sculptured Egyptian cat or Peruvian mummy, moving nothing but his black eyes and looking absolutely non-human. This image and my fear entered into a species of combination with each other. *That shape am I*, I felt, potentially. Nothing that I possess can defend me against that fate, if the hour for it should strike for me as it struck for him. . . After this the universe was changed for me altogether. I awoke morning after morning with a horrible dread at the pit of my stomach, and with a sense of the insecurity of life that I never knew before and that I have never felt since.[37]

William James clearly saw the parallel between his experience of panic fear and his father's "vastation." In a footnote in the *Varieties*, after the description of his own experience, he wrote "for another case of fear equally sudden, see Henry James: *Society the Redeemed Form of Man*, Boston, 1879, pp. 43ff."[38]

Central Place for Religion in the Lives of Henry James and William James

Another way in which the influence of Henry James is apparent in the factors leading to William's affirmation of God is the central place that religion played in both their lives. Even though Henry declared himself to be opposed to all "ecclesiasticisms," nonetheless William interpreted his father's thought as being essentially theological and essentially simple. Henry James was constantly attempting to formulate and express "what the true relation is between mankind and its Creator."[39]

William James also was, like his father, a profoundly religious person. As he said to one of his correspondents: "Religion is the great interest of my life...."[40]

When Henry James attempted to express his theological viewpoint, his ideas were centered on a doctrine of creation, or better, a conception of God as Creator. This doctrine was discussed at the dinner table among father and sons in the James household. William James, whose education, after several false starts, was devoted to the science of medicine, could not accept his father's unreasoned assumption of the existence of God. William's scientific formation trained him to look for evidence, to search for proof. Nevertheless, while he could not accept the existence of God as a postulate, William did affirm the existence of God. In addition, William formed an idea of God as finite, a position he shared with his father. William described his father's conception of God as "monistic enough to satisfy the philosopher, and yet warm and living and dramatic enough to speak to the heart of the common pluralistic man."[41]

Choice Between Monism and Pluralism

Both Henry James and William considered the choice between monism and pluralism as a fundamental problem of natural theology. It seems clear that William was influenced by his father in his statement of this problem.

William James interpreted his father's thought as logically implying monism, but he knew that his father was struggling to avoid the pantheistic implications of that choice. William points out that the first principle of monistic metaphysics, given such names as "One and Only Being," "The Universal Substance," "The Soul and Spirit of Things," "The First Principle of Monistic Metaphysics," is a "pale, abstract, and impersonal conception compared with that of the Eternal Living God, worshipped by the incalculable majority of our race."[42]

William James described his father's thoughts as "monistic enough to satisfy the metaphysician" since it made of God the one and only active principle. At the same time he saw a certain ambivalence in his father's thought and described it as anything but a "bald monism."[43]

William pointed out that, for his father, there is an *other* of God in our own selfhood. That selfhood however has no positive existence, "being really *naught*, a provisional phantom-soul breathed by God's love into mere logical negation."[44]

William commented that a monism, thus mitigated, can speak to the common heart, and he referred to those pages of his father which portray "creation on God's part as part of an infinite passion of self-surrender to his opposite."[45]

Skepticism of William James (1867)

This conception of reality as monistic gave rise to a philosophical correspondence between William James and his father in 1867, while William was in Europe. At that time William described himself as "drifting towards a sensationalism closed in by skepticism."[46]

In one letter, William said that he could not understand what his father meant by the "descent of the creator into nature." In a second letter written three weeks later, however, William indicated to his father that his materialism and skepticism were vacillating. He described his first letter as rather "a description of the natural sag of my mind when left to itself, than as its deliberate opinion when active. Then it becomes wholly skeptical."[47] He immediately adds, "I do not despair, however, of finding bottom somewhere, and it may be where you stand, if I ever fully understand you. I see much better what you are driving at now than I ever did before, however."[48]

In that same correspondence, Henry James diagnosed William's trouble in understanding his father's thought as arising mainly from the purely scientific cast of William's thought at that time. He saw science as a temporary blight exerted upon William's metaphysic wit.

William James' Criticism of His Father's Position on Creation/Pantheism

In another letter in the series, William pointed out a difficulty that he saw in his father's position. Creation has at all times been opposed to pantheism. From the scorn with which his father always mentioned pantheism, it was evident that Henry placed a broad gulf between creation and pantheism. Nevertheless, if the essence of the pantheistic conception consists in there being a necessary relation between Creator and creature, so that both are the same fact viewed from opposite sides, the conception really opposed to pantheism must necessarily refuse to admit any equation between Creator and creature. But this creates the other part of the dilemma, since whenever one imagines a non-pantheistic creation, in which, from an absolute first, a second appears, this process must be described as magical. William James then complains to his father that he fails to understand why, on the one hand, Henry has such an aversion to pantheism, and yet, on the other hand, such an aversion to "arbitrary creation." When Henry insists that a creature attains "an absolute being," William sees this as transcending the limits of his creatureship.[49] Returning to the same idea later in the same letter, William adds that he cannot understand how "you ever come out with more than you put in, namely the sole creator. He, in the last resort bears the whole expense of the operation."[50]

R. B. Perry's Comment on the Exchange of Letters Between William James and Henry James

Perry described William James' mind in this series of letters as follows:

> His own mind was as yet unformed, and he was predisposed by early influences as well as by the state of his health to acceptance of his father's saving faith. His dissent, prompted by scientific studies and proclivities which had already given him a standard of critical judgment, is therefore the more notable.[51]

William James' Last Letter to His Father (1882)

By December 1882, Henry James was at the point of death. William wrote his last letter to his father from London. The letter was written with the realization that Henry might be in his last illness. There is a kind of resignation to the approach of death. William said:

> You are old enough, you've given your message to the world in many ways and will not be forgotten; you are here left alone, and on the other side, let us hope and pray, dear, dear old Mother is waiting for you to join her.[52]

This profession of belief in immortality apparently seemed a bit too strong for William, for later in the same letter he said: "As for the other side, and Mother, and all our possibly meeting, I *can't* say anything. More than ever at this moment do I feel that if that *were* true, all would be solved and justified."[53]

In his final letter to his father, William assured Henry of the importance of the father's religious thought upon the son.

> In that mysterious gulf of the past into which the present soon will fall and go back and back, yours is still for me the central figure. All my intellectual life I derive from you; and though we have often seemed at odds in the expression thereof, I'm sure there's a harmony somewhere, and that our strivings will combine. What my debt to you is goes beyond all my power of estimating, — so early, so penetrating and so constant has been the influence.[54]

William James' Letter to His Wife on the Influence of His Father

The elder Henry James died on December 19, 1882. William, still in London, was notified by cablegram. William then wrote a letter to his wife in which he pointed out again the influence of his father on his own religious thought. He said:

> For me, the humor, the good spirits, the humanity, the faith in the divine, and the sense of his right to have a say about the deepest reasons of the universe, are what will stay by me. I wish I could believe I should transmit some of them to our babes.[55]

Summary of the Influence of Henry James on William James' Affirmation of God

How should one then sum up the influence of the elder Henry James on William James' religious philosophy with regard to the affirmation of God? It seems clear that there is a profound sympathy between father and son, and a close psychological resemblance. From his father, William James learned to make religion the deepest interest of his life. Like his father, William developed a philosophy of religion which was rooted in spiritual and religious experience. William followed his father in focusing his thought about God on the idea of God as Creator. Like his father, however, the all-powerful Creator was subject to limitations, a finite God. Just as Henry James did not base his belief in God on metaphysics and the traditional proofs for the existence of God, so William remained skeptical about the value of such proofs.[56]

William spoke of his father's affirmation of God as a postulate or an assumption. One might agree with Frederick Harold Young that we do not have in Henry James a philosopher of religion or a systematic theologian in the technical, academic, or scientific sense of those terms.[57]

Nevertheless, there is a quality of personal religious experience at the base of Henry James' affirmation as an arbitrary decision. When William James looks to religious experience to ground his affirmation of God, his position does not seem very far removed from that of his father. William had difficulty describing his father's thought as either monistic or pluralistic. He recognized that his father rejected pantheism because of his experience of selfhood. Henry James seemed to be unable to harmonize the pull of his logic to absolute monism with his personal experience of evil and freedom. The same philosophical problem continued to worry William James until the end of his life.

The influence of Henry James on William James' thought concerning the affirmation of God was so profound and enduring that one can hardly appreciate the thought of William James without realizing that it developed in an often vigorous dialogue with his father.

Notes

1 Ralph Barton Perry, *The Thought and Character of William James*, 2 vols. (Boston and Toronto: Little, Brown & Co., 1935) (henceforth referred to as Perry). After fifty years, Perry's book is still the best biography of James. It is also a primary source for about 500 letters written by William James which were not included in *The Letters of William James*, edited by his son Henry James. In addition, Perry has included about fifty letters written by Henry James the elder, the father of William James, and about thirty letters written by Henry James, William's novelist brother. Many letters written to William James or his father are also included in Perry's two-volume work. That work will be used both as a primary source for these materials and as a secondary source for Perry's biographical comments. For a laudatory evaluation of Perry's biography of William James see Morton White, *Pragmatism and the American Mind* (New York: Oxford University Press, 1973), pp. 32-34. For a nuanced criticism of Perry's work, see Henry Samuel Levinson, *The Religious Investigations of William James* (Chapel Hill: The University of North Carolina Press, 1981), pp. 275-277.

2 Perry, 1:xi.

3 Jean Strouse, *Alice James: A Biography* (New York: Bantam Books, 1982), p. 5.

4 Strouse, p. 6.

5 William James, ed., *The Literary Remains of the Late Henry James* (Boston: James R. Osgood & Co., 1885), p. 145f (henceforth referred to as *Literary Remains*).

6 Strouse, pp. 7f.

7 Strouse, p. 10.

8 *Literary Remains*, p. 185f.

9 Leon Edel, *Henry James*, 5 vols. (Philadelphia: J. B. Lippincott Company, 1953-1972); reprint ed., vol. 1: *The Untried Years: 1843-1870* (New York: Avon Books, 1978), p. 27. See also Leon Edel, *Henry James: A Life* (New York: Harper & Row Publishers, 1985), p. 6.

10 Edel, *Henry James, The Untried Years*, p. 28.

11 *Literary Remains*, p. 124.

12 William James, *The Letters of William James*, ed. Henry James, 2 vols. (Boston: The Atlantic Monthly Press, 1920), 1:8 (henceforth referred to as *Letters*).

13 Henry James, *Notes of a Son and Brother* (New York: Charles Scribner's Sons, 1914); reprint ed., with *A Small Boy and Others* and *The Middle Years*, as Henry James, *Autobiography* (Princeton, N.J.: Princeton University Press, 1983), p. 278.

14 *Literary Remains*, p. 59.

15 *Literary Remains*, p. 62.

16 *Literary Remains*, p. 64f.

17 *Literary Remains*, p. 66.

18 Dwight W. Hoover, *Henry James, Sr., and the Religion of Community* (Grand Rapids, Mich.: William B. Eerdmans Publishing Company, 1969), p. 42.

19 William James noted that many disciples of Swedenborg held that there is no warrant in Swedenborg's works for Henry James' interpretations. See *Literary Remains*, p. 112.

20 *Literary Remains*, p. 9.

21 *Literary Remains*, p. 12.

22 *Literary Remains*, p. 13.

23 *Literary Remains*, p. 13, citing J. A. Kellogg, *Philosophy of Henry James: A Digest* (New York: J. W. Lovell Company, 1883).

24 *Literary Remains*, p. 13f.

25 *Literary Remains*, p. 15.

26 *Literary Remains*, p. 18.

27 *Literary Remains*, p. 19.

28 *Literary Remains*, p. 19.

29 *Literary Remains*, p. 21.

30 *Literary Remains*, p. 21.

31 *Literary Remains*, p. 33.

32 *Literary Remains*, p. 41f, quoting from Henry James, *Society the Redeemed Form of Man* (Boston: Houghton, Osgood and Company, 1879), p. 33f.

33 Quoted without citation in Warren, *The Elder Henry James*, p. 252.

34 Perry, 1:128f. This observation is not an attempt at psycho-history. No attempt is made to interpret symptoms to disclose a meaning hidden from the agent and from common observers. On psycho-history, see Jacques Barzun, *Clio and the Doctors: Psycho-History, Quanto History and History* (Chicago: University of Chicago Press, 1974) for a negative judgment. For a more positive appraisal, focused on Erik Erikson's *Young Man Luther: A Study in Psycho-Analysis and History* (New York: W. W. Norton and Co., Inc. 1958), see Roger A. Johnson, ed., *Psycho-History and Religion: The Case of Young Man Luther* (Philadelphia: Fortress Press, 1977).

35 Perry, 1:129.

36 *Varieties*, p. 138f.

37 *Varieties*, p. 138. For the information that William James was the subject of this experience see *Letters*, 1:145.

38 *Varieties*, p. 139. Cf., Gay Wilson Allen, *William James: A Biography* (London: Rupert Hart-Davis, 1967), p. 165; and Perry, 1:322.

39 *Literary Remains*, p. 9.

40 *Letters*, 2:58.

41 *Literary Remains*, p. 115.

42 *Literary Remains*, p. 114.

43 *Literary Remains*, p. 115.

44 *Literary Remains*, p. 115.

45 *Literary Remains*, p. 115.

46 Perry, 2:705.

47 Perry, 2:706.

48 Perry, 2:706.

49 Perry, 2:712.

50 Perry, 2:713.

51 Perry, 2:155.

52 *Letters*, 1:219.

53 *Letters*, 1:220.

54 *Letters*, 1:219.

55 *Letters*, 1:221.

56 *Varieties*, p. 342f.

57 Young, p. 283.

Chapter II

Charles Renouvier

Renouvier's Life and Work

The second philosopher whose influence was crucial in the development of William James' philosophy of the affirmation of God was Charles Bernard Renouvier (1815-1903). He was born in Montpellier and was educated at the Ecole Polytechnique, where he specialized in mathematics and natural science. At the school, he came under the influence of the work of Antoine Cournot and of Auguste Comte, who at that time was an instructor in higher mathematics there. Renouvier never held an academic position, but he worked as a private scholar. In 1867, he began the publication, with his friend Francois Pillon, of a monthly periodical, *L'Annee Philosophique*. Renouvier published manuals of ancient and modern philosophy. A second group of works, which contains the center of his doctrine, presents a position called "neocriticism." The third and final part of his philosophic production was centered on the notion of personalism.[1]

Renouvier has left an enormous philosophical production, enough to fill about fifty volumes. Because of the quantity of his production and the various positions which he espoused, it is not feasible to include a firsthand study of his thought in this work. Our concern is with his influence on William James, which can better be studied through James' references to Renouvier.[2]

William James' First Contact with Renouvier

The first allusion to Renouvier in the writings of William James occurs in a letter to his father dated October 5, 1868. The letter was probably written in Divonne, France. William said:

> I got a little book by a number of authors, "L'Annee 1867 Philosophique," which may interest you if you have not got it already. The introduction, a review of the state of philosophy in France for some years back, is by one Charles Renouvier, of whom I have never heard before but who, for vigor of style and compression, going to the core of half a dozen things in a single sentence, so different from the namby-pamby diffusiveness of most Frenchmen, is unequaled by anyone. He takes his stand on Kant. I have not read the rest of the book.[3]

William James' Review of Essais de Critique

An important element in Renouvier's neocriticism is his theory of free will.[4] William James reviewed the *Essais de Critique Generale* in the *Nation* in 1876. James wrote that Renouvier's polemic against the metaphysical notions of Substance, of Infinite in existence, and of abstract ideas, "seems to us more powerful than anything which has been written in English."[5]

In the review, James pointed out that Renouvier rejected psychical determinism. He held that the only logical enemy of free will is the doctrine of Substance, or Pantheism. In the view of William James, Renouvier clarified the question by stating in simple phenomenal terms that it is a question as to those human acts which are preceded by *deliberation*.

> A representation arises in the mind, but ere it can discharge itself into a train of action, it is inhibited by another which confronts it. This, on the point of discharging itself, is again checked by the first, which returns with a reinforced intensity, and so for a time the pendulum swings to and fro, till finally one or the other representation recurs with such a degree of reinforcement that the tumult ceases, and an act, a decision for the future, or the arrest of a passionate impulse takes place. This stable survival of one representation is called a volition. The whole question of its predetermination relates to the intensity of the degree of reinforcement with which the triumphant representation recurs.[6]

James cites Helmholtz for the view that science must assume an unalterable principle of determination, even when the proximate causes of phenomena are alterable themselves. James, however, suggests that the contrary assumption of an ultimate law of indetermination might be a moral postulate. There is no possibility of deciding the question empirically.

> Must one remain forever uncertain, or shall one anticipate evidence and boldly choose one's side? . . . Doubt itself is an active state, one of voluntary inhibition or suspense, so that whichever plan one adopts, one's state is the result of other facts than pure receptivity of intelligence.[7]

In other words, the possibility of doubting or suspending one's response is evidence of indetermination or freedom.

James points out that Renouvier moves from an analysis of doubt to a vigorous and original discussion of the ultimate grounds of certitude and of belief in general. Renouvier said:

> The radical sign of will, the essential mark of that achieved development which makes a man capable of speculating on all things and raises him to his dignity of an independent and autonomous being, is the possibility of doubt.[8]

James holds that Renouvier moves from doubt to certitude, which is a state and an act of man,

> . . . a state in which he posits his consciousness, such as it is, and stands by it. Properly speaking, there is no certitude; all there is is men who are certain . . . certitude is thus nothing but belief . . . a moral attitude.[9]

William James comments that in every wide theoretical conclusion, we must seem more or less arbitrarily to *choose* our side. This reflection, which is here made in the context of a discussion of freedom or determinism, is significant as an early statement by James on the role of free choice in the quest for truth. In certain circumstances one must make a choice, and suspension of choice itself would be a choice, "a most practical one, since by it we should forfeit the possible benefits of boldly espousing a possible truth. If this *be* a moral world, there are cases in which any indecision about its being so must be death to the soul."[10] If there is no freedom, there would be only the delusion of liberty.

> But if our choice is truly free, then the only possible way of getting at that truth is by the exercise of the freedom which it implies. Here the act of belief and the object of belief coalesce, and the very essential logic of the situation demands that we wait not for any outward sign, but, with the possibility of doubting open to us, voluntarily take the alternative of faith.[11]

Such a position on freedom and certitude implies that freedom must be chosen. Renouvier says: "Let our liberty pronounce on its own real existence." Since freedom and necessity are alike in that neither can be demonstrated, both freedom and determinism must be postulated if taken at all. James then challenges those who hold for determinism to admit that "unless they deduce it *a priori* from the existence of a metaphysical substance, they *choose* it . . . because on the whole they prefer it."[12] Thus James holds that freedom is carried into the very heart of our theoretic activity and becomes the cornerstone of Renouvier's philosophy.[13]

William James Helped Out of Despondence by Renouvier's Book

This theoretical statement of Renouvier's philosophy of freedom came about six years after William James had been helped out of a deep period of despondence by that same philosophy of freedom. That period seems to have begun in 1869. In December of that year, William wrote in his diary, "Nature and life have unfitted me for any affectionate relations with other individuals."[14] Allen comments on this passage that William obviously felt the necessity of controlling his emotional longing and his desire for love and marriage.

> Given the condition of his nervous system, whatever the cause of his back pains and frequent headaches, it is not difficult to understand his conviction that he must and *ought* to deny himself the affectional relations which his nature craved and his conscience rejected.[15]

During this period of trial, William could not actively participate in life, and he had trouble even reading. On New Year's Day 1870, he thought he sensed some real improvement on the condition of his ailing back. By February 1, 1870, however, the back problem got worse. In his diary William wrote:

> Today I about touched bottom, and perceived plainly that I must face the choice with open eyes: Shall I *frankly* throw the moral business overboard, as one unsuited to my innate aptitudes, or shall I follow it, and it alone, making everything merely stuff for it.[16]

During this period of mental and emotional turmoil, while William James was groping for something to believe in, he suffered a great emotional shock. His cousin, Minny Temple, died on March 8, 1870. William received the news the following day. His diary reveals that he drew a tombstone at the notice of her death. He was stunned by the news, and this experience of grief plunged him further into depression. It was probably while he was in this condition that he suffered from a traumatic experience of panic. This experience, which was similar to his father's "vastation," has already been described from James' report in *The Varieties of Religious Experience*.[17]

Despite his despair, William could not discuss his unbearable fears with his mother; he could not even turn to his father, who could have been more sympathetic. He could not even share his terror with his brother Henry who was in England.[18]

It was out of this condition of panic fear and terror that William turned to Charles Renouvier. He had discovered Renouvier's works two years earlier, and now he found in the French philosopher the help he needed. This help provided the basis for a notebook entry dated April 30, 1870:

> I think that yesterday was a crisis in my life. I finished the first part of Renouvier's second "Essais" and see no reason why his definition of Free Will — "the sustaining of a thought *because I choose to* when I might have other thoughts" — need be a definition of an illusion. At any rate, I will assume for the present — until next year — that it is no illusion. My first act of free will shall be to believe in free will. . . . Hitherto, when I felt like taking a free initiative, suicide seemed the most manly form to put my daring into; now I will go a step further with my will, not only act with it but believe as well. . . . Life shall be . . . doing and suffering and creating.[19]

The death of Minny Temple made a profound impact both on William James and his brother Henry. Henry James wrote that, "We felt it together as the end of our youth."[20]

William James' choice of free will may also be seen as making an end to his youthful indecision and aimlessness. That definitive choice of freedom made under the inspiration of Renouvier seems never to have been retracted. It not only marked the beginning of a new stage in William James' emotional life but it set the course for his future development as a philosopher of religion. The choice made in 1870 was an important step toward the affirmation of God.

William James' Later Philosophic Interest in Renouvier

William James continued his philosophic interest in Charles Renouvier. In 1879-1880, James taught a course at Harvard on Renouvier in which Renouvier's untranslated works were used as texts. He continued to follow Renouvier's later works and re-editions of earlier works, and this interest continued to the very end. The book *Some Problems of Philosophy*, which was left behind in manuscript form when James died in 1910, was edited and published in 1911 by James' student, Horace M. Kallen. The dedication printed at the head of the work was taken from within the text:

> He (Charles Renouvier) was one of the greatest of philosophic *characters*, and but for the decisive impression made on me in the seventies by his masterly advocacy of pluralism, I might never have got free from the monistic superstition under which I had grown up. The present volume, in short, might never have been written. This is why, feeling endlessly thankful as I do, I dedicate this text book to the great Renouvier's memory.[21]

Ralph Barton Perry said:

> That Renouvier's was the greatest individual influence upon the development of James' thought cannot be doubted. Renouvier's phenomenalism, his pluralism, his fideism, his moralism, and his theism were all congenial to James' mind, and in them James found support and confirmation. On the other hand he dissented from Renouvier's intellectualism, from his monadism, and from certain of his speculative extravagances.[22]

Personal Relationship of William James and Renouvier

The relationship between William James and Charles Renouvier was not merely that of reader and author. James wrote his first letter to Renouvier in 1872. He said:

> Thanks to you I possess for the first time an intelligible and reasonable conception of freedom. I accept it almost entirely. On other points in your philosophy I still have doubts, but I can say that through that philosophy I am beginning to experience a rebirth of the moral life; and I assure you, Monsieur, that this is no small thing![23]

The final letter from William James to Charles Renouvier was written on August 4, 1896. James wrote:

> I sent you a *New World* the other day, ... with an article in it called "The Will to Believe," in which (if you took the trouble to glance at it) you probably recognized how completely I am still your disciple. In this point perhaps more fully than in any other; and this point is central.[24]

Charles Renouvier died in 1903. After his death, William James gave his final verdict on his friend: "He will remain a great figure in philosophic history...."[25]

Renouvier is a significant figure in James' approach to God. Renouvier's doctrine of freedom seems to have led James to a moral and religious experience of choice; which may be seen as a paradigm for the religious thought of *The Varieties of Religious Experience*. That is, from his own experience of choosing to be free, James was ultimately to develop a theory in which moral and religious experience were presented as the basis for an approach to God.

Notes

1. Paul Edwards, ed., *The Encyclopedia of Philosophy*, eight volumes bound as four (New York: Macmillan Publishing Co., Inc., and The Free Press, 1967; reprint edition, 1972), 7:180ff. See also Etienne Gilson, gen ed., *History of Philosophy*, 4 vols. (New York: Random House, 1962-1966), vol. 4: *Recent Philosophy: Hegel to the Present*, by Etienne Gilson, Thomas Langan, and Armand A. Maurer, C.S.B., pp. 318-321, 796f.

2. For a listing of the works of Renouvier in William James' library, see William James, *Essays in Philosophy* (Cambridge, Mass.: Harvard University Press, 1978), p. 199.

3. *Letters*, 1:138. See also Perry, 1:654.

4. Cf., Charles Renouvier, *Essais de Critique Generale* (Paris: Librairie Armand Colin; reprint ed., 1912), pp. 301-330.

5. William James, *Collected Essays and Reviews* (New York: Longmans, Green and Company, 1920; reprint ed., New York: Russell and Russell, 1969), p. 29.

6. *Collected Essays and Reviews*, pp. 30f.

7. *Collected Essays and Reviews*, p. 32.

8. *Collected Essays and Reviews*, p. 33. (No citation is given to Renouvier's work.)

9. *Collected Essays and Reviews*, p. 33.

10. *Collected Essays and Reviews*, p. 34.

11. *Collected Essays and Reviews*, p. 34.

12. *Collected Essays and Reviews*, p. 35.

13. *Collected Essays and Reviews*, p. 35.

14. Allen, *William James*, pp. 163, 531.

15. Allen, *William James*, p. 163.

16. Allen, *William James*, p. 164.

17 *Varieties*, p. 139.

18 Allen, *William James*, p. 167.

19 *Letters*, 1:147f.

20 Henry James, *Autobiography*, p. 544.

21 William James, *Some Problems of Philosophy*, (Cambridge, Mass.: Harvard University Press, 1979), pp. 3, 85.

22 Perry, 1:655.

23 Perry, 1:662. The French original is in *Letters*, 1:163f.

24 *Letters*, 2:44.

25 *Letters*, 2:204. The letter dated June 12, 1904, is to Renouvier's collaborator, Francois Pillon.

Chapter III

Chauncey Wright

Wright's Life

> If power of analytic intellect pure and simple could suffice, the name of Chauncey Wright would assuredly be as famous as it is now obscure, for he was not merely the great mind of a village — if Cambridge will pardon the expression — but either in London or Berlin he would, with equal ease, have taken the place of master which he held with us.[1]

This piece appeared in *Nation* in 1875 (p. 194), shortly after Chauncey Wright's death, which occurred on September 12, 1875. These words of William James on the death of his close friend give an idea of the esteem for Wright's intellect on the part of his close friends.

Chauncey Wright (1830-1875) was born in Northampton, Massachusetts. His father, Ansel Wright, was a deputy sheriff and merchant of Northampton. His mother, Elizabeth Boleyn, came originally from Enfield, Connecticut. Ansel Wright was a member of the Unitarian church in Northampton, and Chauncey was brought up as a Unitarian. In nineteenth century America, Unitarianism still accepted many of the tenets of Christianity. While Unitarians denied the doctrine of the Blessed Trinity, they believed that Christ was a messenger from God, supernaturally and uniquely endowed, and sent as a special, indispensable revelation to man.[2]

After attending the Northampton District schools and high school, Chauncey attended the Select High School, an experimental school in which twenty or thirty students were brought together for advanced work. In this school one of his teachers was David S. Sheldon, who explained the movements of the heavenly bodies, and who inspired Chauncey to construct some astronomical instruments. Sheldon not only fixed Chauncey's interest unalterably in scientific matters but introduced him to the concept of biological evolution — then "in the air" — which came to play a dominant role in his later intellectual interests. Through the promptings of a friend, Mrs. Ann Lyman, Chauncey entered Harvard College in 1848. In both high school and college he was brilliant in mathematics and science, but he had difficulty with the classical languages, and he took little interest in the study of languages or literature.[3]

While at Harvard, Chauncey Wright began his interest in philosophy. He began by reading Emerson's *Essays*, and this started him on a journey away from his early Unitarianism. Wright was particularly impressed with Emerson's criticism of historical Christianity, focused on the person of Christ. At Harvard, Chauncey continued his interest in evolution. This was years before the publication of Darwin's *On the Origin of Species* in 1859.

After his graduation from Harvard in 1852, his reputation in mathematics led to his being hired as a computer by the director of the *Nautical Almanac*. The work on the almanac was a kind of mathematical piecework which did not involve regular hours of work. "He invented new ways of computing which cut his labor tremendously and gave him ample time for what turned out to be his real career, namely, being Socratic sage or scourge (depending on one's viewpoint) to the inhabitants of old Cambridge."[4]

Four Periods in Wright's Intellectual Life

Edward Madden has recognized four periods in Chauncey Wright's life, 1830-1852, 1852-1864, 1864-1869, and 1870-1875. From 1852, after his Harvard days, "philosophy more and more occupied his interests until there was little room for anything else. His intellectual interests in the 1850's can be indexed under the names Francis Bacon, William Hamilton, and John Stuart Mill."[5]

The earlier enthusiasm for Emerson's thought was succeeded by an interest in the philosophy of Bacon and Hamilton because of their greater powers of critical analysis. Wright was particularly influenced by Mill's views on scientific evidence and proof. On the basis of his reading of them, Wright concluded that: "One ought continually to test and correct his beliefs by the facts of concrete experience of a kind common to all and not by emotions, intuitions or unaided ratiocinations."[6]

In 1860, Wright first read Darwin's *On the Origin of the Species*. He accepted not only Darwin's evolutionary thesis but also his theory of natural selection. During this period Chauncey Wright was a member of The Club or The System. Other members were James Thayer, William Ware, Ephraim Gurney, Charles Dunbar, Darwin Ware, and George Shattuck. The club met from 1856 through February 1859. Wright became the central figure of the club and his quarters became the unofficial headquarters.[7]

The second period in Chauncey Wright's adult life began in 1864 when he found a new friend, Charles Eliot Norton. Norton, with his wife Susan, his mother, his sisters Grace and Jane, came to fill Chauncey's hunger for family life. The years from 1864-1869 were fruitful ones for him, and he began to produce articles and reviews for the *Nation* and *The North American Review*.

The most notable of Wright's longer articles for *The North American Review* during these years are on *Natural Theology, The Philosophy of Herbert Spencer*, and *A Physical Theory of the Universe*. His "Philosophy of Herbert Spencer" is the place, many commentators believe, where he clearly prefigures some elements of the pragmatisms of C. S. Peirce, William James, and John Dewey.[8]

During this period, his friends Ephraim Gurney and Charles Eliot Norton were his most favored conversational partners. In 1865, Gurney suggested the revival of The Club, which continued for another two or three years.

The fourth and final period of Wright's life lasted from 1870 to 1875. This was the period of his most significant philosophical work and the flowering of his philosophical ability in conversation. Wright became the senior member of a famous discussion group called The Metaphysical Club. It was during this period that William James was under the influence of Wright. James found in Wright the debating opponent he needed to sharpen his ideas. Wright became for James the very model of the scientific thinker. Wright's criticism of Herbert Spencer's evolutionary philosophy led James to see its weaknesses. Finally, Wright's experimental approach to psychology and philosophy was adopted by James in his own work.

During this period Wright published many articles in *Nation* and *The North American Review*. Among his articles in the *Nation* were several dealing with the theory of evolution and Darwinism. His most important productions of this period were published in *The North American Review*. Four articles dealt with a defense of Darwinism against the writings of biologists such as Alfred Russel Wallace and St. George Mivart. Wright's article on "The Evolution of Selfconsciousness" is considered to have given a fresh impetus to empirical psychology in America, and influenced William James' views on reasoning in his *Principles of Psychology*. Wright also influenced James' thinking on radical empiricism and on the concept of pure experience. During these years Chauncey taught twice at Harvard. In 1870 he taught psychology and in 1874 he taught mathematical physics.

On Saturday, September 11, 1875, Chauncey Wright suffered a stroke while writing at his desk. This was followed by another stroke shortly afterwards and Chauncey died.

Thayer's Criticism of Wright

After Wright's death, J. B. Thayer collected letters from Wright's oldest and dearest friends. In that volume, Gurney described him as "calm, gentle, unassuming; ready to be pleased; demanding little of friends . . . deficient in ambition; devoid of jealousy and envy; perfectly honorable, and perfectly amiable. . . ."[9] J. B. Thayer had one reservation about his friend Chauncey Wright. He felt that Chauncey had permitted the scientific habit of thought, which refused to take side when sufficient evidence is lacking, to creep into the realm of conduct and action. But "conduct of some sort is forced on men, and even inaction is made to count for action."[10]

Madden comments that William James "was much impressed with Thayer's criticism of Wright and used the idea in his view about the Will to Believe. James spent most of his life trying to fight his old friend's agnosticism."[11]

Gay Wilson Allen comments that Wright's philosophical skepticism had pushed James to the limits of his forensic and emotional strength. James never felt satisfied with his answers to Wright's criticisms. "Not until his own empiricism had matured did he gain sufficient confidence in his own thinking to cease worrying about the holes that Chauncey Wright has torn in his immature logic."[12]

Wright's Philosophical Discussions

When one turns from the life of Chauncey Wright to his philosophical positions, one must recognize with Charles Eliot Norton that Wright had justly won recognition from competent judges as a philosophical thinker of a high order.[13]

After graduating from Harvard College, Wright became a close student of the philosophical writings of Sir William Hamilton (1805-1865). Wright read everything Hamilton had written, and became a defender of Hamilton's views, a curious combination of Realism and Kantianism. Wright's earliest orientation in philosophy was toward empiricism. He had been interested in the theory of evolution from his high school days, and when Darwin's *The Origin of Species* appeared in 1859, Wright became an enthusiastic defender of Darwin's position. Most of Wright's intellectual labors were devoted to the defense of evolution, and some of his most philosophical work was developed in that context.[14]

Wright defended the evolutionary theory of Darwin, attacking the Natural Theology of the anti-Darwinian theologians. One fruit of this effort was the publication of an article on "Natural Theology as a Positive Science."[15] In the article, he attacked the basic assumptions of those theologians who were opposed to evolution. For example, William Paley (1734-1805) held that the works of nature proceed from intelligence and design. They resemble what intelligence and design are constantly producing and what nothing we know except intelligence and design ever produce at all. In reply, Wright denied that cause and effect in natural phenomena can be interpreted to support the claims of natural theology by any key which science itself affords.

> By what criterion . . . can we distinguish among the numberless effects, that are also causes, and among the causes that may, for ought we can know, be also effects, — how can we distinguish which are the means and which are the end?[16]

After denying that science can furnish an argument from design, however, Wright points out that the objections to such an argument are not objections to the spiritual doctrine of final causes or to the belief that final causes exist.[17] Wright goes a step further in stating that:

> The practical influences and effects of such philosophizing are, we believe, more obnoxious to the true interests of religion than its methods are to the true principles of philosophy, and fully justify an examination of its arguments.... Not only do the peculiar doctrines of natural theology add nothing to the grounds of a faith in final causes; they, in effect, narrow this faith to ideas which scarcely rise in dignity above the rank of superstitions.... It is from the illegitimate pretensions of natural theology that the figment of a conflict between science and religion has arisen; and the efforts of religious thinkers to counteract the supposed atheistical tendencies of science, and to give a religious interpretation to its facts, have only served to deepen the false impression that such a conflict actually exists, so that revolutions in scientific theories have been made to appear in the character of refutations of religious doctrines. That there is a fundamental distinction between the natures of scientific and religious ideas ought never to be doubted; but that contradiction can arise, except between religious and superstitious ideas, ought not for a moment be admitted.[18]

From these remarks it is clear that Wright distinguishes between religious faith in God and a natural theology understood as an arrangement of arguments for the existence of God based on the physical sciences. It is only the latter which he attacked. He considers progress in science to be a progress in religious truth, not because any new reasons are discovered for the doctrines of religion but because advancement of knowledge frees us from the errors of both ignorance and of superstition. Thus, when a proof of special design is invalidated by the discovery that a particular effect in nature is really a result of the general properties of matter, such as the law of universal gravitation, any harm that might be done is the result of the theologians' mistake rather than the enmity of science to religion. Nevertheless, attempting to do away with weak scientific arguments for religious truth should not be considered as weakening a legitimate faith in final causes. In Wright's words: "Even the Newtonian mechanism of the heavens, simple, primordial, and necessary as it seems, still discloses to the devout mind evidence of a wisdom unfathomable, and of a design which transcends interpretation...."[19]

While Wright is firm in supporting objections to a philosophy which assigns physical reasons to support a faith in final causes,[20] nevertheless, he does not dispute the legitimacy of religious faith in final causes, nor the disclosure to the devout mind of the evidences of a design which transcends scientific interpretation.

In 1871, Wright developed his position in a more explicitly Christian way in a review article on the work of St. George Mivart (1827-1900), *On the Genesis of Species*. He pointed out that Mivart's area of exploration has a bearing on the doctrine of final causes. Wright proposed, however,

> not only to distinguish between this branch of theology and the theories of inductive science on one hand, but still more emphatically, on the other hand, between it and the Christian faith in divine superintendency, which is very liable to be confounded with it. The Christian faith is that even the fall of a sparrow is included in this agency, and that as men are of more value than many sparrows, so much more is their security. So far from weakening this faith by showing the connection between value and security, science and the theory of Natural Selection have confirmed it.[21]

From this text, it is clear that Chauncey Wright, while he espoused philosophical agnosticism, still accepted a Christian view of the world.

Wright's Influence on William James

Wright as a Model of the Scientific Thinker

What influence did Chauncey Wright have on William James' philosophy of religion and, in particular, on his position on the affirmation of God? First of all, for James, Wright was a kind of model of the scientific thinker. Wright was not an academic specialist but, in the best sense of the word, an amateur in various branches of science. It has already been noted that Harvard University invited him to lecture on psychology and also to conduct a course in mathematical physics. William James commented that had Wright early in life concentrated on making himself a physicist; for example, "there is no question but that his would have ranked today as one of the few first living names."[22]

In the controversy over Darwin's theory of evolution, Wright replied to criticisms of the biologists Alfred Russel Wallace and St. George Mivart by providing an analysis of the concepts of "scientific explanation," "accident," "irregularity," "novelty," "species," "fixity," and so on. Darwin himself was much impressed by this philosophical contribution to the discussion, and cited one of Wright's articles in his "Descent of Man." At his own expense, Darwin had a second article reprinted and distributed.[23]

Perry acknowledged William James' admiration for Wright as a scientist. He wrote:

> James felt him to be a master in the field of scientific thought and tended to accept him as an authoritative exponent of scientific aims and methods. To some extent, like Jeffries Wyman, he represented the ideal scientific temper, restrained, impersonal, and scrupulous.[24]

Wright's Criticism of Herbert Spencer's Evolutionary Philosophy

A second way in which Chauncey Wright had an influence on William James' approach to the problem of God was through Wright's telling criticism of the evolutionary philosophy of Herbert Spencer (1820-1903) of which James was enamored as a young man. James began to read philosophy in the 1860s and the writings of Spencer were the most important part of his early philosophical reading. In 1904, in a review of Spencer's *Autobiography*, James said:

> I read this book (*First Principles*) as a youth when it was still appearing in numbers, and was carried away with enthusiasm by the intellectual perspective which it seemed to open. . . .
>
> Later I have used it often as a text book with students, and the total outcome of my dealings with it is an exceedingly unfavorable verdict. Apart from the great truth which it enforces, that everything has evolved somehow, and apart from the inevitable stimulating effect of any such universal picture, I regard its teachings as almost a museum of blundering reasoning.[25]

The early influence of Herbert Spencer on James was undermined by the criticisms by Charles Sanders Peirce and Chauncey Wright. Wright criticized Spencer's work in several articles, beginning in 1860, and continuing till shortly before Wright's death. Edward Madden comments that Wright attacked Spencer's claim to have a *scientific* philosophy. Wright held that Spencer did not understand the logical structure of science itself.[26]

It is most likely that Wright's opposition to Spencer both in his articles and in his conversation helped William James to recognize the fundamentally unscientific character of Spencer's work. In the end, James rejected Spencer's doctrine of the Unknowable. In his lecture notes for the course on The Philosophy of Evolution, in which he used Spencer's *First Principles* as a text, James held that the "Unknowable" had a dozen vague and mutually inconsistent meanings. "All that Spencer's chapters prove is that self-contradictory nonsense does not exist.... To ward off the approach that his philosophy does not explain things, he says: 'Everything I don't know is unknowable.'"[27]

James also denied Spencer's claim to have provided in the "Unknowable" a simple object of religious faith. Rejecting this in the name of religion, James said, "Mere existence commands no respect whatever, or any other emotion, until its quality is specified."[28]

Wright's Experimental Approach to the Philosophy

Another way that Chauncey Wright influenced William James' approach to God was in his adherence to an experimental approach to philosophy and his confirmation of a similar tendency in James.[29] Both were empiricists. Wright's essay on the "Evolution of Self-Consciousness," which was published in 1873, contributed to James' view of the biological aspects of thought. James set forth his positions in an essay entitled "Brute and Human Intellect" in 1878. The substance of this essay later appeared in the *Principles of Psychology*.[30]

Edward Madden pointed out that Chauncey Wright as a Harvard undergraduate had already defended the naturalistic thesis of continuity in the development of the brute and human intellect.[31] In the 1873 article, Wright developed the view that there is a continuity between the instinct found in animals and human intelligence. He described how the latter emerges from mental powers such as memory and attention, and he points out that such powers are common in different degrees to human beings and the lower animals.[32] William James acknowledged the definition of man as a rational animal, but, contrary to the traditional intellectualist philosophy, James said that it is by no means easy to decide what is meant by reason, or how the peculiar thinking process called reasoning differs from other thought-sequences which may lead to similar results.[33] Despite the influence of Wright, however, James develops his position differently, and attempts to bring out "the intellectual contrast between brute and man."[34]

Wright as Debating Opponent

Ultimately, the influence of Chauncey Wright on William James is not that of a master teaching a doctrine to a disciple; rather, it is the subtle influence of an amiable personality with great powers of analytical intellect with whom William James loved to spar in conversation, especially in the company of their mutual friends. During the period when William James was beginning to move into philosophy as a professional discipline, Wright, the scientific genius, provided James with a powerful logical and analytical debating opponent against whom he tried to defend the reasonableness of religion.

William James' Final Estimate of Wright

William James, in the conclusion of his notice in the *Nation* of Chauncey Wright's death, summed up his estimate of Wright:

> Mr. Wright belonged to the precious band of genuine philosophers, and among them few can have been as completely disinterested as he. Add to this eminence his tireless amiability, his beautiful modesty, his affectionate nature and freedom from egotism, his childlike simplicity in worldly affairs, and we have the picture of a character of which his friends feel more than ever now the elevation and the rarity.[35]

Notes

1 William James, *Collected Essays and Reviews*, p. 20.

2 Edward H. Madden, *Chauncey Wright and The Foundations of Pragmatism* (Seattle: University of Washington Press, 1963), p. 3f.

3 Madden, pp. 5f.

4 Madden, p. 8.

5 Madden, p. 8.

6 Madden, pp. 8f.

7 For a study of the introduction of Darwin's ideas in the United States, and their permeation of American culture, see Cynthia Eagle Russett, *Darwin in America: The Intellectual Response, 1865-1912* (San Francisco: W. H. Freedman & Co., 1976). Her excellent bibliographical essay, hidden under the title "Suggestion for Further Reading," is on pp. 221-224. For a more narrowly focused study of the introduction of Darwinian thought in America, see Philip P. Weiner, *Evolution and the Founders of Pragmatism* (New York: Harper and Row, Publishers, 1949; reprint ed., Harper Torch Books, 1965).

8 Madden, pp. 14-16.

9 Madden, p. 29.

10 Madden, pp. 29f, citing Thayer, *Letters of Chauncey Wright*, p. 320.

11 Madden, p. 30.

12 Allen, *William James*, p. 202.

13 Chauncey Wright, *Philosophical Discussions*, ed. with a biographical sketch of the author by Charles Eliot Norton (New York: Henry Holt and Company, 1877), p. vii.

14 Elizabeth Flower and Murray G. Murphey, *History of Philosophy in America* (New York: G. P. Putnam and Sons, 1977), 2:535-537.

15 *Philosophical Discussions*, pp. 35-42. (The article appeared in the *North American Review* for January 1865.)

16 *Philosophical Discussions*, p. 36. Cf., Flower and Murphey, 2:538.

17 *Philosophical Discussions*, p. 37.

18 *Philosophical Discussions*, pp. 39f.

19 *Philosophical Discussions*, p. 41.

20 *Philosophical Discussions*, p. 39.

21 *Philosophical Discussions*, p. 160.

22 *Collected Essays and Reviews*, p. 2.

23 Madden, p. 23.

24 Perry, 1:521.

25 William James, *Essays in Philosophy* (Cambridge, Mass.: Harvard University Press, 1978), p. 116.

26 Madden, p. 74.

27 Perry, 1:484.

28 Perry, 1:486.

29 Perry, 1:521.

30 William James, *The Principles of Psychology*, 2 vols. (New York: Henry Holt and Company, 1890; reprint ed., Cambridge, Mass.: Harvard University Press, 1983), Chapter XXII. Wright's article is cited on p. 982. That article is included in *Philosophical Discussions* (pp. 199-266).

31 Madden, p. 183.

32 Madden, p. 128.

33 James, *The Principles of Psychology*, p. 952.

34 James, *The Principles of Psychology*, p. 973.

35 *Collected Essays and Reviews*, p. 25.

Chapter IV

Charles Sanders Peirce

Peirce's Life

On Sunday afternoon, September 16, 1861, William James, who had just started at the Lawrence Scientific School of Harvard University, wrote to his family. At one point in the long letter he described one of his fellow students, Charles Sanders Peirce, whom he had just met. He said, "In last year's 'class' there is a son of Professor Peirce, whom I suspect to be a very smart fellow with a great deal of character, pretty independent and violent though." This first mention of Peirce marks the beginning of a friendship which extended for the rest of James' life, a friendship which had a significant influence on James' philosophy of religion and his position on the affirmation of God.

Charles Sanders Peirce (1839-1914) was an extraordinary genius in both science and philosophy. He has been described by one student of his work as "the most versatile, profound, and original philosopher that the United States has ever produced."[1]

Charles Sanders Peirce was born on September 10, 1839, in Cambridge, Massachusetts. His father, Benjamin Peirce, was a professor of mathematics and natural philosophy, and later of astronomy, at Harvard. He was among America's foremost scientists in the nineteenth century, a respected scholar and teacher. The influence of Benjamin on his son was profound but not altogether beneficial. On the one hand, he supervised his son's education, with emphasis on mathematics, philosophy, the experimental sciences, and logic. On the other hand, he seems to have forced the intellectual training of his son, and he neglected to provide a balanced education for the boy. Famous scientists and literary personalities were frequent visitors at the Peirce home, among them were Louis Agassiz, Asa Gray, Henry Wadsworth Longfellow,

Oliver Wendell Holmes, Ralph Waldo Emerson, and Margaret Fuller.

Benjamin Peirce was a theist and a Unitarian. Charles remained a theist throughout his life, but he became an Episcopalian.[2]

Charles entered Harvard when he was sixteen years of age. He completed his courses there without distinction, being seventy-first in the class of ninety graduates. He then entered the Lawrence Scientific School at Harvard, and, in 1863, he was the first person to receive the degree of Bachelor of Science in Chemistry from Harvard, *summa cum laude*. He then joined the United States Coast and Geodetic Survey, and he remained with that agency until 1891.

The Metaphysical Club

In the early 1870s, Peirce continued his work at the Harvard Observatory in the field of astronomy, and this led to the publication of the only book published during his lifetime, *Photometric Researches*, in 1878. In the late sixties or early seventies, Peirce began to meet with some of his friends to discuss philosophy. This may have been the result of a suggestion made by William James in 1868, when from Berlin he wrote to Oliver Wendell Homes, Jr.: "When I get home, let's establish a philosophical society to have regular meetings and discuss none but the very tallest broadest questions."[3] Peirce later described the group as follows:

> It was in the earliest seventies that a knot of us young men in Old Cambridge, calling ourselves, half-ironically, half-defiantly, "The Metaphysical Club" — for agnosticism was then riding its high horse, and was frowning superbly upon all metaphysics — used to meet, sometimes in my study, sometimes in that of William James . . . . (The club included Oliver Wendell Holmes, Jr., and Joseph Warner, a Harvard trained lawyer.) Nicholas St. John Green was one of the most interested fellows, a skillful lawyer and a learned one, a disciple of Jeremy Bentham. His extraordinary power of disrobing warm and breathing truth of the draperies of long worn formulas was what attracted attention to him everywhere. In particular, he often urged the importance of applying Bain's definition of belief as "that upon which a man is prepared to act." From this definition, pragmatism is scarce more than corollary; so that I am disposed to think of him as the grandfather of pragmatism. (Peirce then mentioned as other members of the club Chauncey Wright, John Fiske and Francis Ellingwood Abbot.)[4]

Peirce also described the Metaphysical Club in a letter of 1905 to his former student at Johns Hopkins, Christine Ladd Franklin (1847-1930):

> In the sixties I started a little club called the Metaphysical Club. It seldom if ever had more than a half dozen present. Wright was the strongest member and probably I was the next. Nicholas St. John Green was a marvelously strong intelligence. Then there was Frank Abbot, William James and others. It was there that the name and doctrine of pragmatism saw the light.[5]

In 1908, Peirce referred to the Metaphysical Club in an article. He tried to distinguish his form of pragmatism (which he called pragmaticism) from that of William James:

> In 1871, in a Metaphysical Club in Cambridge, Massachusetts, I used to preach this principle as a sort of logical gospel, representing the unformulated method followed by Berkeley, and in conversation about it I called it "pragmatism." ... Of course, the doctrine attracted no particular attention, for, as I had remarked in my opening sentence, very few people care for logic. But in 1897, Professor James remodelled the matter, and transmogrified it into a doctrine of philosophy, some parts of which I highly approved, while other and more prominent parts I regarded, and still regard, as opposed to sound logic.[6]

Philip Wiener, after studying the writings and letters of the members of Peirce's Metaphysical Club, had doubts as to the actual existence of the Club.[7] More recently, however, Max H. Fisch has examined the evidence anew and concluded that there really was such a club.[8] Whether or not one believes there was a formal club or merely a regular gathering of philosophically minded friends, it is clear that Peirce was in close contact with some of the most important philosophical thinkers in America during this period in his life. It was through these meetings that Peirce's friendship with William James developed, and that James became familiar with Peirce's thought.

Peirce at Johns Hopkins

In 1876, the Johns Hopkins University was founded in Baltimore, Maryland, with an endowment from Johns Hopkins, a Baltimore banker. Daniel Coit Gilman became the first president of the University, and he organized it as primarily a graduate school. Gilman appointed Peirce part-time lecturer in logic in 1879, and he reappointed Peirce annually for four more years. Then, in January 1884, Gilman abruptly dismissed Peirce from Hopkins. Bruce Kuklick comments: "No one knows why.... After 1884 he never held another scholarly post, and the notoriety of having been dismissed from Hopkins did much to destroy his chances in American academe."[9]

During his years at Johns Hopkins, Peirce was associated with a number of persons who later became prominent in American intellectual life, including Christine Ladd Franklin (1847-1930), John Dewey (1859-1952), and Thorstein Veblen (1857-1929).

In 1891, Peirce was asked to resign from the Coast and Geodetic Survey. He received a small inheritance on the death of his mother in 1887, and he moved to Milford, Pennsylvania. Despite some real estate speculation, he and his second wife were able to manage until the depression of 1893 brought him to bankruptcy. Peirce had to sell his land and, after 1905, he survived on the charitable donations of his friends. In 1907, William James helped to establish a fund which barely provided Peirce with enough money to live on. During the last years Peirce's philosophical work suffered. Without the regular stimulus of a teaching schedule, Peirce completed very little in the years after he left Hopkins. "Everything remained in the chaos of fragmentary manuscripts."[10]

Murray Murphey's Theory of Peirce's Philosophical Development

Recent studies of Peirce have attempted to arrange his work in chronological order, and to see a succession of philosophical positions in his writings. This approach was pioneered by Murray G. Murphey. His position is summarized in a recent article.[11]

According to this analysis, Peirce developed his first system between 1859 and 1861. That system is a form of extreme post-Kantian idealism. In 1862, Peirce began the serious study of logic and he began to use the works of the medieval scholastics, especially Duns Scotus (c. 1266-1308). This was a transitional period in which Peirce began to move away from Kant. In 1867, Peirce published a paper introducing his second system. The paper was entitled "On a New List of Categories." This second system also proved inadequate, and, by 1870, Peirce propounded his third system. This third system involved certain revisions in Peirce's theories of meaning and inquiry. The results of these revisions were published in six articles on the philosophy of science which appeared in 1877-1878 in *Popular Science Monthly*. It was during this period that Peirce was in the closest philosophical contact with William James, and several of these articles were influential in the development of James' philosophy of religion. Peirce was not satisfied with his third system, and by 1855 he began to attempt a radical reformulation of his position. His fourth system was based on new developments in logic and mathematics, especially the theory of quantification and Cantor's set theory. Peirce first presented this metaphysics in a series of articles in *The Monist* in 1891-1893. Peirce called his final system "Synechism," or the Philosophy of Continuity, and claimed that it was a new form of extreme scholastic realism.

This fourth system of Peirce was never completed. When he died, only the general outline of the system had been worked out, since Peirce saw that the structure would have to remain incomplete until he had been able to solve the problem of the logic of continuity.[12]

Peirce's Influence on William James

Since the purpose of this study is to explore the influences on William James which have helped to shape his philosophy of religion, and, in particular, his approach to the affirmation of God, it is not necessary to deal with developments in the systematic architectonics of Peirce's thought. It is necessary, however, to investigate the ways in which the work and conversation of Peirce were significant in the development of James' thought.

Peirce Helped to Free William James from Herbert Spencer

First of all, Peirce helped to free James from the influence of Herbert Spencer. The early period of William James' development was during the time of Spencer's greatest popularity. Spencer was the thinker who brought the general idea of evolution, together with the genetic and comparative method in science, to the minds of the reading public in England and the United States. At the time that William James began to read philosophy seriously in the 1860s, the writings of Spencer furnished the most important part of his early philosophical reading. James tells us that he first read

Spencer's *First Principles* in his youth, "when it was still appearing in numbers." Perry estimates that this would be between 1860 and 1862.[13] James wrote, in a notice of Spencer's death for the New York *Evening Post* in 1903:

> I read this book as a youth when it was still appearing in numbers, and was carried away with enthusiasm by the intellectual perspectives which it seemed to open. When a maturer companion, Mr. Charles Peirce, attacked it in my presence, I felt spiritually wounded, as by the defacement of a sacred image or picture, though I could not verbally defend it against his criticisms.[14]

James' disenchantment with Spencer's works grew until, by 1886, he was able to write: "How can an adult man spend his time in trying to torture an accurate meaning into Spencer's incoherent accidentalities? It is so much more easy to do the work over for oneself."[15]

By 1892, James had so far removed away from Spencer's thought that he was willing to help Peirce "stone Uncle Spencer." James expressed it in a verse.

> "'He left a Spencer's name to other times,
> Linked with one virtue and a thousand crimes.'
> The one virtue is his belief in the universality of evolution — the 1000 crimes are his 5000 pages of absolute incompetence to work it out in detail."[16]

Despite their finally negative judgments on the work of Spencer, both Peirce and James continued to have a grudging admiration for him. Peirce, in 1897, noted in an autobiographical paper that he had learned little from the evolutionary philosophers, but he added that, "however antiquated and ignorant Spencer's *First Principles* and general doctrines, yet they are under the guidance and influence of a great and true idea, and are developing it by methods that are in their main features sound and scientific."[17]

William James summed up his views on Herbert Spencer in 1904, when he reviewed Spencer's autobiography for *The Atlantic Monthly*. In a post card to Bliss Perry, the editor of *The Atlantic Monthly*, James said of his views: "I fear it will please Sp's enemies more than his disciples, but the last couple of pages will be very sympathetic."[18] In that review, James agreed with Peirce in paying homage to Spencer.

> To Spencer is certainly due the immense credit of having been the first to see in evolution an absolutely universal principle. If anyone else had grasped its universality, it failed at any rate to grasp him as it had grasped Spencer.[19]

In summary, it seems fair to say that, while Peirce helped to deliver William James from the spell of Herbert Spencer, Spencer continued to be a recurring figure in the dialogue between James and Peirce. In the words of Ralph Barton Perry, "Spencer served James in the role of a punching bag, and for many years he kept him in his intellectual gymnasium!"[20]

Peirce's Idea of Pragmatism as a Key to Philosophical Method

A second way in which Charles Sanders Peirce influenced the development of William James' philosophy of religion and, in particular, his approach to the affirmation of God, was in his introducing the idea of pragmatism as a key to philosophic method. In 1898, in an address delivered before the Philosophical Union of the University of California, James credited Peirce with effecting this development twenty years earlier.[21]

James wrote that he would try to define what seemed to him to be the most likely direction in which to start upon the trail of truth. He said that the clue or compass to this direction had been given to him years ago by Peirce, who had called it the principle of pragmatism.[22] James wrote:

> Peirce's principle, as we may call it may be expressed in a variety of ways, all of them very simple. In *Popular Science Monthly* for January 1878, he introduces it as follows: The soul and meaning of thought, he says, can never be made to direct itself towards anything but the production of belief, belief being the demicadence which closes a musical phrase in the symphony of our intellectual life. Thought in movement has thus for its only possible motive the attainment of thought at rest. But when our thought about an object has found its rest in belief, then our action on the subject can firmly and safely begin. Beliefs, in short, are really rules for action; and the whole function of thinking is but one step in the production of habits of action. If there were any part of a thought that made no difference in the thought's practical consequences, then that part would be no proper element of the thought's significance.... Thus to develop a thought's meaning we need only determine what conduct it is fitted to produce; that conduct is for us its sole significance.[23]

After expressing Peirce's principle of pragmatism, James expressed his belief that the principle should be expressed more broadly than Mr. Peirce expressed it. James said:

> The ultimate test for us of what a truth means is indeed the conduct it dictates or inspires. But it inspires that conduct because it at first foretells some

particular turn to our experience which shall call for just that conduct from us.... The effective meaning of any philosophical position can always be brought down to some particular consequence....[24]

James was convinced that to understand the importance of the pragmatic principle one would have to get accustomed to applying it to concrete cases. He provided an example of this:

Suppose there are two different philosophical definitions, or propositions, or maxims, or what not, which seem to contradict each other, and about which men dispute. If, by supposing the truth of the one, you can foresee no conceivable practical consequence to anybody at that time or place, which is different from what you would foresee if you supposed the truth of the other, why then the difference between the two positions is no difference, — it is only a specious and verbal difference, unworthy of further contention. Both formulas mean radically the same thing, although they may say it in such different words.[25]

After stating the principle of pragmatism as conceived by Peirce, James then illustrated that principle by applying it to the controversy over the existence of God. James stated the question in terms of the principle of pragmatism as follows:

If there be a God, it is not likely that he is confined solely to making differences in the world's latter end; he probably makes differences all along its course. Now the principle of practicalism says that the very meaning of the conception of God lies in those differences which must be made in our experience if the conception be true.[26]

James tests this formulation of the principle by applying it to the inventory of the perfections of God as elaborated by dogmatic theology. According to the principle, these statements of God's perfections either mean nothing, or they imply certain definite things in our feelings and actions, things which we would not feel or do were there no God. For example, God is:

... a being existing not only *per se*, or by himself, as created beings exist, but *a se* or from himself; and out of this *"aseity"* flow most of his perfections. He is, for example, necessary; absolute; infinite in all respects; and single.... Now in which one of us pratical Americans here assembled does this conglomeration of attributes awaken any sense of reality? And if in no one, then why not? Surely because such attributes awaken no responsive active feelings and call for no particular conduct of our own.... The attributes which I have quoted have absolutely nothing to do with religion, for religion is a living practical affair. Other parts, indeed, of God's traditional description do have practical connection with life, and have owed all their historic importance to that fact. His omniscience, for example, and his justice. With the one he sees us in the dark, with the other he rewards and punishes what he sees.[27]

The address just quoted was given in 1898. Later, in his Lowell Lectures, William James commented that

> Peirce's principle of pragmatism lay entirely unnoticed by anyone for twenty years until I, in an address before Howison's Philosophical Union at the University of California, brought it forward again and made a special application of it to religion. By that date the times seemed ripe for its reception.[28]

James pointed out that many philosophical disputes collapse into insignificance the moment they are subjected to the simple test of tracing a concrete consequence.

> There can *be* no difference anywhere that doesn't *make* a difference elsewhere — no difference in abstract truth that doesn't express itself in a difference in concrete fact and in conduct consequent upon that fact, imposed on somebody, somehow, somewhere and somewhen. The whole function of philosophy ought to be to find out what definite difference it will make to you and me, at definite instants of our life if this world-formula or that world-formula be the true one.[29]

Affinity Between Peirce's Philosophy and William James' "Will to Believe"

It seems clear, therefore, that the principle of pragmatism of Charles Sanders Peirce provided a stimulus for the philosophy of religion of William James. In addition, it would seem that an affinity can now be seen to exist between the epistemology and metaphysics of Peirce and the "will to believe" of William James.[30]

William Gavin has pointed out that, for James, one has a right to believe in a hypothesis when the situation is unsolvable, yet forced, living, and momentous.

> Going further, James' metaphysics of "pure experience" involves more than just theoretical knowledge. He held the position that the human being is capable of experiencing dimensions of reality not completely reducible to the knowable, in the strong sense of that term. "Pure experience" is not an objective ground which can be demonstrated with certainty. In this sense, Jamesian metaphysics demands an element of "commitment."
>
> In this paper I want to suggest that these same elements, the affective and/or the will to believe play an important role in Peirce's position.[31]

Gavin indicated that Peirce added to his understanding of pragmatism an element of conviction or commitment.

In addition, Peirce's pragmatism is not metaphysically neutral; it is to be associated with a metaphysical stance of scholastic realism, a realism which advocates the reality of universal ideas.[32] It is only by employing an epistemological method which allows for the reality of general ideas that Peirce can say that we are subject to constraint by a reality which exhibits independence in some sense.[33] When the members of a scientific community are slowly and correctly arriving at a shared belief, Peirce held that the members of that community are driven by a "cheerful hope" that their investigations would ultimately terminate in truth, if only they utilized the method of pragmatism. Pragmatism was seen as the required method because it is self-criticizing. The proof of the method involves an application of the method. This method avoids the possibility of scientific investigations "fixing by convention" what the truth would be. The pragmatic method forces individuals to be constrained by experience, by independent real beings. In taking this position, Peirce made an act of faith in the scientific method. Gavin holds that "in the last analysis, Peirce's 'cheerful hope' involves a Jamesian 'will to believe' in a *situation* that is forced, living, and momentous."[34]

It seems clear, therefore, that there is an intrinsic similarity between Peirce's pragmatic epistemology and William James' "will to believe." Since Peirce began his work in this area before James, it is most probable that it was Peirce who influenced James. In addition, the possibility of a mutual influence of Peirce and James on each other would seem likely in the development of their understanding of the principle of pragmatism.[35]

In exploring the various ways in which Charles Sanders Peirce influenced William James in the development of his philosophy of religion and, in particular, in his approach to the affirmation of God, it is necessary to note that Peirce, like James, was interested in the nature of doubt and belief. As early as 1868, both Peirce and James were interested in the problem of belief in God. It was largely on account of this shared concern that James found Peirce interesting and relevant.[36]

Peirce's "Neglected Argument" for the Reality of God

Peirce's interest in the reality of God continued through his lifetime. Toward the end of his life he published "A Neglected Argument for the Reality of God."[37] This argument is worth considering in some detail in this dissertation because of its similarities to James' argument in *The Varieties of Religious Experience*. James' argument will be considered in PART TWO of this study. It is not clear whether Peirce influenced James' argument or James influenced Peirce's argument. Perhaps some form of mutual influence could be seen here.

In the article, Peirce began by defining the word "God." "The word 'God' so 'capitalized' (as we Americans say), is *the* definable proper name, signifying *Ens necessarium*; in my belief really creator of all three universes of experience."[38]

Peirce explains what these three universes of experience are. The first universe "comprises all mere Ideas, those airy nothings to which the mind of poet, pure mathematician, or another *might* give local habitation and a name within that mind."[39] Peirce calls the second universe that of the brute actuality of things and facts. ". . . the third universe comprises everything whose being consists in active power to establish connections between different objects in different universes. Such is everything which is essentially a Sign."[40]

Peirce then defines "arguments" as "any process of thought reasonably tending to produce a definite belief."[41] Peirce then commends:

> If God really be, and be benign, then in view of the generally conceded truth that religion, were it but proved, would be a good outweighing all others, we should naturally expect that there would be some argument for his reality that should be obvious to all minds, high and low alike, that should earnestly strive to find the truth of the matter; and further, that this argument should present its conclusion, not as a proposition of metaphysical theology, but in a form directly applicable to the conduct of life, and full of nutrition for man's highest growth. What I shall refer to as the N.A. — the Neglected Argument — seems to me best to fulfill this condition. . . . [42]

Peirce then begins to describe this "Neglected Argument." The first step in the argument is "a certain agreeable occupation of mind" which one might call reverie, if one removes from that word any connotation of vacancy and dreaminess. When this reverie considers some wonder in one of the universes, Peirce calls it "musement." It is this which may in time flower into the "Neglected Argument."[43] At first, this musement may involve psychological speculations, but these speculations will naturally lead on to musings upon metaphysical problems proper. Some of these problems can be solved by logical analysis; other problems will involve "universe-wide aggregates of unformulated but partly experienced phenomena."[44] The Muser should not be too impatient to analyze these, but should ponder them from every point of view "until he seems to read some truth beneath the phenomena."[45]

The first step in an examination of the truth of one's interpretation must be a logical analysis of the theory. From speculations on the homogeneities of each universe, for example on the phenomena of growth, which consists in the homogeneities of small parts, one enters into certain lines of reflection which "inevitably suggest the hypothesis of God's Reality."[46]

This hypothesis is not a substitute for the explanations of the physical sciences, which remain necessary. Such explanations, however, are insufficient. Peirce holds that:

> . . . in the Pure Play of Musement the idea of God's Reality will be sure sooner or later to be found an attractive fancy, which the Muser will develop in various ways. The more he ponders it, the more it will find response in every part of the mind, for its beauty, for its supplying an ideal of life, for its thoroughly satisfactory explanation of his whole threefold environment.[47]

This hypothesis of God, Peirce holds, is a peculiar one, in that it supposes an infinitely incomprehensible object. Peirce contrasts such a hypothesis with Zeno's argument about Achilles and the tortoise,[48] which he describes as "nothing but a contemptible catch."[49] Peirce, on the contrary, holds that:

> . . . any normal man who considers the three universes in the light of the hypothesis of God's Reality, and pursues that line of reflection in scientific singleness of heart, will come to be stirred to the depths of his nature by the beauty of the idea and by its august practicality, even to the point of earnestly loving and adoring his strictly hypothetical God, and to that of desiring above all things to shape the whole conduct of life and all the springs of action into conformity with that hypothesis. Now to be deliberately and thoroughly prepared to shape one's conduct into conformity with a proposition is neither more nor less than the state of mind called Believing that proposition, however long the conscious classification of it under that head be postponed.[50]

After giving this sketch of what he calls the "Neglected Argument," Peirce shows its roots in the principle of pragmatism or, rather, pragmaticism. He points out that it is the course of meditation upon the three Universes which gives birth to the hypothesis of God's Reality and ultimately to the belief that these Universes have a Creator independent of them.[51] For Peirce, pragmatism meant believing in God.[52]

Peirce's argument for the Reality of God is based on the effort to see himself as part of the universal cosmos. The same effort made of him a scientific man and fashioned him into a contemplative and religious man. The reason is that he did not take a narrow view of science but tried to open himself to an awareness of all the dimensions of human experience. Where some scientific thinkers had tried to set limits on the methods that science may use, Peirce advocated a return to the data of concrete experience. "He asks man to open his eyes, and also his heart — for it, too, is a perceptive organ — and to be awake to what is within and without."[53]

Peirce was interested in the macrocosm and admired the vast vault of the stars and planets. That interest in the macrocosm however was complimented by his fascination with the tiniest elements of the microcosm. Reflecting on the animal world, he saw in man the culmination and perfection of the harmony of nature. The process of evolution was the unifying element relating the macrocosm and the microcosm. From a consideration of this, Peirce concluded that the idea of God's reality would ultimately be found to be an attractive hypothesis. The more one ponders that hypothesis, the more it will appear as a satisfactory explanation of the world.[54]

The strength of this argument consists in the fact that there is in human nature a tendency toward belief in God, and this belief is the natural result of contemplating the universe. Belief in God is a fundamental ingredient of the soul. In Peirce's mind, without God the world would be ultimately unintelligible.[55]

Peirce's thought is that of a religious man and his thought was developed out of his own religious experience.[56] This gave him a firm basis for his belief in God. He wrote:

> When a man has that experience with which religion sets out, he has as good reason — putting aside metaphysical subtilties [sic] — to believe in the living

personality of God as he has to believe in his own. Indeed *belief* is a word inappropriate to such direct perception.[57]

On the basis of such an affirmation of God, religion becomes more than a mere belief: "Religion is a life, and can be identified with a belief only provided that belief be a living belief — a thing to be lived rather than said or thought."[58]

It is clear that Peirce's idea of the experiential basis of religion is very similar to the views of William James, especially in his *Varieties of Religious Experience*. Is this another way in which Peirce may be seen as an influence on James? It would be very difficult to determine whether Peirce influenced James or James influenced Peirce in this regard. Their familiarity with one another's work and their conversations, beginning in the 1870s, seem to indicate a mutual influence in their ideals of the religious life.

William James' Appreciation of Peirce

When William James published his first philosophical book, *The Will to Believe*, he acknowledged the influence of Peirce on his thought. In the dedication of the book, James expressed a general indebtedness to Peirce. His words may appropriately be used to conclude this chapter on Peirce's influence in the development of James' philosophical approach to the affirmation of God. James wrote:

> To
> My Old Friend,
> Charles Sanders Peirce,
> To whose philosophic comradeship in old
> times and to whose writings in more recent years I owe more incitement and
> help than I can express or repay.

Notes

1. Philip P. Wiener, ed., *Charles S. Peirce: Selected Writings (Values in a Universe of Chance)* (Garden City, N.Y.: Doubleday and Company, Inc., 1958; reprint ed., New York: Dover Publications, Inc., 1966), p. vii.

2. Francis E. Reilly, S.J., *Charles Peirce's Theory of Scientific Method* (New York: Fordham University Press, 1970), pp. 3, 158.

3. Bruce Kuklick, *The Rise of American Philosophy: Cambridge, Massachusetts, 1860-1930* (New Haven and London: Yale University Press, 1977), p. 47.

4. Charles Sanders Peirce, *Collected Papers of Charles Sanders Peirce*, vols. 1-6, ed. Charles Hartshorne and Paul Weiss (Cambridge: Harvard University Press, 1931, 1932, 1933, 1935); vols. 7-8, ed. Arthur Burks (Cambridge: Harvard University Press, 1958) (henceforth cited as *CP* with the indication of the volume and the paragraph number), 5.12.

5. Philip P. Wiener, *Evolution and the Founders of Pragmatism* (Cambridge: Harvard University Press, 1949; reprint ed., New York: Harper and Row Publishers, Inc., 1965), p. 20.

6. Charles Sanders Peirce, "A Neglected Argument for the Reality of God," in *CP*, 6.482.

7. Wiener, *Evolution and the Founders of Pragmatism*, pp. 24f.

8. Max H. Fisch, "Was There a Metaphysical Club in Cambridge?" in *Studies in the Philosophy of Charles Sanders Peirce*, 2nd series, ed. Edward C. Moore and Richard S. Robin (Amherst: University of Massachusetts Press, 1964), pp. 3-32.

9. Kuklick, *The Rise of American Philosophy*, p. 123.

10. Kuklick, *The Rise of American Philosophy*, p. 123.

11. *The Encyclopedia of Philosophy*, s.v. "Peirce, Charles Sanders" by Murray G. Murphey. See also the chapter on Peirce in the *History of American Philosophy* by Flower and Murphey, 2:567-631.

12. Flower and Murphey, *History of Philosophy*, 2:620.

13. Perry, 1:474.

14. William James, *Essays in Philosophy*, p. 116.

15 *Letters*, 1:254.

16 Perry, 1:475.

17 Peirce, "Concerning the Author," in *CP*, 1.5.

18 William James, *Essays in Philosophy*, p. 263.

19 William James, *Essays in Philosophy*, p. 114.

20 Perry, 1:475.

21 William James, "Philosophical Concepts and Practical Results," in *Collected Essays and Review*, pp. 406-437. The address was reprinted in *The University Chronicle* (Berkeley, Calif.), September 1898. It was reprinted with slight verbal revision, and with the omission of the first three pages and the concluding paragraph in *Journal of Philosophy, Psychology and Scientific Methods* 8 (December 1908): 673-687, under the title "The Pragmatic Method." In that form the essay is reprinted in James, *Essays in Philosophy*, pp. 123-139. Part of the essay was used in *The Varieties of Religious Experience* (1902), and in *Pragmatism* (1907). This article is seen as the beginning of the pragmatist movement.

22 James, *Collected Essays and Reviews*, p. 410.

23 James, *Collected Essays and Reviews*, pp. 410f. Peirce's article, "How to Make Our Ideas Clear," is in *CP*, 5.398-410. The passage paraphrased by James is at *CP*, 5.396. For a later statement of Peirce on the meaning of pragmatism, which Thayer describes as "the clearest and most complete single statement of what pragmatism is that Peirce ever wrote," see *CP*, 8.191. See H. S. Thayer, *Meaning and Action: A Critical History of Pragmatism*, 2nd ed. (Indianapolis: Hackett Publishing Co., 1981), pp. 493-495.

24 *Collected Essays and Reviews*, p. 412.

25 *Collected Essays and Reviews*, pp. 412f.

26 *Collected Essays and Reviews*, p. 424.

27 *Collected Essays and Reviews*, pp. 424-426.

28 William James, *Pragmatism: A New Name for Some Old Ways of Thinking* (New York and London: Longmans, Green and Co., 1970; reprinted, Cambridge: Harvard University Press, 1978), p. 29. The Lowell Lectures were delivered in Boston in 1906, and at Columbia University in New York in 1907.

29 *Pragmatism*, p. 30.

30 Cf., William J. Gavin, "Peirce and 'The Will to Believe,'" *The Monist* 63 (July 1980): 342-349. This entire number of *The Monist* is devoted to "The Rele-

vance of Charles Peirce." (Gavin's article will be cited as Gavin, "The Will to Believe.")

31 Gavin, "The Will to Believe," p. 342.

32 Gavin, "The Will to Believe," p. 343.

33 Gavin, "The Will to Believe," p. 344.

34 Gavin, "The Will to Believe," pp. 345-346.

35 For a detailed comparison of Peirce and James in their understanding of pragmatism see: Justus Buchler, *Charles Peirce's Empiricism* (London: Kegan Paul, Trench, Trubner & Co., Ltd., 1939; reprint ed., New York: Octagon Books, 1980), pp. 166-174.

36 Perry, 1:542.

37 *CP*, 6.452-493.

38 *CP*, 6.452.

39 *CP*, 6.455.

40 *CP*, 6.455.

41 *CP*, 6.456.

42 *CP*, 6.457.

43 *CP*, 6.458.

44 *CP*, 6.463.

45 *CP*, 6.463.

46 *CP*, 6.465.

47 *CP*, 6.465.

48 Zeno of Elea (born c. 490 B.C.) is well known as the author of several ingenious arguments such as the riddle of Achilles and the Tortoise to prove the impossibility of motion. Zeno's arguments on the subject of motion have been preserved by Aristotle. The argument of Achilles is as follows: Achilles will never overtake the tortoise. He must first reach the place from which the tortoise started. By that time the tortoise will have got some way ahead. Achilles must make up that, and again the tortoise will be ahead. He is always coming nearer but he never makes up to it. See John Burnet, *Early Greek Philosophy*, 4th ed. (Cleveland and New York: The World Publishing Co., 1969), p. 318. The reference is to Aristotle's Physics, Z, 9 (239 b 11).

49 *CP*, 6.467.

50 *CP*, 6.467.

51 *CP*, 6.483. For a good treatment of this argument for the Reality of God, see James K. Feibleman, *An Introduction to the Philosophy of Charles S. Peirce* (Cambridge, Mass.: The M.I.T. Press, 1970), pp. 422-425.

52 Feibleman, *Introduction*, p. 420.

53 Robert J. Roth, *American Religious Philosophy* (New York: Harcourt, Brace and World, Inc., 1967), p. 70.

54 *CP*, 6.465.

55 Roth, *American Religious Philosophy*, p. 71.

56 *CP*, 6.435.

57 *CP*, 6.436.

58 *CP*, 6.439.

Chapter V

Josiah Royce

Life

Josiah Royce (1855-1916) was a close friend and protege of William James and their philosophical dialogues were helpful to James in the development of his approach to the affirmation of God.

At a dinner in his honor, at the Walton Hotel in Philadelphia on December 29, 1915, Royce gave a brief address which was largely autobiographical in character. He said: "I was born in 1855 in California. My native town was a mining town in the Sierra Nevada, a place five or six years older than myself."[1] The small town was Grass Valley, and his parents had arrived there as "forty-niners."[2]

In 1875, at the age of nineteen Royce was awarded the degree of Bachelor of Arts at the University of California. The president of the University of California (1872-1875) was Daniel Coit Gilman (1831-1908). At his urging, a group of San Francisco businessmen set up a fund to support Royce's post-graduate studies in Germany.[3]

After some language study at Heidelberg, Royce registered at the University of Leipzig for courses with Wilhelm Wundt and Wilhelm Windelband. In April 1876, he left Leipzig and enrolled at the Georg-Augusts University in Göttingen where his principal professor was Rudolf Lotze. In the meantime, Daniel Coit Gilman had become President of the new Johns Hopkins University in Baltimore, and he offered Royce a fellowship for graduate studies in philosophy. The fellowship involved teaching a course each semester, and Royce taught courses on Schopenhauer, the "Return to Kant," Spinoza, and German Romanticism. It was at Johns Hopkins that Royce met William James, who was lecturing there.

Royce's First Meeting with William James

At a dinner held at William James' house in 1910, Royce told of his first meeting with James:

> My real acquaintance with our host began one summer day in 1877 when I first visited him in the house on Quincy Street, and was permitted to pour out my soul to somebody who really seemed to believe that a young man might rightfully devote his life to philosophy if he chose. I was then a student at the Johns Hopkins University.[4]

Royce received his Ph.D. degree at Hopkins in 1878. He was unable to obtain a position teaching philosophy and, reluctantly, he accepted an instructorship in English at the University of California. There, under the direction of Edward Rowland Sill (1841-1887), he would teach elementary courses in composition and literature. His annual salary would be $1200.

Royce's Call for Help from California

Despite the fact that he would have an opportunity to teach an occasional course in philosophy, Royce was burdened by a sense of isolation in California. On January 14, 1879, in a letter to William James, he described the barrenness of his situation:

> There is no philosophy in California from Siskiyou to Ft. Yuma, and from the Golden Gate to the summit of the Sierras there could not be found brains enough (to) accomplish the formation of a single respectable idea that was not a manifest plagiarism. Hence the atmosphere for the study of metaphysics is bad. And I wish I were out of it.[5]

James responded sympathetically to his young friend:

> Your letter was most welcome. I had often found myself wondering how you were getting on, and your wail as the solitary philosopher between Behrings' Strait and Tierra del Fuego has a grand lonesome picturesqueness about it. But recollect your extreme youth and the fact that you are making a living and practicing yourself in the pedagogic art, Uberhaupt.[6]

William James Arranges for Royce to Come to Harvard

In 1878, Royce met Katharine Head, a student at the University of California. Kitty was the daughter of Edward Head, a prominent San Francisco lawyer and judge. Josiah and Kitty were engaged by January 1880, and they were married on October 2,

1880. William James continued his efforts to find a way to get Royce to Harvard. The opportunity came when James decided to take a one year leave of absence at half pay, and he had to find a substitute to do his work for the remaining half-salary of $1200. On April 23, 1882, James wrote to Royce to ask whether Royce would be interested enough to drop his permanent appointment at Berkeley and come to Cambridge for $1200 without a guarantee of anything beyond the one year. James encouraged Royce to take the risk, since the person on the scene would have the inside track for a permanent position upon the expected retirement of Professor Francis Bowen (1811-1890). (That retirement in fact did not take place until 1889.) Royce wasted no time in telegraphing his affirmative reply to the offer. On May 2, 1882, he wrote to James:

> I am very willing to run risks and make sacrifices to get a permanent foothold East. Even if they offered me something definite here, I should regard an egg in Cambridge as worth more than a brood of chickens here.[7]

Writing to Daniel Coit Gilman on July 12, 1882, Royce said:

> The position is surely a very modest one, but I feel very glad of it, for it means a chance, for a time at least, to live in a studious community and to do my own work. What becomes of me and my family after the end of the year does not appear but I am very willing to take risks in a good cause.[8]

Royce made the trip East with his wife and their infant son. When Professor George H. Palmer (1842-1933) took a leave from Harvard the following year, Royce's appointment was renewed. He was able to remain at Harvard for a third year only by accepting part-time work in the English department. In 1885, when he published his first major treatise, *The Religious Aspect of Philosophy*, Royce received a five year appointment as assistant professor. Five years later, under the pressure of an offer to Royce from Stanford University, Harvard promised him an early promotion, and in 1892 named him Professor of the History of Philosophy.

In 1889 Royce was encouraged to present a series of public lectures on some prominent thinkers. This led to the publication of *The Spirit of Modern Philosophy* in 1892. In 1894 Royce received an invitation from George Holmes Howison (1834-1916) to lecture at the University of California during the summer of 1895. The lecture was entitled "The Conception of God." The lecture was then published, with comments by S. E. Mezes, J. LeConte, and G. H. Howison, in 1895. A second edition, with a supplementary essay by Royce, appeared in 1897.

In that same summer of 1897, Royce was invited to deliver the Gifford Lectures at the University of Aberdeen in 1899 and 1900. Royce appreciated the importance of the invitation. He described the lectures in a letter to Mary Dorr on August 7, 1898, as follows: "They are, or ought to be, in a purely technical or academic sense the effort of my life. . . . This trust concerning a very sacred task has been put upon me; and now I must live up to it."[9]

Royce's Gifford lectures were published as *The World and the Individual*. In commenting on this comprehensive statement of Royce's philosophical system, John Clendenning said that Royce "had, quite indisputably, earned a permanent place in the history of philosophy."[10]

Royce's Poor Health and Death

After interrupting his studies for a time after the death of his son, Royce began work again, but in February of 1912, he suffered a stroke. The illness was a slight one, however, and Royce continued his writing. Clendenning notes that: "Incredible though it may seem, Royce — fifty-seven years old and recovering from apoplexy — produced *The Problem of Christianity* in less than a year."[11]

Royce was deeply moved emotionally by the beginning of the First World War. When a German U-boat sank the steamship Lusitania, Royce abandoned nonpartisanship and described the war as a struggle between Germany and humanity. John Clendenning observed that,

> . . . from this time until his death sixteen months later, the conflict became his daily obsession. His physical deterioration was rapid, and his early death was supposed by many to have been hastened by the torment that the war caused him.[12]

After a short period of confinement to bed, Royce died on September 14, 1916.

Royce's Intellectual Development

Frank M. Oppenheim, S.J., of Xavier University, Cincinnati, has been described as "The man at the center of the contemporary

Royce community."[13] Father Oppenheim has recently published a book on Royce's intellectual development[14] which views the growth of Royce's thought under the influence of three profound insights. These insights occurred in the pivotal years of 1883, 1896, and 1912. A brief review of that development will prepare the way for an understanding of Royce's influence on William James' philosophy of religion, and in particular, of his affirmation of God.

At California, Royce was influenced philosophically by two of his professors, Joseph LeConte (1823-1901), a physician and professor of geology, and Edward Rowland Sill (1841-1887), Royce's English teacher. In addition, Royce began to read John Stuart Mill (1806-1873) and Herbert Spencer (1820-1903), the most popular English philosophers. Royce later said, "I became through (John Stuart) Mill's influence a decidedly skeptical empiricist."[15]

After graduating from Berkeley, Royce continued his study of philosophy in Germany for one year and at Johns Hopkins for two years. Royce's doctoral dissertation at Johns Hopkins was entitled "Of the Interdependence of the Principles of Knowledge, an Investigation of the Problems of Elementary Epistemology, in Two Chapters, with an Introduction on the Principal Ideas and Problems in Which the Discussion Takes Its Rise."[16] The dissertation dealt with what we do when we make true judgments. Royce continued his investigations of the problem of knowledge and, in 1883, he broke through to his fundamental religious insight: that is, that there is One Thought and it is infinite, and all truth is known to that Infinite Thought. That Infinite is greater than humanity, and truly to serve humanity is to serve this infinite.[17] He later wrote that by the time he was working on his *Religious Aspect of Philosophy*, "I had definitely passed over from my earlier skeptical position to the constructive idealism that I have ever since endeavoured to work out...."[18]

Royce's "religious insight" was based on his reflections about the possibility of logical, ethical, and religious error. In Chapter XI of *The Religious Aspect of Philosophy*, Royce held that "the conditions that determine the logical possibility of error must themselves be absolute truth."[19]

Royce's second maximal insight was achieved in 1896 under the influence of F. H. Bradley and G. H. Howison who "jarred Royce into taking individuals seriously and into preserving human individuals from being absorbed by the Absolute."[20] The fruit of this second insight emerged in Royce's book *The World and the Individual* and in his study *The Philosophy of Loyalty* (1908).

Royce was conscious that the philosophy of religion embraced more than the study of the argument from design in the light of modern science and more than the description of the religious experience of humanity. For Royce, in *The World and the Individual*, the central problem is the question: What is reality?[21]

In *The Philosophy of Loyalty*[22] Royce attempted to deal with some of the principles of ethics. In response to the modern revolt against moral traditions, Royce was intent on finding "the true meaning that was latent in old traditions."[23]

Royce's third maximal insight was achieved in 1912, under the influence of C. S. Peirce, and after a study of the letters of St. Paul. The result of this achievement was his book *The Problem of Christianity*.[24] In this book, the idea of Spirit moved to a central place in Royce's thought. He saw the Spirit as a living bond between the individual and the community, and as the Great Interpreter who mediates between the individuals and the communities in which they participate.[25]

In summary, then, the work of Royce may be seen as a development beginning from his religious insight into the reality of God. He then worked out a philosophy of loyalty. With loyalty as the basis of his ethics, Royce was able to safeguard individuality and ultimately to acknowledge the idea of community as the integrating idea in his philosophy and in his religion. A study of the development of Royce's thought seems to show the ideas of Community, Individuality and Spirit working within a process and taking shape progressively. Thus there is a unity in Royce's thought which did not stifle his creativity but rather allowed him to say: "I myself have spent my life in revising my opinions."[26]

Royce's *The Religious Aspect of Philosophy*

William James' Review of the Work on Its Publication (1885)

The beginning of the relationship between William James and Josiah Royce was the interest that the young Harvard assistant professor showed in the promising graduate student at Johns Hopkins University. However, by the time that Royce published *The*

Religous Aspect of Philosophy, the relationship had become that of friendly neighbors, university colleagues, and partners in a continuing philosophical dialogue. The evidence of the beginnings of this dialogue can be seen in James' review of Royce's *The Religious Aspect of Philosophy*.[27] In the review, James gave high praise to the work. He said:

> And here again, from the very depths of the desert of skepticism, the flower of moral faith is found to bloom. Everything in Dr. Royce is radical. There is nothing to remind one of the dreary fighting of each step of a slow retreat to which the theistic philosophers of the ordinary commonsense school have accustomed us. For this reason the work must carry a true *sursum corda* into the minds of those who feel in their bones that man's religious interests must be able to swallow and digest and grow fat upon all the facts and theories of modern science, but who yet have not the capacity to see with their own eyes how it may be done.... California may feel proud that a son of hers should at a stroke have scored so many points in a game not yet exceedingly familiar on the Pacific slope.[28]

Later Praise from William James

James also praised *The Religious Aspect of Philosophy* in *The Principles of Psychology*. James described Chapters IX and X of Royce's work as "on the whole the clearest account of the psychology of belief with which I am acquainted."[29] Royce himself saw Chapter XI as the central theory and insight of the book, and the argument of that chapter continued to hold his allegiance.[30]

James was not satisfied with Royce's argument, since it implied a philosophy of monism. At the same time, however, he was not able to devise a logical argument to refute Royce's argument.

In 1887 he described the book to Carl Stumpf as

> ... a new argument for monistic idealism, an argument based on the possibility of truth and error in knowledge, subtle in itself, and rather lengthily expounded, but seeming to me to be one of the few big original suggestions of recent philosophical writing. I have vainly tried to escape from it. I still suspect it of inconclusiveness, but I frankly confess that I am unable to overthrow it.[31]

In a letter to Renouvier a year later, James indicated that he still accepted the argument. He wrote:

> To go straight to the point, either I have misunderstood you, or you have failed to grasp the full force of his argument from "error" for an absolute mind. I believe the latter; for I find that very few persons grasp it, and I

> myself should not have grasped the depth and importance of it without many an oral discussion with Royce himself — who, by the way, is a regular little Socrates....[32]

Finally, under the influence of Professor D. S. Miller, James found an answer to Royce's argument.[33]

It seems clear, then, that Royce's *The Religious Aspect of Philosophy* played an important role in the development of James' approach to God, and that the book deserves a closer look.

The Argument of *The Religious Aspect of Philosophy*

The work grew out of lectures on religious questions which Royce delivered to the students of Harvard College. It sketches the basis of a system of philosophy, and it applies the principles of that system to religious problems. Royce acknowledged that he chose religious problems for the study because they first "drove the author to philosophy, and because they, of all human interests, deserve our best efforts and our utmost loyalty."[34]

In propounding his doctrine of philosophic idealism, Royce used a method of universal doubt as a necessary element for his philosophic reflections. He considered that the doubts of the time were not to be "refuted" in an old-fashioned apologetic style. He held that doubts, taken as such, will upon analysis be found to contain and imply a positive religious creed and an ethical system.[35]

Royce used this method of universal doubt in an attempt to establish religion as a moral code and as a theory. What was his conception of religion? First of all, religion has to do with moral action. Religion is impossible without some appearance of moral purpose, and all religions teach right conduct. Religion, however, "gives us more than a moral code.... A religion adds something to the moral code. And what it adds is, first, 'enthusiasm.' ... A religion not only commands the faithful, but gives them something that they are glad to live for, and if need be to die for."[36]

Religion has another element which makes it especially interesting to a student of philosophy. As a means of teaching devotion to a moral code, religion includes a more or less complete theory of things. "Religion says not merely *do and feel*, but also *believe*."[37]

With this understanding of religion, it is easy to see that philosophy must be concerned about the problems of religion. "Kant's fundamental problems: What do I know? What ought I to do? are of religious interest no less than of philosophic interest."[38]

Royce thought that one could not be considered as a sincere thinker if one should undertake to pay attention to philosophy but to neglect these religious problems on the ground that there is no time for them. "Surely he has time to be not merely a student of philosophy but also a man, and these things are among the essentials of humanity...."[39]

The method Royce chose to develop his religious philosophy was the method of doubt.

> The skeptical method is not only a good, but also a necessary beginning of religious philosophy. Doubt is a duty for the religious philosopher and it has a curious and very valuable place in philosophy. Philosophic truth, as such, comes to us first under the form of doubt; ... First, then, the despair of a thorough-going doubt, and then the discovery that this doubt contains in its bosom the truth that we are sworn to discover, however we can, — this is the typical philosophic experience.[40]

Royce uses the method of doubt to deal with the ethical problem. Book One of *The Religious Aspect of Philosophy* is entitled "The Search for a Moral Ideal." The culmination of this effort to attain moral truth by way of universal skepticism is found in Chapter VI: "The Moral Insight." Absolute ethical skepticism was seen by Royce to lie in "the neutrality that would result from a provisional acceptance of all the conflicting aims in the world of action."[41]

The way of achieving the moral insight is to consider the world of ends. This world of ends should be considered not in detail but as a whole. Royce then asks: "What highest end is suggested, we ask, to him who realizes for himself this whole world of ends?" A person who realizes or attempts to realize the whole world of ends becomes conscious of the conflict among them. He feels "the bitterness of the universal strife" which leads him to pessimism. "This warfare cannot be ended" is the despairing cry. Royce however refuses to accept a pessimistic answer. He pushes the reflection a step further:

> But has he thus uttered the final word? For he has not yet added the reflection that we are here insisting upon. Let him say: "then I too have an end, far-off and unattainable though it seems, and so my will is not aimless. I desire to realize these aims all at once. Therefore I desire their harmony." This is the one good that comes up before my fancy as above all the various

conflicting individual goods of the various separate aims. This Higher Good would be attained in a world where the conflict ceased. That would be the Ideal World, where all possible aims were pursued in absolute harmony.[42]

This insight is an ideal toward which one can direct one's efforts. Royce said, "... my Ideal very simply means the Will to direct my acts *towards* the attainment of universal Harmony. It requires me to act with this my insight always before me."[43] This insight, for Royce, sets up a new moral principle which transcends skepticism with regard to the special moral aim. This principle is:

> *So act as thou wouldst will to act if all the consequences of thy act for all the aims that are anywhere to be affected by this act, could be realized by thee now and in this one indivisible moment.* Or more briefly put: *Act always in the light of the completest insight into all the aims that thy act is to affect.*[44]

Thus Royce claims to have found a moral doctrine in the very heart of skepticism itself. This moral doctrine would at first appear to be an absolute individualism. Royce, however, points out that the highest good would be realizable only if the aims of all the conflicting wills in the world were brought in conformity to his insight. "And all the world of individuals would act as one Being, having a single Universal will. Harmony would in fact be attained." Royce's Ideal thus has another precept to give. It says: "Act in such wise as to extend this moral insight to others. Here is a definite practical aim, and it justifies us in saying to all the conflicting wills: You should respect one another."[45]

For Royce, then, the moral insight involves the will to harmonize as far as possible all the conflicting wills that are in the world. Where there is a conflict, the moral insight involves "the will to act as if my neighbor and myself were one being that possessed at once the aims of both of us."[46]

Royce points out that salvation from ethical skepticism and the attainment of truth is not reached by dreading doubt but by accepting it and absorbing it until, as an element of one's thought, it becomes also an element in a higher truth. But this ethical ideal must work in the real world and solve concrete moral problems which actually trouble human beings. The first demand of moral idealism, therefore, concerns the moral education of the race. Royce said: "The first demand that the moral insight makes of us so soon as we get it is: so act so as to increase the number of those who possess the insight."47

Royce explains that harmony cannot be even partially attained until a very great number of persons have developed the power to see things in proper perspective with the help of the moral insight. In the meantime, the provisional aim should be to produce the moral mood. In other words, the moral insight helps us to see that *"Whatever the highest human good may be, we can only attain it together, for it involves harmony."*48

This quest for happiness through harmony has to be distinguished from the effort of the hedonist whose highest law would be: "Get the most happiness, all of you." After considering such an ideal of a peaceful society of universal good humor, Royce is disappointed and contemptuous. He says: "That harmless company of jolly good fellows is unspeakably dull."49

Individual satisfaction cannot be the ultimate moral norm. Anyone who has tried to realize that ideal ultimately discovers what a hollow and worthless business it all is. We cannot be satisfied with individual contentments as such, but we must work for the destruction of all our individual limitations. Royce said:

> Our ideal of life must then be the notion of a life where no one being could fairly criticize any other at all. But such a life would be no longer a life of separate individuals, each limited to his petty sphere of work. It would be a life in which self was lost in a higher unity of all the conscious selves.50

Royce uses his moral insight to determine what the relationship must be between each person and one's neighbor. It is not enough to treat each other as mere masses of happy or miserable feelings. Royce held that "we must live united with each other and the world."51

How is this to be accomplished. Royce holds that we should seek to develop every form of life that brings us into oneness. He says: "Our vocation, whatever it be, must not end simply in increasing what people call the aggregate happiness of mankind, but in giving human life more interconnection, closer relationship."52

This moral ideal of life brings out the need for a support for moral acts. Royce looks for more than a reward for moral goodness. He expresses it in this way. "We want to know that, when we try to do right, we are not alone; that there is something outside of us that harmonizes with our own moral efforts by being itself in some way moral."[53]

Royce recalls the example of Job. He did not look for a reward. In the words of Royce, Job "wants a vindicator, a righteous, all-knowing judge, to arise, that can bear witness how upright he has been; such a vindicator he wants to see face to face, that he may call upon him as a beholder of what has actually happened."[54]

Royce's moral insight is thus at bottom a religious insight. This same religious insight is discovered by Royce in the gospel of Matthew. The judgment scene has a moral force because of the concluding words of the judge: "In as much as ye did it unto the least of these, ye did it unto me."[55]

The religious knowledge supporting moral consciousness is in fact the knowledge that there is in the universe

> some consciousness that sees and knows all reality, including ourselves, for which therefore all the good and evil of our lives is plain fact.... The knowledge that there is a being that is no respecter of persons, that considers all lives as equal, and that estimates our acts according to their true value, — this would be a genuine support to the religious need in us, quite apart from all notions about reward and punishment. A thinking being, a seer of all good and evil, is thus desired.[56]

Royce is evidently thinking of a being which would merit the name "God." This concept of God, however, would be an impoverished one. There would be a properly religious value in such a being, but it would be lacking in affection, sympathy, or any power to act in the world, even to avenge wrong-doing. Royce would not want to be understood as accepting such a limited idea of God. Royce insists on continuing the search for an understanding of God that will represent the very best that can be obtained, "some reality that our ideal aims can lead us to regard as of Infinite Worth."[57]

At the end of Royce's study of morality, he has concluded to the need of a Supreme Reality as "the religiously valuable reality in the world" and as an ultimate aspect of things. Such a power must be able to support the realization of our particular ideal and to bring about the unity of our lives.[58]

The Second Book of *The Religious Aspect of Philosophy* is entitled "The Search for a Religious Truth." As he did in the search for a moral ideal, Royce begins his religious quest with a thorough-going and uncompromising skepticism. He does not want his work to be considered an apology for any religious truth. Such a defensive attitude he considers to be an insult to genuine religion. A truly philosophic doubt is of the very essence of Royce's thought, and religious truth is concealed within the doubt. This doubt is focused first on the existence of an external world and on evolutionary progress. The result of Royce's methodical doubt is the conclusion: it is "not what the present world has come from, not what it is becoming, not what it will be by-and-by, but what it eternally is, (that) must furnish us with the deepest religious aspect of reality."[59]

This same doubt extends to the argument for the existence of God from design. It is not enough to say that design is compatible with evolution. The proof of the existence of God from design is not conclusive since the analysis of experience still leaves serious doubt as to what powers, intelligent or not intelligent, are the sources of all our experience. Royce adds: "And the more we know about nature, the less inclined we feel to dogmatize on the basis of mere experience about what powers are behind the scenes."[60]

Royce next explores the possibility of finding religious truth in a non-demonstrative way. "Possibly religion may be content to rest on postulates."[61]

Royce describes a postulate as a voluntary determination to act in a given way, without being rationally forced to do so, and with an understanding of the risk. Postulates are not mere blind faith, but they are voluntary assumptions of a risk, made for the sake of a higher end. Where blind faith says: "I dare not question," the postulate says: "I dare to be responsible for making the assumption." This postulating activity is closely related to our knowledge of reality. Much of our thought rests upon unavoidable postulates. Science itself makes such assumptions in forming its ideal of a universal theory. Royce admits that he would like something much better than a postulate as the basis of religion, if it is obtainable. One would want any postulates made to be justified by some ultimate religious certainty. However, if postulates are interpreted rightly, it is clear "that they ought to be regarded as beliefs, taken for the first on risk, and because the risk is worth taking."[62]

It is sometimes said that beliefs are independent of the will. Royce holds, however, that beliefs have resulted from a sort of struggle between the person and the surrounding world and thus he involves the will in the struggle. The man of energy controls the current of his belief or thought, and he is responsible for the results.[63]

This responsibility is seen particularly in the choice of objects of attention and recognition. Beliefs, then, are not just forced on the person, but they are developed by the voluntary decisions of the person. Religion and science may be considered alike in this. Just as science is based on the postulates of the unity and intelligibility of an external world, so religion may be seen as based on the postulates that "the highest reality is not against us but for us," and that "universal goodness is somehow at the heart of things."[64] In both cases one must take the risk, and one takes the risk because it is worth taking.

Nevertheless, even though postulates are necessary, Royce is still looking for a more excellent way. The postulates must be confirmed, if possible. It takes courage to form postulates, but religion is more than courage. "We must have if possible some external Truth that is not a postulate to rest upon."[65]

In Chapter X, Royce looks to the philosophical Idealism of the past as a path to eternal truth. The idealist philosophers of the past have maintained that the Eternal is a world of spiritual life. Above and beyond the warring powers of this world, they have held that there is a higher spiritual life that includes them and watches over them. The idealists have asserted that through all the evil powers and the good powers in the world, and in them all, there dwells a higher spirit that constitutes them to be what they are. In such a philosophy, evil may be, after all, a partial view of an all-embracing goodness. Can such a view of the eternal be affirmed as more than a postulate?

Royce is willing to start with an absolute skepticism. "Everything is doubtful. We may be in error everywhere. Certainty about the real world beyond is unattainable."[66]

When this skepticism is analyzed however, its implications begin to appear. "*It implies that we can be in error about an external world.* Therefore this extreme skepticism assumes that *there is a difference* between true and false statements about nature."[67]

There must be real and genuine error, or even skepticism itself fails to make sense. The alternative is an utterly irrational chaos. But if there is such a thing as error, what is necessary to explain the possibility of such error?[68]

Royce holds that even the commonplace that not all assertions are equally true is based on an assumption. That assumption is so fundamental that all thinking, all controversy, all science, and all morality depend on it. Royce formulates this assumption as follows:

> *That the agreement or disagreement of his judgments with their intended objects exists and has meaning for an actual thought, a consciousness, to which both these related terms are present, namely, both the judgment and the object wherewith it is to agree.*[69]

Royce then pursues the analysis. If a thought has objects outside of it with which it can agree or disagree, those objects and that agreement can have meaning and be possible only if there is an inclusive thought which includes both the thought and the object with which it agrees. In other words, once one holds that a statement can either agree or fail to agree with a real object other than the thought itself, a further judgment is made implicitly, namely, "that all reality, spiritual and material, is present in its true nature to an all-embracing intelligent thought, of which mine is simply one subordinate part or element."[70]

In Chapter XI, Royce continues to explore the implications of the possibility of error. He holds that the only possible solution to the problem of error is the existence of "an infinite unity of conscious thought to which is present all possible truth."[71] With error, then, as a starting point, Royce holds that "there is no stopping place short of an Infinite Thought."

For Royce this Infinite Thought is not a mere conclusion of logic or an abstract principle. It has a religious value:

> The Infinite Thought, must, knowing all truth, include also a knowledge of all wills, and of their conflict. For him all this conflict, and all the other facts of the moral world, take place. He then must know the outcome of the conflict, that Moral Insight of our first book. In him then we have the Judge of our ideals and the Judge of our conduct . . . we have found not only an infinite Seer of physical facts, but an infinite Seer of the Good as well as of the Evil.[72]

Royce then expresses his philosophical discovery in the words of Emerson's poem "Brahma."

> They reckon ill that [*sic*] leave me out;
> When they fly, I am the wings,
> I am the doubter and the doubt. — 73

The final chapter of *The Religious Aspect of Philosophy*, "The Religious Insight," draws out the implications of Royce's affirmation of the infinite. If the infinite exists, there is a moral imperative to put oneself at the service of the Highest. This is the foundation of a genuinely religious faith and life.

Effect of *The Religious Aspect of Philosophy* on William James

In this first book, Royce establishes himself as one of the masters of philosophy. It is to the credit of William James that, even before this book was written, he recognized Royce's potentialities, and laid the groundwork for Royce's coming to Harvard. That professional act of charity was repaid many times over by Royce, as he became a colleague and neighbor and a partner in philosophical dialogue. As indicated earlier, Royce's argument for the existence of an Infinite Thought was reluctantly accepted by William James, and it took James more than eight years to withdraw himself from his allegiance to it. In a note added to his paper "The Function of Cognition," James expressed the argument that liberated him from Royce's position as follows:

> This powerful book (i.e., *The Religious Aspect of Philosophy*) maintained that the notion of *referring* involved that of an inclusive mind that shall own both the real q and the mental q, and use the latter expressly as a representative symbol of the former. At the time I could not refute this transcendentalist opinion. Later, largely through the influence of Professor D. S. Miller (see his essay "The Meaning of Truth and Error," in the *Philosophical Review* for 1893, vol. 2, p. 403) I came to see that any definitely experienceable workings would serve as intermediaries quite as well as the absolute mind's intentions would.[74]

Whatever the philosophical worth of this argument of refutation, it would seem that the effect of it on James was to move him toward a dependence on religious experience as the basis of his affirmation of God.

The Religious Aspect of Philosophy of Royce played an important role in the development of William James' approach to the affirmation of God. At a difficult time in his life, just after the deaths of his mother and father, James was confronted with a thoroughly modern philosophical work which was unabashedly religious. The book changed the role of Josiah Royce from being a discovery and protege of James to that of being a professional of the first rank who, as James' colleague, neighbor, and close friend could not be disregarded. The book also contained a proof for the existence of God which James was unable to refute for eight years from 1884 to 1893. In addition, *The Religious Aspect of Philosophy* presented James with the model of a religious philosophy which was not agnostic but which was not developed as an apology for any religious communion. It should be noted that James did not meekly become a disciple. He was influenced by Royce's book to enter a period of intense intellectual activity, in order to liberate himself from the grip of Royce's argumentation. Furthermore, Royce, following Peirce, seems to have strengthened in James the insight into the place of the will in the establishment of a philosophical position. It seems clear, therefore, that on the strength of *The Religious Aspect of Philosophy* alone, Royce should be acknowledged as a major influence on William James in the development of his approach to the affirmation of God.

The Later Influence of Royce on William James and James' Eventual Emancipation

In September 1894, Josiah Royce received an invitation from George Holmes Howison to lecture at the University of California during the summer of 1895. Howison suggested that, after the University's Philosophical Union had studied *The Religious Aspect of Philosophy* during the academic year 1884-1885, Royce would then appear in August to discuss some feature of philosophical theism. Howison, Sidney E. Mezes (1863-1931) and Joseph LeConte would engage in a philosophical dialogue on the basis of Royce's paper. Royce agreed to the proposal and acknowledged that he still held the central core of ideas of the book, but he proposed to restate his position in a wholly new way.[75]

The result of that restatement is Royce's address entitled "The Conception of God." Since this book provided matter for the continuing dialogue between Royce and James, some attention should be given to the book. Unfortunately, the dialogue was largely oral, so it is not possible to reconstruct it here. All that can be done now is to summarize Royce's arguments in their published form and James' ultimate judgment on the work as found in his letters.

Royce begins the address by pointing out that a fruitful philosophical study of the conception of God must be linked with an attempt to estimate the evidence for the existence of God, the central mystery of our existence.[76]

Royce defines the word "God" in terms of omniscence or divine wisdom. The knowledge of the Omniscient Being is not just a knowledge of ideas but a knowledge of the facts of experience. This knowledge would therefore include a knowledge of the value and the meaning of all particular experiences. The knowledge of an Omniscient Being would thus be more than a "universally clear but absolutely passionless insight."[77]

For Royce, the attribute of omniscience would involve far more than the word at first suggests. Royce holds that in order to have the attribute of omniscience, "a being would necessarily be conceived as essentially world-possessing — as the source and principle of truth, — not merely as an external observer of a world of foreign truth."[78]

In contrast with the experience of human beings, which is incomplete, the experience of an Omniscient Being would be complete and self-contained, and not a mere part of some large whole. Such a being would possess an Absolute Thought; that is, "a self-contained thought, sufficient unto itself, and needing no further comment, supplement, or correction. A being uniting in itself both Absolute Thought and Absolute Experience may be named simply the Absolute."[79]

Royce holds that to assert the reality of any absolute is the same as to assert an absolute experience for which the absolute reality exists. Any effort to assert that the whole world of experience is a world of fragmentary and finite experience involves a contradiction.[80]

Royce then presents in summary form his argument for the reality of the Omniscient Being. This argument starts with human experience which is seen as fragmentary. An experienced fragment is contained within some more organized whole of experience, in whose unity the fragment finds its organic place. To speak of a fragmentary experience as real is to see the reality as the content of a more organized experience.[81] Royce thus places himself squarely within the tradition of Idealism when he locates all realities as contents of the experience of the absolute.

Royce saw his conception of God as absolute experience to be essentially identical with the conception of God developed by Aristotle. Historically, Aristotle's position was distinct from the idea of God as absolute or perfect reality. The identification of these two understandings of God is the result of recent philosophical thought. It is to the rich experience of Christian mysticism that the historical honor belongs, of having bridged the gulf that seemed to separate, and that to many minds still separates, the God of practical faith from the God of philosophical definition.[82]

James continued to grapple with Royce's idea of the absolute. Much of this dialogue was in the form of conversations as James and Royce walked home from Harvard. Royce described one of these discussions in his diary. On the way home they got "into an argument on the external world, which we at last discussed by the gate, ankle deep in nasty, damp March snow."[83] After one such discussion, James summarized his position in a brief note to Royce. James wrote:

> ... I confess that my worm-on-the-hook despair came less from my assimilation of what you said than from the ease and assurance of your manner in saying it! If you had never been born, this trouble would not have come upon me....
>
> (5) your fundamental plea is that the mutual knowledges of A and B are T's consciousness of the pair of them. This consciousness does not *produce*, *ab extra*, A's knowledge of B, for example, but is all there is "to" either A or A's knowledge.
>
> (6) In what sense then can A, B, and T, with their several knowledges, possibly be distinct?
>
> (7) In no sense, if T be a unit, for then they are only distinguished *by* it, not distinct from it. There is *then* no A-consciousness, no B-consciousness. There is only the T-consciousness of $(A+B)$, taken integrally and as such, a true psychic monism....
>
> (8) *Ergo*, your fundamental plea (see 5) cannot hold with T a monism, so long as A and B are distinct.

> (9) But here my empiricism comes in. They *are* distinct, both from each other and from T — three different subjective facts. Neither knows *as* the other knows. . . . [84]

In this 1895 note, James has overcome the force of Royce's logic. If idealism still remains as an option for James, it is as an hypothesis which is worth trying rather than as a principle which is logically coercive. Perry observed the change and wrote:

> It is clear, furthermore, that he is now carrying the war into the enemy's country, and accusing Royce — the heavily armed and heavily armored dialectician — of breaches of logic! From this time forth he cites Royce's arguments for purposes of exposition and he has ceased to fear them. He has ceased, in fact, even to be impressed by them.[85]

By 1899, James had definitely removed himself from Royce's idea of the Absolute. Writing to Dickinson S. Miller, he praised Miller's study of Royce and said:

> Since teaching the "Conception of God," I have come to perceive what I didn't trust myself to believe before, that looseness of thought is Royce's *essential* element. He *wants* it. There isn't a tight joint in his system; not one. And yet I thought that a mind that could talk me blind and black and numb on mathematics and logic, and whose favorite recreation is works on these subjects, must necessarily conceal closeness and exactitudes of ratiocination that I hadn't the wit to find out. But no! He is the Rubens of philosophy. Richness, abundance, boldness, color, but a sharp contour never, and never, never any *perfection*. But isn't fertility better than perfection?[86]

James' encounter with Royce's "The Conception of God" seems clearly to have been the definitive move by James away from Royce's conception of God as the absolute. Royce's Gifford lectures[87] were his most important systematic work, and James read and criticized the work very carefully; but he was no longer under the spell of Royce. In a letter to Royce of January 21, 1900, James expressed his predominating impression

> Of its *charming* character in being a presentation so light and flowing, of a complex and weighty *Weltanschauung*. Its ease, its unfailing clearness, its sincerity and affability so over-spread its subtlety and intricacy as to disguise them. All this is said without the slightest prejudice to my hard-heartedness in the matter of belief, for I find the arguments you use as incoercive as ever, and the Absolute still remains for me a hypothesis to be tested by its uses, rather than a doctrine to be submitted to for its credentials.[88]

Perhaps the best text to bring out the importance of Royce's influence on William James is James' letter to Royce of September 26, 1900. James wrote:

> You are still the centre of my gaze, the pole of my mental magnet. When I write, it is with one eye on the page, and one on you. When I compose my Gifford lectures mentally, it is with the design exclusively of overthrowing your system, and ruining your peace.... Different as our minds are, yours has nourished mine, as no other social influence ever has, and in converse with you I have always felt that my life was being lived importantly.... I don't believe that we shall dwell apart forever, though our formulas may.[89]

Notes

1 Josiah Royce, *The Basic Writings of Josiah Royce*, ed. with an introduction by John J. McDermott, 2 vols. (Chicago and London: The University of Chicago Press, 1969), 1:31.

2 John Clendenning, Introduction to *The Letters of Josiah Royce*, ed. John Clendenning (Chicago and London: The University of Chicago Press, 1970), p. 12. John Clendenning's *The Life and Thought of Josiah Royce* (Madison, Wisconsin: The University of Wisconsin Press, 1985) appeared too late to be used in this study.

3 *Letters of Josiah Royce*, pp. 16, 45.

4 Perry, 1:779.

5 *Letters of Josiah Royce*, p. 66.

6 *Letters*, 1:202.

7 *Letters of Josiah Royce*, p. 112.

8 *Letters of Josiah Royce*, p. 114.

9 *Letters of Josiah Royce*, pp. 34, 378.

10 *Letters of Josiah Royce*, p. 35.

11 *Letters of Josiah Royce*, p. 37.

12 *Letters of Josiah Royce*, p. 39.

13 John J. McDermott, *The Basic Writings of Josiah Royce*, p. ix.

14 Frank M. Oppenheim, *Royce's Voyage Down Under: A Journey of the Mind* (Lexington: The University Press of Kentucky, 1980). This was preceded by an article by Father Oppenheim, "Josiah Royce's Intellectual Development: A Hypothesis," *Idealistic Studies* 6 (January 1976): 85-102. Oppenheim's major work, *Royce's Mature Philosophy of Religion* (Notre Dame, Indiana: University of Notre Dame Press, 1987) appeared too late to be used in this study.

15 Oppenheim, *Voyage*, p. viif. Oppenheim is here quoting from "Last Lectures in Metaphysics, Notes of lectures delivered by Josiah Royce in Phil. 9, Metaphysics, 1915-1916)" (lecture of January 11, 1916, p. 130, Richard C. Cabot

Papers, Harvard Archives, Cambridge, Mass.). Cabot (1869-1933) taught in the Harvard University Medical School (1899-1933), and held the chair of Social Ethics, 1920-1934. He was a close personal friend of Royce and frequently participated in Royce's seminars.

16 Royce, *Basic Writings*, 2:1174.

17 Oppenheim, *Voyage*, p. viii. See Josiah Royce, *The Religious Aspect of Philosophy: A Critique of the Bases of Conduct and of Faith* (Boston: Houghton Mifflin, 1885; reprint ed., Gloucester, Mass.: Peter Smith, 1965), especially Chapters XI and XII. (This book will be referred to as *R.A.P.*, with the page number.)

18 Josiah Royce, *The World and the Individual*, 2 vols. (New York: The Macmillan Co., 1899, 1901), 2:vii.

19 Josiah Royce, *R.A.P.*, p. 385.

20 Oppenheim, *Voyage*, p. xii.

21 Royce, *World*, pp. 3-6.

22 Josiah Royce, *The Philosophy of Loyalty* (New York: The Macmillan Co., 1908); reprinted in full in *Basic Writings*, 2:855-1013.

23 *Basic Writings*, 2:859.

24 Josiah Royce, *The Problem of Christianity*, 2 vols. (New York: The Macmillan Co., 1913; reprint ed. in a single volume with an introduction by John E. Smith, Chicago and London: The University of Chicago Press, 1968).

25 Oppenheim, *Voyage*, p. xv.

26 Royce, *The Philosophy of Loyalty, Basic Writings*, 2:858. See Oppenheim, "Royce's Intellectual Development . . . ," p. 87.

27 William James, "The Religious Aspect of Philosophy," *The Atlantic Monthly*, 1885, pp. 840-843; reprinted in William James, *Collected Essays and Reviews*, pp. 276-284.

28 William James, *Collected Essays and Reviews*, p. 284.

29 William James, *The Principles of Psychology*, p. 945, n. 29. This note is of interest because of a quotation from *The Religious Aspect of Philosophy* (pp. 303f). Royce wrote: "The ultimate motive (for the existence of an external world) with the man of every-day life is *the will to have an external world.* . . . The popular assurance of an external world is *the fixed determination to make one*, now and henceforth." James was struck by this involvement of the will in the judgment of the existence of the external world.

30 See, for example, Royce's letter to George Holmes Howison, 23 September 1894, in *The Letters of Josiah Royce*, pp. 324-326.

31 *Letters of William James*, 1:265.

32 Perry, 1:703.

33 William James, *The Meaning of Truth* (Cambridge, Mass.: Harvard University Press, 1975), p. 23.

34 Royce, *R.A.P.*, p. ix.

35 Royce, *R.A.P.*, p. xi.

36 Royce, *R.A.P.*, p. 2f.

37 Royce, *R.A.P.*, p. 3.

38 Royce, *R.A.P.*, p. 4.

39 Royce, *R.A.P.*, pp. 4f.

40 Royce, *R.A.P.*, p. 14.

41 Royce, *R.A.P.*, p. 138.

42 Royce, *R.A.P.*, p. 140.

43 Royce, *R.A.P.*, pp. 140f.

44 Royce, *R.A.P.*, p. 141.

45 Royce, *R.A.P.*, pp. 145f.

46 Royce, *R.A.P.*, pp. 168f.

47 Royce, *R.A.P.*, pp. 171-173.

48 Royce, *R.A.P.*, p. 175.

49 Royce, *R.A.P.*, pp. 185-187.

50 Royce, *R.A.P.*, p. 200.

51 Royce, *R.A.P.*, p. 216.

52 Royce, *R.A.P.*, p. 216.

53 Royce, *R.A.P.*, p. 219.

54 Royce, *R.A.P.*, p. 219.

55 Royce, *R.A.P.*, p. 220, citing Mt. 25:40.

56 Royce, *R.A.P.*, pp. 220f.

57 Royce, *R.A.P.*, p. 221f.

58 Royce, *R.A.P.*, p. 222.

59 Royce, *R.A.P.*, p. 251.

60 Royce, *R.A.P.*, p. 282.

61 Royce, *R.A.P.*, p. 297.

62 Royce, *R.A.P.*, p. 305.

63 Royce, *R.A.P.*, p. 305f.

64 Royce, *R.A.P.*, pp. 324-331.

65 Royce, *R.A.P.*, p. 332.

66 Royce, *R.A.P.*, p. 372.

67 Royce, *R.A.P.*, p. 372.

68 Royce, *R.A.P.*, p. 376.

69 Royce, *R.A.P.*, p. 377.

70 Royce, *R.A.P.*, p. 378.

71 Royce, *R.A.P.*, p. 424.

72 Royce, *R.A.P.*, pp. 433f.

73 Royce, *R.A.P.*, p. 434. Cf., *Selected Writings of Ralph Waldo Emerson*, ed. William H. Gilman (New York: New American Library, 1965), p. 471. (*Who leave me out.*)

74 William James, *The Meaning of Truth; A Sequel to "Pragmatism"* (New York and London: Longmans, Green & Co., 1909; reprint ed., Cambridge, Mass., and London: Harvard University Press, 1975), p. 23.

75 Royce, *Letters*, pp. 32, 324-326.

76 Royce, *Basic Writings*, 1:357.

77 Royce, *Basic Writings*, 1:361.

78 Royce, *Basic Writings*, 1:361.

79 Royce, *Basic Writings*, 1:362.

80 Royce, *Basic Writings*, 1:379.

81 Royce, *Basic Writings*, 1:379f.

82 Royce, *Basic Writings*, 1:383f.

83 Perry, 1:808.

84 Perry, 1:808f.

85 Perry, 1:810.

86 *Letters*, 2:86.

87 Josiah Royce, *The World and the Individual*.

88 Perry, 1:812f. For a more technical criticism by James of Royce's doctrine of the Absolute see the memorandum from James to Royce reprinted by Perry as Appendix V. Royce's reply, with James' comments, is included in the Appendix, Perry, 2:726-734.

89 *Letters*, 2:136.

PART TWO

THE REALITY OF GOD FOR WILLIAM JAMES

The introduction of this work provided a brief intellectual biography of William James and a survey of the most important literature dealing with his philosophy and his theory of religion. In PART ONE, five thinkers were studied who were most influential in the development of James' approach to God. With this as a background, this part of the study will present James' position on the affirmation of God more directly.

This part of the work will first clarify the problem facing William James. In CHAPTER VII, an attempt will be made to show the importance of determining a philosopher's "centre of vision" to avoid misunderstanding of his work. Henry Samuel Levinson tried to determine William James' "centre of vision." A critique of Levinson's efforts is given in CHAPTER VIII. Then in CHAPTER IX, an attempt will be made to reconstruct James' "centre of vision."

In CHAPTER X, James' theory of truth will be examined to bring out his "pragmatic realism" and to show the importance for James of the influence of the "passional nature" in all knowing.

When James used the word "faith," he did not understand it as Catholic theologians do, as an assent to the word of God. In CHAPTER XI, James' idea of faith will be studied and its nature as "working hypothesis" will be explored.

In CHAPTER XII, a type of example used by James will be considered, the so-called "outcome cases."

James uses Pascal's Wager Argument in his essay "The Will to Believe." In the first part of CHAPTER XIII, the Wager Argument will be studied in Pascal. In the second part, the criticisms of the argument will be considered. In the third part, the true meaning and value of the argument for Pascal will be investigated. Finally, in the fourth part, the place of the Wager Argument in "The Will to Believe" will be set forth.

In CHAPTER XIV, the concept of practical or moral certitude in philosophy will be studied. First of all, Kant's use of "practical certitude" will be considered. In the second section, Cardinal Newman's position on the value of probable reasoning will be investigated. In the third part, a comparison will be made between Newman and James on moral certitude.

CHAPTER XV will deal with William James' paper "The Will to Believe." In the first section, the state of the question will be set out, with reference to the article of W. K. Clifford. The Wager Argument will be considered next, and then an indirect argument from the nature of science. In the fourth section, the role of the Passional Nature will be studied and shown to be at the root of all our convictions including religious convictions.

In CHAPTER XVI, the argument of *The Varieties of Religious Experience* will be set forth. First of all, the rich descriptions of religious experiences given by James will be briefly summarized. In the second section, one possible error in the interpretation of James' position will be indicated; it is not a form of Ontologism. The third section asks what philosophy can do for religion. This is followed by a fourth section which gives James' idea of a "Science of Religions." James' "reconciling hypothesis" will be presented in the fifth section. The final section will be devoted to James' "philosophical postscript."

After exploring so many of the aspects of James' thought on the affirmation of God, James' position will be stated briefly and simply in CHAPTER XVII by way of conclusion.

Chapter VI

Statement of the Problem

What is the basic question that James attempted to deal with in *The Will to Believe* and *The Varieties of Religious Experience*? Edward H. Madden has pointed out that the general theme underlying all the essays in *The Will to Believe* is that "intellectual decisions unaffected by the volitional and passional natures of man are pure fictions."[1]

Madden holds that the basic question considered by James in the first four essays of *The Will to Believe* is: "What then, on insufficient evidence, does a person have a right to believe?"[2]

This theme and this basic question are both somewhat broader than the question studied in this work, which is limited to James' approach in the affirmation of God. The question as stated by Madden also is misleading. From James' point of view the insufficiency of the evidence is to be measured against scientific standards of demonstration rather than against reasonable standards for affirming the reality of God. It is the latter point which is the concern of this study. For James, therefore, the question should be posed as follows: "Does one have a right to adopt belief in God in spite of the fact that the evidence is not sufficient to coerce our merely logical intellect?"[3]

Notes

1 Madden, Introduction to William James, *The Will to Believe*, p. xi.
2 Madden, Introduction to William James, *The Will to Believe*, p. xv.
3 See William James, *The Will to Believe*, p. 13.

Chapter VII

The Philosopher's "Centre of Vision"

The task of historical interpretation of a philosopher's work cannot be achieved merely by the making of accurate summaries of the individual arguments in his writings. Two further dimensions have to be explored by the interpreter. First of all, one must place the philosopher's writings in the context of his own life and development under the influence of thinkers with whom he was in dialogue. In addition to that, it is also necessary to interpret a thinker's work by identifying its focus. Every major philosopher does his work within a horizon and under the guidance of a comprehensive vision of life. This vision serves to modify and unify all his statements, so much so that the responsive interpreter must construct a purposive unity of meanings in order to achieve an historical re-envisioning of a philosophy.[1]

Henri Bergson (1859-1941) expressed this same insight using the concept of "philosophical intuition." Bergson pointed out that a philosophical system at first appears as a complete edifice with commodious lodgings for all problems. In contemplating its aesthetic form, one may experience a joy in finding order in complexity. As one identifies the materials of the building, and recalls their origins in previous philosophies, one establishes a more or less original synthesis of the philosopher's ideas. Nevertheless, as one begins to penetrate more fully into the philosopher's thought, instead of just circling around it from the outside, the doctrine is transformed for us. It no longer seems as complicated. The various parts fit into one another.

Finally, the whole philosophy is brought together into a single point. This point may be something so simple, so extraordinarily simple, that the philosopher has never succeeded in saying it. That is why he had to keep on talking all his life. Bergson summed up his insight by saying, "A philosopher worthy of the name has never said more than a single thing: and even then it is something he has tried to say rather than something actually said."[2]

In other words, at the heart of every great philosopher's thought is a central intuition which is never completely conceptualized. In order to elaborate an account of that system, one must grasp that central intuition. To understand the work of a great thinker, it is not enough to collect quotations from various works and to string them together according to some design. One must instead place oneself at the center of the philosopher's vision of life.[3]

This comparison of views of philosophers such as James Collins, Henri Bergson, and Edmund Husserl is helpful in understanding a similar theme which is developed by William James, and which has to be taken into consideration in interpreting James' work.

In James, the theme is set out in a letter to an unnamed woman who had just completed a doctoral dissertation on James' work. James praised the "objective and dispassionate" way in which the work was done and the carefully subdivided and articulated structure of the dissertation. Nevertheless, James criticized the work for too much philological method. James described the flaw in this method, and its remedy, in the following passage:

> You take utterances of mine written at different dates, for different audiences, belonging to different universes of discourse, and string them together as the abstract elements of a total philosophy which you then show to be inwardly incoherent. This is splendid philology, but is it live criticism of anyone's *Weltanschauung*? Your use of the method only strengthens the impression I have got from reading criticism of my "pragmatic" account of "truth" that the whole Ph.D. industry of building up an author's meaning out of separate texts leads nowhere, unless you have first grasped his centre of vision, by an act of imagination.[4]

James Collins comments that this text should be understood not as an obscurantist's blast against doctoral dissertations "but a philosopher's living cry that justice be done to his central vision and the organic unity of this thought."[5]

This same concept of a center of vision was used by James in *A Pluralistic Universe* in order to clarify the philosophy of Hegel. James wrote:

> In no philosophy is the fact that a philosopher's vision and the technique he uses in proof of it are two different things more palpably evident than in Hegel. The vision in this case was that of a world in which reason holds all

The Philosopher's "Centre of Vision" 127

things in solution and accounts for all the irrationality that superficially appears by taking it up as a "moment" into itself.[6]

James then stated again the importance of this concept. He said: "Any author is easy if you can catch the centre of his vision."[7]

James uses the concept of vision again in the same chapter in discussing the work of Harold Henry Joachim (1868-1938). After indicating that Joachim held to a theory despite logical problems with that theory, James commented:

> Not only empiricists, but absolutists also, would all, if they were as candid as this author, confess that the prime thing in their philosophy is their vision of a truth possible, which they then employ their reasoning to convert as best it can, into a certainty or probability.[8]

These texts from Collins, Bergson, Husserl, and James express in different language the same basic insight, that is, that the historian of philosophy must approach a philosopher's work by first trying to grasp his "centre of vision." The historian must construct a unique explanatory perspective from which all the philosopher's work can be seen to form an intelligible whole.

The search for the center of vision is particularly important for one who studies the thought of William James. The reason for this is that James is such a quotable writer that one is often tempted, as John McDermott says, to "join together a series of brilliant asides and avoid commenting at all."[9] He quotes with approval the comment of Julius Bixler that: "The isolated reference from James is always unreliable."[10]

In attempting to determine William James' approach to the reality of God, then, it is important not to be satisfied with stringing together isolated texts but to see his position as grounded upon his vision of life. James expressed this in these words:

> Let me repeat once more that a man's vision is the great fact about him. Who cares for Carlyle's reasons, or Schopenhauer's, or Spencer's? A philosophy is the expression of a man's character, and all definitions of the universe are but the deliberately adopted reactions of human characters upon it.[11]

Notes

1 See James Collins, *Interpreting Modern Philosophy* (Princeton, N.J.: Princeton University Press, 1972), pp. 298f.

2 Henri Bergson, *The Creative Mind*, trans. Mabelle L. Andison (New York: Philosophical Library, 1946), pp. 126-132. A similar conception of the importance of a comprehensive vision for a philosopher is found in Edmund Husserl (1859-1938), the founder of Phenomenology. See E. Husserl, *The Crisis of European Sciences and Phenomenology* (Evanston: Northwestern University Press, 1970), p. 102.

3 See also Peter Gay, ed., *The Question of Jean-Jacques Rousseau*, by Ernst Cassirer (Bloomington: Indiana University Press, 1963), p. 22; and Albert Dondeyne, *Contemporary European Thought and Christian Faith*, trans. Ernan McMullin and John Burnheim (Pittsburgh, Pa.: Duquesne University Press, 1963), pp. 25-27.

4 William James, *Letters*, 2:354f.

5 James Collins, *Interpreting Modern Philosophy*, p. 402.

6 William James, *A Pluralistic Universe* (New York and London: Longmans Green & Co., 1909; reprint ed., Cambridge, Mass. and London: Harvard University Press, 1977), p. 43.

7 *A Pluralistic Universe*, p. 44.

8 *A Pluralistic Universe*, p. 59.

9 John J. McDermott, Introduction to *The Writings of William James*, p. xxi.

10 Julius Seelye Bixler, *Religion in the Philosophy of William James*, p. xi.

11 William James, *A Pluralistic Universe*, p. 14.

Chapter VIII

Levinson's Reconstruction of James' "Centre of Vision"

Before attempting to construct an interpretive perspective on James' work, it is necessary to consider Henry Samuel Levinson's attempt to formulate James' center of vision. In his Princeton doctoral dissertation, submitted in 1976,[1] Levinson acknowledges the need for an interpretive viewpoint. He writes:

> Indeed, there are so many William James' that it becomes appropriate to ask why we need yet another one. If we take the major interpretations of James alone, we have James the pragmatic realist (Perry); James the existential phenomenologist (Wild); James the proto-transcendental phenomenologist (Wilshire); and James the forerunner of logical empiricism (Ayer).[2]

Levinson holds that all the interpreters just mentioned have made a crucial error in method, since each has arranged his interpretation of James according to an understanding of how James asks and answers questions of philosophical import. Levinson agrees that it is necessary to determine James' philosophical method to gain an adequate understanding of his work. Levinson claims, however, that

> ... no major James scholar has centered his arguments and claims about James either on *what* questions James asked or on what James construed to be the sorts of circumstances and conditions that generate those questions. It will be my intention to interpret James from these latter points of view.[3]

When Levinson expresses his "act of imagination" concerning the center of James' vision, he does not begin with a question but rather begins with a doctrinal position. Levinson says: "I claim that the possibility of salvation or what James calls 'the chance of salvation' stands at the center of his vision."[4]

I believe that this is very significant since it negates Levinson's previous point that James should be interpreted through his methodology. Even the questions that James asks reflect his religious beliefs rather than an abstract philosophical method. Levinson implicitly accepts this insight, for he says: "I propose to argue to the thesis that James' work must be taken as that of a religious thinker."[5]

Levinson however immediately returns to the level of methodology when he notes that James' work is informed by three key questions: "Is life worth living? Can people effect changes they intend? Are there gods, or unseen powers that cooperate with us as agents and patients of communities?"[6]

Levinson sees these questions as those that James thinks he must ask if he is to resolve the issue "whether our outstanding problems as persons are solvable problems."[7]

Levinson claims that James is a religious thinker rather than a theologian. He defines the two as follows:

> As I see it, a religious thinker asks esoteric questions and tries to determine their answers. But he has no such answers in store, and, indeed, is open to the possibility that there simply are none to be found. A theologian, to the contrary, asks "secular questions" — ethical, epistemological, metaphysical questions — and provides theological answers according to theological methods developed within a particular religious tradition based on some particular revelation or other.[8]

It is clear that Levinson thinks that James' questions are more significant than his answers. In fact he goes on to say:

> I need to admit from the outset that, *as a thinker* at least, James demonstrates no interest in defending either the necessity or actuality of salvation. Indeed he precludes both options by argument. James intends to consider and defend the possibility of salvation. In other words, he will argue that people are such, and the universe is such, as to allow for a chance of salvation. In support of his contention that things generally may admit to solutions, he will generate a synoptic philosophy equally critical of those who claim on the one hand, either the necessity or actuality of salvation, and of those on the other who claim the impossibility of salvation.[9]

This understanding of James comes perilously close to the claim of George Santayana that "James did not really believe; he merely believed in the right of believing that you might be right if you believed."[10]

In his later book, Levinson rejected Santayana's position, and he said: "James made it crystal clear in his lectures on the value of saintliness that he believed."[11]

It seems clear therefore that Levinson's reduction of James' center of vision to three key questions does not do justice to James' position. One need look only at James' lecture "Is Life Worth Living?" to see how much more positive his position is than Levinson seems to think. He appeals to religious faith and tries to sweep away any views that might keep the springs of religious faith compressed. He wants to hold up to the light of day those considerations which may let loose those springs of religious faith.[12]

There is a spirit in things to which we owe allegiance. James was convinced that "there stretches beyond this visible world an unseen world of which we now know nothing positive, but in relation to which the true significance of our present mundane life consists."[13]

Moreover, in the *Varieties*, James commits himself to the proposition that religious experience unequivocally testifies that we can experience union with *something* larger than ourselves and in that union find our greatest peace.[14]

This is belief rather than methodology, and it is this belief which dominated James' quest to show that life is worth living. It is this belief which provides the "chance of salvation" toward which James directed his work.

As an added note, it is somewhat ironic that James, who wrote "The Will to Believe" as a response to William K. Clifford's "The Ethics of Belief," should now have the "centre of vision" of his word reduced by Levinson to three questions, much as Clifford in that same essay had reduced "the sacred tradition of humanity" to "questions rightly asked," "conceptions which enable us to ask further questions," and "methods of answering questions."[15]

Notes

1. Henry Samuel Levinson, *Science, Metaphysics and the Chance of Salvation: An Interpretation of the Thought of William James* (Missoula, Montana: Scholars Press, 1978) (henceforth referred to as *The Chance of Salvation*).

2. Levinson, *The Chance of Salvation*, p. 1.

3. Levinson, *The Chance of Salvation*, p. 1.

4. Levinson, *The Chance of Salvation*, p. 3.

5. Levinson, *The Chance of Salvation*, p. 3.

6. Levinson, *The Chance of Salvation*, p. 4.

7. Levinson, *The Chance of Salvation*, p. 4.

8. Levinson, *The Chance of Salvation*, p. 4.

9. Levinson, *The Chance of Salvation*, pp. 4f.

10. George Santayana, *Character and Opinion in the United States* (New York: W. W. Norton, 1967), p. 77.

11. Levinson, *Religious Investigations*, p. 123.

12. James, *The Will to Believe*, p. 40.

13. James, *The Will to Believe*, p. 48.

14. William James, *Varieties of Religious Experience*, p. 143.

15. *The Ethics of Belief Debate*, ed. Gerald D. McCarthy (Atlanta, Ga.: Scholars Press, 1986), p. 33.

Chapter IX

A Reconstruction of William James' "Centre of Vision"

How then can James' "centre of vision" be expressed? The unique explanatory perspective from which all of his work can be seen to form an intelligible whole was expressed clearly in the conclusion of his talk to the Harvard Young Men's Christian Association on April 25, 1895:

> These then, are my last words to you: Be not afraid of life. Believe that life *is* worth living, and your belief will help create the fact. The "scientific proof" that you are right may not be clear before the day of judgment (or some stage of being which that expression may serve to symbolize) is reached. But let the faithful fighters of this hour, or the beings that then and there will represent them, may then turn to the fainthearted, who here decline to go on, with words like those which Henry IV greeted the tardy Crillon after a great victory had been gained: "Hang yourself brave Crillon! We fought at Arques, and you were not there."[1]

James' basic message is that life, with its hopes and ambitions, trials and struggles, cannot be ultimately meaningless.[2]

In a lecture on "What Makes a Life Significant," James tried to give heart to students by assuring them that "No outward changes of condition in life can keep the nightingale of its eternal meaning from singing in all sorts of different men's hearts."[3]

The grasp of eternal meaning, which was the central insight of William James' philosophy, implied personal immortality. James said:

> The reader would be in accord with everything that the text of my lecture intended to say, were he to assert that every memory and affection of his present life is to be preserved, and that he shall never *in saecula saeculorum* cease to be able to say to himself: "I am the same personal being who in old times upon the earth had those experiences."[4]

William James' philosophy has been described by John McDermott as "meliorism."[5] For James, philosophy helps a person to make a difference. This quality should certainly be included as an aspect of James' centre of vision. Meliorism is an expression of the contemporary philosophical radical reffirmation of time. In opposition to the static determinism of Spinoza, some nineteenth-century thinkers rejected determinism. Among those opting for freedom rather than determinism were Charles Renouvier and Charles Sanders Peirce. James rejected determinism in his essay "The Dilemma of Determinism" in 1884.[6]

Meliorism is exemplified by James' 1897 oration upon the unveiling of the monument in Boston to Robert Gould Shaw. The black soldiers commanded by Shaw were depicted realistically in the monument. "There they march, warm-blooded champions of a better day for man." In other words, one can make a difference in the world, one can make it better, and this gives meaning to life — and death![7]

James' horizon is not limited, and his hopes for salvation are focused on a life beyond the grave. His commitment to personal immortality supports his theism and is in turn supported by it. James saw God as one who has an infinite desire for the salvation of all the persons he has created. James wrote:

> God, we can then say, has so inexhaustible a capacity for love that his call and need is for a literally endless accumulation of created lives. He can never faint or grow weary, as we should, under the increasing supply. His scale is infinite in all things. His sympathy can never know satiety or glut.[8]

It is clear then that for William James, God is not a mere wish but a reality to which he committed himself, and that theism is at the very heart of James' center of vision. James himself put it very simply in 1897, in a letter to Henry W. Rankin: "Religion is the great interest of my life...."[9]

This judgment as to James' center of vision developed in his paternal home, with the discussions and arguments with his father, Henry James the Elder. James' decision to choose to be free, under the influence of Charles Renouvier, kept religion at the center of James' vision. The religious life of Chauncey Wright and Charles Sanders Peirce, James' logician-opponents, kept his religious interest from being submerged in his scientific efforts. The religious thought of Josiah Royce also was a stimulus and encouragement to James to keep religion at the center of his vision. Any interpretation of James which puts religion on the periphery of his vision is not faithful to his life or thought.

Notes

1 William James, *The Will to Believe*, p. 56. The reference at the end of the quotation is to a letter of Henry IV (1553-1610) in a traditional form as expressed by Voltaire. See *The Oxford Dictionary of Quotations*, 2nd ed. (London: Oxford University Press, 1955), p. 242.

2 See Robert J. Roth, *American Religious Philosophy* (New York: Harcourt, Brace & World, 1967), p. 40.

3 William James, *Talks to Teachers on Psychology and to Students on Some of Life's Ideals* (New York: Holt, 1899; reprint ed., with Introduction by Paul Woodring, New York: W. W. Norton & Co., Inc., 1958), p. 191.

4 William James, *Human Immortality: Two Supposed Objections to the Doctrine*, 2nd ed. (Boston and New York: Houghton Mifflin, 1899); reprinted in William James, *Essays in Religion and Morality* (Cambridge, Mass.: Harvard University Press, 1982), p. 76.

5 John McDermott, Preface to *The Writings of William James*, p. xv.

6 Reprinted in *The Will to Believe*, pp. 114-140.

7 William James, *Essays in Religion and Morality* (Cambridge, Mass.: Harvard University Press, 1982), p. 65.

8 "Human Immortality," in *Essays in Religion and Morality*, by William James, p. 100.

9 *Letters of William James*, 2:58.

Chapter X

William James' Theory of Truth

A Global View of James' Theory of Truth

After reconstructing William James' center of vision, which dominated all his philosophical work, there is one area of his philosophy which has to be considered in order to understand properly James' approach to God. That area is the meaning of truth for James.

The bibliography on the question is extensive, and it would take a book-length study to review the work of the principal critics of James' pragmatic theory of truth. The most important contributors to this discussion are cited in the bibliographical essay appended to Levinson's *Religious Investigations*.[1]

A recent brief summary of James' position, and of the criticism of it, is given in H. S. Thayer's introduction to the Harvard edition of *The Meaning of Truth*. Thayer provides a schematic outline of James' position. He holds that for James,

> For an idea (belief, judgment, statement) to be pragmatically true three conditions are to be fulfilled. The idea must:
>
> 1. Be cognitively true.
> 2. Be compatible with the older body of truths.
> 3. Work. It must provide some satisfaction of a need or purpose (recalling the two aspects of "working" just discussed). In short, "thoughts are true which guide us to *beneficial* interaction with sensible particulars" (M. T., p. 51).

In this schematic form we are given a general definition of James' conception of truth.[2]

What is meant by the first condition, cognitive truth? Thayer holds that: "This is dictionary truth in its simplest abstract form, namely, as the agreement (or correspondence) between beliefs and statements and what these may be said to be about."[3]

This summary of James' theory of truth raises a question. Was James a realist?

Pragmatic Realism

In attempting to answer the question whether James was a realist, Thayer contrasts cognitive truth with pragmatic truth, without attempting to describe the latter. At this point it is sufficient to note that, for an idea or judgment or statement to be true or false, it must at least be *cognitively* true or false; it either will or will not correspond with reality. Thayer notes that James does not deny this, and calls his critics mistaken in this regard. It is clear that Thayer's interpretation of James is correct on this point. James himself responded to a criticism by Marcel Hebert as follows:

> Having previously written that truth means "agreement with reality," and insisted that the chief part of the expediency of any one opinion is its agreement with the rest of acknowledged truth, I apprehended no exclusively subjectivistic reading of my meaning. My mind was so filled with the notion of objective reference that I never dreamed that my hearers would let go of it; and the very last accusation I expected was that in speaking of ideas and their satisfactions, I was denying realities outside.[4]

For James there can be no truth if there is nothing to be true about.

> Ideas are so much flat psychological surface unless some mirrored matter gives them cognitive lustre. This is why as a pragmatist I have so carefully posited "reality" *ab initio*, and why, throughout my whole discussion, I remain an epistemological realist.[5]

There is no doubt, therefore, that James' theory of truth is properly called realism. It is not just a mere laboring of the point to emphasize the realistic nature of James' theory of truth. This provides the context within which James' position on the influence of the will on cognition must be considered.

As Susan Haack has brought out well, William James is entirely willing to grant that truth is agreement, or correspondence, with reality. She adds, however, that what is distinctive about the pragmatist approach to truth is the understanding that if a belief is true, it will stand the test of experience. A true belief, therefore, is one that works, that makes a difference.[6]

The Influence of the "Passional Nature" on Knowing

William James' most famous essay is entitled "The Will to Believe." Much of the controversy since the publication of the essay in 1896 has concerned the right to believe religious doctrines when the evidence for them is not logically compelling. James, however, did not limit his theory on the influence of the will, or the "passional nature," to matters of religious truth.

As early as 1879, James, in his essay "The Sentiment of Rationality," held that subjective factors of choice are involved in every kind of knowledge. In that essay, James said:

> We started by calling every concept a teleological instrument. No concept can be a valid substitute for a concrete reality except with reference to a particular interest in the conceiver. The interest of theoretic rationality, the relief of identification, is but one of a thousand human purposes.[7]

When this essay was revised for publication in *The Will to Believe* in 1897, James revised the passage to make the original message even clearer: "Every way of classifying a thing is but a way of handling it for some particular purpose. Conceptions, 'kinds,' are teleological instruments."[8]

This aspect of James' thinking has only recently been brought to the fore by students of James. For example, Edward H. Madden has written that, for James,

> Intellectual decisions unaffected by the volitional and passional natures of man are pure fictions. All philosophies carry the badge of their professors' preferences. James . . . never retracts his blunt statement that the intellect is subordinate to the affections.[9]

One recent writer, Robert O'Connell, has developed this understanding of James' theory of truth in an excellent book-length study.[10] O'Connell has shown that James held that the "passional" side of human nature intervenes from the first movements of the intellect and not only from the moment when the intellect's survey of the evidence has reached an impasse. Such a position implies that only the thinker of developed moral character can be expected to "see" the universe in appropriate moral terms. O'Connell adds that one is reminded of Aristotle's warnings about teaching philosophy to the young and Plato's claim that only one "sensibilized" to beauteous forms can glimpse the forms.[11]

O'Connell points out that James took this position in both his earlier and his later writings. The "passional nature" of being is granted license to intervene *prior* to our intellectual survey of the facts, and in a way that governs that intellectual survey.

In James' position, any philosophical study of the world may yield a number of formulae, all consistent with the facts, yet developed for different purposes. This is true in the physical sciences, and there does not seem to be any reason why it should not be true in philosophy.

> Why may there not be different points of view for surveying it (i.e., the world), within each of which all data harmonize, and which the observer may therefore either choose between or simply cumulate one upon another? A Beethoven string quartet is truly, as someone has said, a scraping of horses' tails on cats' bowels, and may be exhaustively described in such terms; but the application of this description in no way precludes the simultaneous applicability of an entirely different description. Just so, a through-going interpretation of the world in terms of mechanical sequence is compatible with its being interpreted teleologically, for the mechanism itself may be designed.[12]

For James, therefore, the element of choice, of will is present in every form of knowledge. But how, then, does one decide among the choices? James answered:

> If, then, there were several systems excogitated, equally satisfactory to our purely logical needs, they would still have to be passed in review, and approved or rejected by our aesthetic and practical nature.[13]

In making such choices, one considers the relationships of one thing with another. One relationship is of greater importance than all the rest. "I mean the relation of a thing to its future consequences."[14]

In other words, the philosopher or the scientist chooses among possible conceptions on the basis of practical considerations, the foremost of which is its ability to "banish uncertainty from the future."[15]

The recognition by William James of the importance of the element of choice in all knowledge formed an important element in James' great work *The Principles of Psychology*, published in 1890. At the very beginning of that work, James noted that: "The pursuance of future ends and the choice of means for their attainment are thus the mark and criterion of the presence of mentality in a phenomenon."[16]

Knowledge is organized into systems, which may conflict among themselves. A choice has to be made, governed by principles. A system, to pass for true, "must at least include the reality of the sensible objects in it. . . ." The system which includes the most of them will prevail. In the meantime, various forms of idealism, or realism, or materialism are devised to deal with the facts which have to be included. James then notes:

> That theory will be most generally believed which, besides offering us objects able to account satisfactorily for our sensible experience, also offers those which are most interesting, those which appeal most urgently to our aesthetic, emotional, and active needs.[17]

In discussing reasoning, James notes again that "classification and conception are purely teleological weapons of the mind." He holds, therefore, that: "The essence of a thing is that one of its properties which is so important for my interests that in comparison with it I may neglect the rest."[18]

Reasoning, therefore, is always for a subjective interest. One extracts "essences" or characters which then serve as equivalents, or surrogates, for the entire original datum. To be able to reason, one must be able to extract "essences" or characters. James notes that some people reason better than others. Everybody has access to the same facts, but it takes a Newton to notice the law of the squares[19] or a Darwin to note the survival of the fittest. James explains that, while all knowledge is vague at first, it is differentiated by those who have experience and training in a particular field.

> A layman present at a shipwreck, a battle, or a fire is helpless. . . . But the sailor, the fireman, and the general know directly at what corner to take up the business. They "see into the situation" — that is, they analyze it — with their first glance. It is full of delicately differenced ingredients which their education has little by little brought to their consciousness, but of which the novice gains no clear idea.[20]

James completes his chapter on reasoning in *The Principles of Psychology* by concluding that it is intimately connected with conception, and hence with the attention paid to particular "essences" or characters. This brings out again the importance of the principle of selection, or, in other words, the influence of the volitional powers, the "passional nature" on all forms of knowing.[21]

Notes

1 Levinson, *Religious Investigations*, pp. 293-294, 296-297.

2 H. S. Thayer, Introduction to William James, *The Meaning of Truth*, p. xxxvii.

3 H. S. Thayer, Introduction to William James, *The Meaning of Truth*, p. xxvii.

4 William James, *The Meaning of Truth*, pp. 126-133. The quotation is found on p. 128.

5 William James, *The Meaning of Truth*, p. 106. See also Perry, *Present Philosophical Tendencies*, pp. 214f.

6 See Susan Haack, "Can James' Theory of Truth be Made More Satisfactory?," *Transactions of the Charles S. Peirce Society* 20 (1984): 269-278. She cites *Pragmatism*, pp. 95f. In this article Haack, rightly I believe, rejects Bybee's position that James' theory of truth is rather a theory of knowledge. See Michael D. Bybee, "James' Theory of Truth as a Theory of Knowledge," *Transactions of the Charles S. Peirce Society* 20 (1984): 253-267.

7 William James, "The Sentiment of Rationality," in *Essays in Philosophy*, p. 56.

8 William James, "The Sentiment of Rationality," in *The Will to Believe*, p. 62 (henceforth cited as SR).

9 Edward H. Madden, Introduction to William James, *The Will to Believe*, p. xi. This same rediscovery has been made by H. S. Thayer. See H. S. Thayer, Introduction to *Pragmatism*, p. xxi.

10 Robert J. O'Connell, S. J., *William James on the Courage to Believe* (New York: Fordham University Press, 1984).

11 O'Connell, p. 3.

12 SR, p. 66.

13 SR, p. 66.

14 SR, p. 67.

15 SR, p. 67.

16 William James, *The Principles of Psychology*, p. 21.

17 William James, *The Principles of Psychology*, p. 940.

18 William James, *The Principles of Psychology*, p. 961.

19 Newton studied the elements of circular motion and then applied his findings to the moon and the planets. He derived the universe square relation, that is, that the radially directed force acting on a planet decreases with the square of its distance from the sun. This was crucial for the law of universal gravitation. See *Encyclopaedia Britannica*, 15th ed. (1974), s.v. "Newton, Sir Isaac," by Richard S. Westfall.

20 William James, *The Principles of Psychology*, p. 969.

21 William James, *The Principles of Psychology*, p. 992.

Chapter XI

The Meaning of "Faith" as Working Hypothesis

In the inquiry into William James' theory of truth, it is helpful to investigate the meaning of James' concept of faith. This word has sometimes caused confusion for James' readers, who might understand the word in its theological meaning. For example, the teaching of the Catholic Church is that faith is a supernatural virtue, a gift from God, by which one gives oneself to God and accepts God's word as revelation. This is a completely different concept from James' concept of faith. For James, "belief" will mean every degree of assurance, including the highest possible certainty and conviction.[1] Faith and belief, for James, are not narrowly religious concepts. James saw faith as a central act of the mind, not only in religious matters but also in secular matters, in science as well as philosophy.

It is interesting that this statement is in the opening paragraph of a chapter entitled "The Perception of Reality." He states that "the true opposites of belief, psychologically considered, are doubt and inquiry, not disbelief."[2]

In both the former states, doubt and inquiry, the content of the mind is in unrest. Belief is the resting of the mind in its conception.

With regard to the acceptance of any kind of theory, that theory will be most acceptable, will be believed, which appeals most to our aesthetic, emotional, and active needs.[3]

For James, faith is not understood as a religious act, or limited to the acceptance of religious theory. Faith extends to all areas of the intellectual life. Wherever there is a judgment about something "concerning which doubt is still theoretically possible, and where one is willing to act, it is proper to speak of faith as belief." James says that: "faith is the readiness to act in a cause, the prosperous issue of which is not certified to us in advance."[4]

James points out that the scientific philosophers of the day, who decry religious faith, make at least one act of faith themselves, namely, that the course of nature is uniform. Of course, this belief is necessary for the very existence of all the sciences. All scientific work demands a certain degree of subjective energy, which in turn calls for a certain amount of faith in the results.

From 1879, therefore, when "The Sentiment of Rationality" was published, and through the years when he was working on *The Principles of Psychology* (published in 1890), and through the last decade of the nineteenth century when he was concerned with *The Will to Believe*, William James was consistent in seeing faith as a central act of the mind in religious and secular matters, in science, and in philosophy.

But, one might ask, is it not immoral, shameful, illogical to take an attitude of faith? James recalls that Professor Huxley holds that faith in a doctrine for which we have no compelling proof is the "lowest depth of immorality." And Professor Clifford calls it "guilt" and "sin" to believe even the truth without "scientific evidence."[5]

The implied premise for thinkers like Huxley and Clifford is that philosophical and religious evidence is available to everyone, without reference to power of intellect or preparation of mind and heart. James says: "But what is the use of being a genius, unless *with the same scientific evidence* as other men, one can reach more truth than they?"[6]

James notes that Clifford himself proclaimed his belief in a psychological theory called "the conscious-automaton theory." On the other hand, George Henry Lewes (1817-1879), a British philosopher, rejected the theory, although the proofs before him were the same which Clifford accepted. For James, this would not present itself as a difficulty because he held that one may be "peculiarly sensitive to evidence that bears in one direction." This sensitivity should not be decried as the intrusion of a subjective factor. Rather, it should be seen as a kind of divination pointing one in the direction of the right answer.

> ... Every philosopher, or man of science either, whose initiative counts for anything in the evolution of thought, has taken his stand on a sort of dumb conviction that the truth must lie in one direction rather than another, and a sort of preliminary assurance that his notion could be made to work.[7]

James shows that what makes people like Clifford or Huxley interesting to us is the very fact that they are determined to be right, and that they throw their resources into the fray to do whatever is necessary to be right. They have a sense, a divination, of where the truth lies, and they go for it with all their might. James sums up in these words:

> In short, if I am born with such a superior general reaction to evidence that I can guess right and act accordingly, and gain all that comes of right action, while my less gifted neighbor (paralyzed by his scruples and waiting for more evidence which he dares not anticipate, must as he longs to) still stands shivering on the brink, by what law shall I be forbidden to reap the advantages of my superior native sensitiveness?[8]

From such passages it is possible to see further what role James assigns to faith. In all areas of intellectual activity, for any real progress, it is necessary that the scientist or philosopher or religious thinker begin his work with some degree of faith. No one would begin any effort to find the truth unless one had some idea where it could be found. Faith, therefore, means, in such cases, the "working hypothesis" which gathers together the intuitions, the experience of the thinker, the first hints of evidence, and uses the working hypothesis to arouse and channel the energy needed to put that hypothesis to the test of action.

Applying this to religious beliefs, when one confronts the great questions such as the reality of God, the immortality of the soul, morality, and free will, the "working hypothesis" may be strong enough to provide a reasonable basis for religious living. James holds out the chance that, ". . . his intimate persuasion (may be) that the odds in its favor are strong enough to warrant him in acting all along on the assumption of its truth."[9]

This understanding of faith, then, as "working hypothesis" is a key element in James' theory of truth and an important insight into process that led James to the affirmation of God.

Notes

1 William James, *The Principles of Psychology*, p. 913.

2 William James, *The Principles of Psychology*, p. 914.

3 William James, *The Principles of Psychology*, p. 940.

4 William James, *TWTB*, p. 76.

5 William James, *TWTB*, p. 77. The references to Huxley and Clifford are found in *The Will to Believe*, pp. 265 and 255.

6 William James, *TWTB*, p. 77.

7 William James, *TWTB*, p. 77f.

8 William James, *TWTB*, p. 78.

9 William James, *TWTB*, p. 79.

Chapter XII

Outcome Cases

In describing his position in *The Will to Believe,* James used several examples to make his point. The examples, however, have sometimes led to confusion, and so it is helpful to examine a couple of them more closely to see what role they play in his approach to God.

The first example is found in the 1879 essay, "The Sentiment of Rationality." The example reads as follows:

> Suppose, for example, that I am climbing in the Alps, and have had the ill-luck to work myself into a position from which the only escape is by a terrible leap. Being without similar experience, I have no evidence of my ability to perform it successfully; but hope and confidence in myself make me sure I shall not miss my aim, and nerve my feet to execute what without those subjective emotions would have perhaps have been impossible.... In this case (and it is one of an immense class) the part of wisdom clearly is to believe what one desires; for the belief is one of the indispensable preliminary conditions of the realization of its object. *There are then cases where faith creates its own verification.* Believe, and you shall be right, for you shall save yourself; doubt, and you shall again be right, for you shall perish. The only difference is that to believe is greatly to your advantage.[1]

A second case used by James in the 1896 essay "The Will to Believe" was that of the train robbers.

> A whole train of passengers (individually brave enough) will be looted by a few highway men, simply because the latter can count on one another, while each passenger fears that if he makes a movement of resistance, he will be shot before anyone else backs him up. If we believed that the whole car-ful would rise at once with us, we should each severally rise, and train-robbing would never even be attempted. There are, then, cases where a fact cannot come at all unless a preliminary faith exists in its coming. *And where faith in a fact can help create the fact*, that would be an insane logic which should say that faith running ahead of scientific evidence is the "lowest kind of immorality" into which a thinking being can fall.[2]

In analyzing these two examples, it is helpful to use terminology which James himself used, the significance of which has been brought out well by Father O'Connell. In a letter to L. T. Hobhouse in 1904, he reacted to Hobhouses's references to "The Will to Believe." First of all, James suggests that the essay "should have been called by the less unlucky title the *Right to Believe*."

James described his effort in the essay as an attempt to give a license to indulge in private over-beliefs,[3] which he claimed to have hedged with many restrictions. O'Connell notes that James leaves the term "over-beliefs" undefined, but nevertheless expects his correspondent to understand it. James also spoke of "Mystical over-beliefs" in notes made during the preparation for the Gifford lectures. There he wrote: "In religion the vital needs, the mystical over-beliefs . . . proceed from an ultra rational region."[4] These over-beliefs are productions of what James calls "the passional nature." The meaning of "over-belief" can be seen more clearly in the light of a 1907 letter from James to Horace M. Kallen. James said:

> Truth is constituted by verification actual or possible, and beliefs, *however* reached have to be verified before they count as true. . . . It is *usually* poor policy to believe what isn't verified but sometimes the belief produces verification — as when it produces activity creative of the fact believed; and again, it may without altering given facts, be a belief in an altered value or meaning for them.[5]

O'Connell points out that in this passage James distinguishes between a first kind of belief which "produces verification, when it produces activity creative of the fact believed," and a second kind of belief which "may without altering given facts be a belief in an altered meaning or value for them."[6] It would seem that the term "over-belief" refers to the same kind of experience as this second kind of belief.

It is the first kind of belief, the belief that produces verification by activity creative of the fact believed, which is illustrated by James' two examples. O'Connell describes these cases as "outcome illustrations." He says:

> For in all of them we are asked to consider a belief as promoting a choice of one alternative over its opposite — jumping for example instead of staying — and in all of them we may judge the soundness of the guiding belief on the

basis of its eventual outcome . . . whether or not it did in fact produce the kind of action "creative of the fact believed."[7]

In the case of the Alpinist, therefore, the belief that one can jump successfully creates the hope and confidence which makes it possible to make the terrible jump, and the belief produces its verification by producing activity creative of the fact believed.

On the contrary, in the case of the train robbery, the absence of the belief on the part of any of the passengers that he can spark a successful resistance of the passengers against the train robbers brings it about that no one of the passengers will make the initial heroic effort. Therefore, the robbers will be successful; or, to reverse the point of view, the belief that one cannot succeed produces the passivity which provides for the verification of the belief.

Two other examples have entered the James literature in recent years, the Street Car Case, proposed by C. J. Ducasse,[8] and the Truck Driver Case, proposed by Stephen T. Davis.[9] In Ducasse's Street Car Case let one suppose himself

> . . . on a street car going down a hill when suddenly the brakes fail. There are then two possible things for a passenger to do: To jump off, or to stay on. But he does not know which of the two is most likely to save him from injury, and he cannot put off deciding which to do until he has consulted the records of other accidents. In such a case decision is and has to be non-rational, in the sense of being instinctive, impulsive, temperamental, instead of based on in your words "a rational gauging of the exigency."[10]

The case proposed by Davis is as follows:

> While entering a steep down grade, a truck driver suddenly discovers that his brakes have failed. The truck begins to pick up speed and the driver sees that he will soon be in real danger. In this situation, the driver is faced with a choice: He can either jump from the truck, risking some bruises and broken bones while escaping the greater danger of a possible crash further down the hill, or he can remain in the truck, risking a crash but hoping eventually to guide the truck down the hill to a level spot. But the driver does not know how far it is till the end of the grade, for this stretch of road is new to him.[11]

When one compares these four examples, it seems clear that the two non-Jamesian examples involve choices that are pure gambles. In the Street Car Case of Ducasse, one must try to add additional factors, such as the driver's skill, or an "instinct of affirmation," to pull the decision out of the category of a pure gamble. This is also true of Davis' case, and both examples illustrate the interpretation given by some of James' approach to God as "wishful thinking." Davis, in fact, has James accept the criticism and say: "All right, but what exactly is wrong with wishful thinking in cases involving genuine options?"[12]

Ducasse describes the street car choice as "pure gamble." The side on which one bets depends on one's temperament. Whatever, however, determines the decision one way or the other is totally non-rational. Ducasse considered that he had developed a defense of "wishful thinking."

Must the same be said of James' two examples? Not, it would seem, for the train robbery case. The fact of an heroic resistance by the passengers cannot come about unless there is a preliminary faith in its coming, and that faith helps to create the fact of resistance. In this case, therefore, the faith of the passengers is not a pure gamble, nor can it be called wishful thinking. The faith of the passengers would presumably be communicated by subtle signs and would call forth similar faith in others, leading to resistance.

What about James' case of the Alpinist? Here again it seems clear that it is not a question of a pure gamble; in this case the faith in one's ability to make the terrible leap creates hope and confidence in oneself and gives one the courage to execute what would otherwise have been impossible.

Father O'Connell sees James' two cases of the Alpinist and the Train Robbers as parallel to the Street Car Case and the Truck Driver Case. O'Connell describes all four cases as "outcome illustrations."[13]

This judgment however cannot be accepted, since it does not distinguish between the nature of the two non-Jamesian cases as pure gamble and James' two cases in which belief-producing activity is creative of the fact believed. With regard to the affirmation of God, however, it does not seem that any of the four cases expresses clearly James' approach. At best, the cases developed by Ducasse and Davis can be used as explanations of an approach based on Pascal's wager argument, an argument which plays a dominant role in "The Will to Believe," as will be shown.

James' two examples on the other hand cannot be used in arguing for the affirmation of God since his existence is not a fact created by one's belief. As O'Connell notes, such examples leave important gaps between what I believe to be the case, that is, that God exists, and what in actuality is the case. Secondly, if the case is now that there is no God, my actions cannot change what is now the case, and make it that God exists.[14]

O'Connell holds therefore that James' way of appealing to such outcome cases as those of the Alpinist or the Train Robbers is seriously misguided when applied to the existence of God.

One may concede this from a strictly logical point of view. Nevertheless, it seems clear that James did not propose these examples as the logical equivalents of his approach to the affirmation of God. What, then, is their role? They may have been used to illustrate James' point that one must make important decisions in life on the basis of the non-logical factors which he calls "our passional nature." If this is so they are not out of place in "The Will to Believe" and "The Sentiment of Rationality."

Notes

1 William James, *TWTB*, p. 80.

2 William James, *TWTB*, p. 29.

3 See William James, *Letters*, 2:207.

4 Perry, 2:328; O'Connell, p. 71.

5 Perry, 2:249.

6 O'Connell, p. 71.

7 O'Connell, p. 71.

8 See Peter H. Hoare and Edward H. Madden, William James, Dickenson Miller & C. J. Ducasse on 'The Ethics of Belief,' *Transactions of the Charles S. Peirce Society* 4, no. 3 (Fall 1969): 115-129. The case is given in O'Connell, p. 61.

9 *Transactions of the Charles S. Peirce Society* 8, no. 4 (Fall 1972): 231-245.

10 Hare and Madden, p. 117, as given in O'Connell, p. 61.

11 Davis, p. 239.

12 Davis, p. 244.

13 O'Connell, p. 71.

14 O'Connell, p. 80.

Chapter XIII

Pascal and the Wager Argument

In his essay "The Will to Believe," Willliam James included a brief treatment of Pascal's wager. The brevity of the treatment, however, is no indication of the importance of the Wager Argument in James' thought. It is surprising, therefore, that Levinson's full scale investigation of James' religious investigation does not mention Pascal or the wager.[1] The even more recent major study by Gerald E. Meyers refers to the Wager Argument in a single sentence.[2]

Blaise Pascal

Blaise Pascal (1623-1662) was a French mathematician, physicist, inventor, philosopher and religious thinker. Pascal was a prodigy educated solely by his father, an excellent mathematician. At sixteen, Pascal wrote his first major work, "An Essay on Conics." At nineteen, Pascal invented the calculating machine, an important contribution to the industrial revolution. His work replicating Torricelli's experiment with a barometer led to Pascal's statement of the conditions for judging a scientific hypothesis, an important description of scientific method.

Pascal had a religious conversion in 1646, and he associated himself with the Jansenists of Port Royal. After a profound religious experience in 1654, Pascal devoted the rest of his life principally to religious activities. He began to jot down brief reflections on religion in the hope of developing a Christian apologetics. These reflections, the *Pensees*, were left unfinished, and have been organized by various editors according to very different plans.[3]

A recent English translation of his *Pensees* is that by A. J. Krailsheimer, Pascal, *Pensees* (Middlesex, England: Penguin Books Ltd., 1966). This edition follows Lafuma's arrangement of the *Pensees*.

The Wager Argument of Pascal

The text of the Wager Argument in the Krailsheimer translation runs five pages. The argument may be abbreviated slightly as follows:

> Let us say: "Either God is or he is not." But to which view shall we be inclined? Reason cannot make you choose either, reason cannot prove either wrong.
>
> Do not then condemn as wrong those who have made a choice, for you know nothing about it. "No, but I will condemn them not for having made this particular choice, but any choice, for, although the one who calls heads and the other one are equally at fault, the fact is that they are both at fault: the right thing is not to wager at all."
>
> Yes, but you must wager. There is no choice, you are already committed. Which will you choose then? Let us see: since a choice must be made, let us see which offers you the least interest. You have two things to lose: the true and the good; and two things to stake: your reason and your will, your knowledge and your happiness; and your nature has two things to avoid: error and wretchedness. Since you must necessarily choose, your reason is no more affronted by choosing one rather than the other. That is one point cleared up. But your happiness? Let us weigh up the gain and the loss involved in calling heads that God exists. Let us assess the two cases: if you win you win everything, if you lose you lose nothing. Do not hesitate then; wager that he does exist.
>
> You want to be cured of unbelief and you ask for the remedy: learn from those who were once bound like you and who now wager all they have. These are people who know the road you wish to follow, who have been cured of the affliction of which you wish to be cured: follow the way by which they began. They behaved just as if they did believe, taking holy water, having masses said, and so on. That will make you believe quite naturally, and will make you more docile.
>
> Now what harm will come to you from choosing this course? You will be faithful, honest, humble, grateful, full of good works, a sincere, true friend. ... It is true you will not enjoy noxious pleasures, glory and good living, but will you not have others?
>
> "I tell you that you will gain even in this life, and that at every step you take along this road you will see that your gain is so certain and your risk so negligible that in the end you will realize that you have wagered on something certain and infinite for which you have paid nothing."[4]

The Meaning of the Wager Argument for Pascal

After reviewing the Wager Argument in the *Pensees*, it is helpful to look into the meaning of the argument for Pascal himself.

Recently, Nicholas Rescher has noted that the strategy of the argument should be viewed against the background of Descartes' revolution in philosophy. "Descartes put man as knower at the center of the stage. Instead of addressing questions regarding the nature of reality *directly*, the issue of our *knowledge* became the pivot point."5

Pascal, however, rejected Descartes' position assigning to God the role of guarantor of our knowledge of the world. He also rejected Descartes' metaphysical proof for the existence of God. Pascal said:

> The metaphysical proofs of God are so remote from human reasoning and so complicated, that they make little impression. If some find them profitable, it is only at the moment when they grasp them; an hour later they fear they have been mistaken.6

Notice that Pascal does not reject the metaphysical proofs but, rather, holds that they are not psychologically effective for apologetic use. What he says of prophecies and miracles may be applied also to proofs for the existence of God from his point of view. Even if one should not think them absolutely convincing, one could not say that is unreasonable to accept them.7

Rescher points out that instead of attempting to demonstrate the existence of God, Pascal attempts to validate *belief* in God. "What we can establish by reasoning is not the direct conclusion that there is a God but only that oblique result that *belief* in God is warranted."8

Pascal is attempting to show uncommitted indifferentists that belief in God is rationally legitimate. Rescher holds that, in doing this, Pascal was following mitigated skepticism, by arguing that belief can be validated "on other than strictly evidential grounds, namely on grounds of *practical* reason — as instrumentality of action rather than theoretical cognition."9

Rescher holds that it is not the task of the Wager Argument to constrain actual belief. No mere argument can achieve that. He also holds that the argument is not to motivate a course of action *as if* one believed. In such a case, belief would be beside the point and hypocrisy.10

Rescher has identified what he calls salient features of Pascal's Wager Argument. First of all, he holds that the argument has its roots in doubt. One might accept this with regard to the person one is trying to convince. It is not true, however, of the person attempting to do the work of persuasion. Rescher also holds that the argument is non-demonstrative. In other words, Pascal, who thought proofs were ineffective, is not attempting another proof for the existence of God. Rescher rightly holds that: "As an instrument of apologetics the Wager Argument is aimed at *motivating* belief in God rather than at *demonstrating* its validity."[11]

The Wager Argument of Pascal should not be cut off from the entire body of his religious thought. That religious thought focuses on God and the human being. "Man is only a reed, the weakest in nature. But he is a thinking reed.... The greatness of man consists in thought."[12]

The Wager Argument is a religious rather than a philosophical argument. As James Collins has noted, from Voltaire onward, the Wager Argument has been subjected to severe criticism.[13]

The most important modern critic of the Wager Argument is the British philosopher Antony Flew.[14] Flew shows that he misunderstands the Wager Argument when he treats it as if it were an attempt at a metaphysical proof for God's existence, when in fact it is not.[15]

Flew's criticisms of the Wager Argument are seriously flawed by his misunderstanding of the Catholic teachings on the knowledge of God and the idea of eternal punishment. It is not necessary to report further on the criticisms here. The most important modern attack on the Wager Argument is beside the point.

Reasons of the Heart

For Pascal, the practical problem: Should I believe in God? is not usually solved by a study of the metaphysical proofs for God's existence; certitude is not attained by means of reasoning; certitudes are attained by the heart.

It is easy to misunderstand Pascal on this point. When he speaks of "the heart," he is not just referring to the emotions, but he means the exercise of the intelligence in a special way. To understand this, one must consider Pascal's distinction between "the spirit of geometry" and the "spirit of finesse." The geometric spirit is hard and inflexible. One and one always add up to two. Once one grasps the principles of mathematics, for example, one sees them clearly, and it is hard to go astray in reasoning about them.

The main problem is to grasp the principles securely. The opposing temper of mind, "the spirit of finesse," deals with principles in common use. They are there for anyone to see. The trouble is that there are so many principles, and they are so hard to see, that many people never grasp those principles.

We have only one mind, but it functions very differently in demonstrating conclusions from geometrical principles, when it functions as reason, and when it tries to grasp subtle principles in a simple and comprehensive vision. It is this latter use of the mind that Pascal calls "the heart." This is almost exactly the classical distinction made between reason and intellect, and it is almost exactly the modern distinction between reason and intuition.[16]

In other words, what Pascal calls "the heart" is the way the mind operates in knowing principles, even the principles of geometry. Feeling may be involved, particularly in moral or religious problems, but this is not necessarily so. The principles of geometry are grasped by the heart, by an intuition, at a glance. They are not the conclusions of reason, but, just as surely, they are not grasped by mere feeling.[17]

Pascal describes this intuitive knowledge of the first principles as being as solid as that which reasoning provides. And it is these knowledges of the heart and what Pascal calls "instinct" that reason builds upon and which serves as the foundation for all its discourse. Pascal holds that it would be as useless and ridiculous for reason to require from the heart proofs of its first principles as it would be for the heart to require from the reason a feeling for all the propositions which it demonstrates.[18]

One additional point which is helpful in interpreting Pascal's Wager Argument is the recognition that, for Pascal, one's grasp of truth is impeded by the passions. Pascal, therefore, encourages his reader to make efforts not in trying to convince oneself by heaping up proofs for God but by trying to reduce the strength of one's passions. One can do this by learning from those who have been entangled in problems but who are now willing to bet everything on God. These are people who know the road you want to follow and who have been cured of the illness that you wish to have cured. Follow them.[19]

The Wager Argument for Pascal is not an attempt at a metaphysical proof for the existence of God. It is an apologetic effort, aimed at persons who have not definitely rejected the existence of God. They are still open to the possibility that there is a God. The argument does not attempt to demonstrate the existence of God but to show that a reasonable person may still affirm the reality of God. As used by Pascal, the argument is helped by the evident faith of its proponent and the witness of his own belief in God. This witness is founded upon reasons of the heart, profound insights into the truth. Those to whom God gives such a belief, founded on reasons of the heart, are indeed happy, and they consider themselves quite legitimately persuaded of His existence.[20]

Practical Certitude: Pascal and Kant

One might describe Pascal's Wager Argument as an attempt to reach a practical certitude of the existence of God. This marked a decisive step in modern philosophy.

Pascal moved the discussion from attempts to prove the existence of God through speculative demonstration to attempts at seeing the existence of God as the conclusion of practical reasoning. Pascal did not reject the metaphysical proofs for the existence of God on the basis of logical or metaphysical reasoning. Rather he held that such proofs are so far removed from man's thinking and so complicated that few are convinced by them, and even they who see the force of these demonstrations shortly afterwards are afraid that they may have been mistaken.[21] Pascal, then, does not attack the philosophical value of the metaphysical proofs but only their apologetic value in leading one to conversion.

The concept of practical certitude based on practical reason is normally associated with Immanuel Kant (1724-1804). Kant turned to practical reasoning only after he had come to the conclusion that speculative reason could not demonstrate the existence of God. Kant, in his greatest work, *The Critique of Pure Reason* (1781),[22] concluded that:

> ... all attempts to apply reason in theology in any merely speculative manner are altogether fruitless and by their very nature null and void. ... Consequently, the only theology of reason which is possible is that which is based upon moral laws or seeks guidance from them.[23]

In his second critique, *The Critique of Practical Reason* (1788), Kant presented the existence of God as a postulate of pure practical reason. Kant said that the condition for the speculative use of reason is its knowledge of the highest *a priori* principles. The condition of the practical use of reason lies in the determination of the will with respect to the final and perfect end.[24]

The first postulate of pure practical reason is the immortality of the soul. Kant held that the achievement of the highest good in the world is the necessary object of the will. Therefore the complete fitness of the will is the supreme condition of the highest good. But the complete fitness of the will is holiness. Holiness can be found only in an endless progress to that complete fitness. This endless infinite progress of the will is possible only if the will is the infinitely enduring existence and personality of the same rational being. Or, in other words, this infinite progress is possible only if the soul is immortal.

The immortality of the soul, therefore, is a postulate of pure practical reason.[25] The same reasoning leads one to affirm also a happiness proportional to the highest good. Therefore one must postulate the existence of God as necessarily belonging to the possibility of the highest good. The existence of God, therefore, is also a postulate of pure practical reason.[26]

When one compares the approach of Kant to that of Pascal, it is notable that Pascal's Wager Argument does not conclude directly to the existence of God. Rather, it is a practical justification of belief in God. The thrust of Pascal's argument is to justify the act of faith in God as a prudent decision. For Pascal, in addition, this prudent choice to believe in God carries in its train belief in the entire Catholic system ("holy water and masses"). Pascal seems to reason that one who bets on God is implicitly betting on the Catholic Church.

Kant, on the other hand, would disdain to bet on anything, and his understanding of Christianity is purely naturalistic. Kant is the enemy of supernaturalism, based on divine revelation, and clericalism, the possession of supernatural powers by men who are officials of a church founded by God. The nature of Kant's religion is expressed in the title of his book, *Religion Within the Limits of Reason Alone*.[27]

The difference between Pascal's approach and Kant's approach is clear. Pascal uses the Wager Argument to bring a prospective convert to the point where he can reasonably make an act of faith. Kant, after having rejected the possibility of a rational demonstration of God's existence, attempts to rationalize his belief in God and immortality by forming postulates on the basis of practical reasoning. If one is to be moral at all, one must accept God and immortality. There is a wall, however, between practical reason and pure or speculative reason, so that one's practical postulates are without any speculative value.

For Kant, then, practical reason can lead to decisions which are significant for one's moral and religious life. For Pascal, on the other hand, the Wager Argument, though not a philosophical argument, can be used as apologetics to bring a person of good faith to accept the existence of God. Pascal does not draw clear lines between speculative and practical reason, and he would be surprised to hear the claim that philosophy should not make a place for our affirmation of God even if it were based on practical reasons.

William James is closer to Pascal than to Kant on this point. While he would not quibble about words, and would allow his field of research to be called "religious science," he puts the affirmation of God at the center of his philosophical vision.

The Place of the Wager Argument in James' "The Will to Believe"

As indicated previously, William James included the Wager Argument of Pascal in his essay "The Will to Believe." James' language in presenting Pascal's argument seems to have a connotation of contempt for the argument. He begins by describing the argument as an attempt "to force us into Christianity by reasoning as if our concern with truth resembled our concern with the stakes in a game of chance."[28]

In *The Will to Believe* James presented Pascal's Wager Argument as follows:

> You must either believe or not believe that God is — which will you do? Your human reason cannot say. A game is going on between you and the nature of things which at the day of judgment will bring out either heads or tails. Weigh what your gains and your losses would be if you should stake all

you have on heads, or God's existence: if you win such a case, you gain eternal beatitude; if you lose, you lose nothing at all. If there were an infinity of chances, and only one for God in this wager, still you ought to stake your all on God; for though you surely risk a finite loss by this procedure, any finite loss is reasonable, even a certain one is reasonable, if there is but the possibility of infinite gain. Go then, and take holy water, and have masses said; belief will come and stupify your scruples — *cela vous fera croire et vous abetira*. Why should you not? At bottom what have you to lose?[29]

After stating the argument James comments:

You probably feel that when religious faith expresses itself thus, in the language of the gaming-table, it is put to its last trumps.... We feel that a faith in masses and holy water adopted willfully after such a mechanical calculation would lack the inner soul of faith's reality; and if we were ourselves in the place of the Deity, we should probably take particular pleasure in cutting off believers of this pattern from their infinite reward.[30]

It is interesting to note, however, that James repeats three times the words "masses and holy water." It seems clear therefore that he had slid imperceptibly from the question of belief in God to that of belief in the Catholic Church, symbolized by the words "masses and holy water." James then tells his audience that Pascal would vainly use his argument on "us, for the hypothesis he offers us is dead."[31]

The casual reader of James' essay would easily conclude that the Wager Argument had been dismissed from consideration. A closer analysis of the essay will show that James himself used an argument very similar to the Wager Argument, but without reference to the Catholic system, masses and holy water. For example, James says, toward the end of "The Will to Believe,"

But sad experience makes me fear that some of you may still shrink from radically saying with me, *in abstracto*, that we have the right to believe at our own risk any hypothesis that is live enough to tempt our will.[32]

The religious hypothesis is a living option, a momentous option and forced option. We cannot merely refuse to decide. A refusal would avoid error if religion is untrue. Nevertheless, we lose the good if the religious hypothesis be true. We are just as badly off as if we positively chose to disbelieve. The skeptic holds that it is better to risk loss of truth than chance of error. It is obvious that this is as much an unproved proposition as its opposite. The skeptic's position should not be described as the intellect against all passions; it is only intellect obeying one passion which lays down the law.

James rejects skepticism and argues in favor of committing oneself to God, even when there is some risk in doing so. He says:

> If religion be true and the evidence for it be still insufficient, I do not wish, by putting your extinguisher upon my nature (which feels to me as if it had after all some business in this matter), to forfeit my sole chance in life of getting upon the winning side — that chance depending, of course, on my willingness to run the risk of acting as if my passional need of taking the world religiously might be prophetic and right.[33]

James, therefore, after criticizing Pascal's Wager Argument, comes around to something very close to it. He goes a step further and criticizes one who refuses to bet on God. According to James:

> One who should shut himself up in snarling logicality and try to make the gods extort his recognition willy-nilly, or not get it at all, might cut himself off forever from his only opportunity to making the god's acquaintance.[34]

James, therefore, cannot see his way clear to accepting the agnostic's rules for truth-seeking. He will not agree to keep his willing nature out of the game. James expresses his position theoretically in a rule of formal logic as follows: *"A rule of thinking which would absolutely prevent me from acknowledging certain kinds of truth if those kinds of truth were really there would be an irrational rule."*[35]

In summary, James at first rejected Pascal's Wager Argument, but then expressed in his own language an argument which is suspiciously similar to that of Pascal.

Notes

1 Levinson, *The Religious Investigations of William James*.

2 Gerald E. Meyers, *William James: His Life and Thought* (New Haven and London: Yale University Press, 1986), p. 452. Much of the recent literature on the Wager Argument is listed in Philip Wainwright, *Philosophy of Religion: An Annotated Bibliography of Twentieth century Writings in English* (New York and London: Garland Publishing, Inc., 1978), pp. 753-766.

3 The currently accepted best one-volume edition of Pascal's works is *Oeuvres Completes*, ed. Louis Lafuma, preface by Henri Gouhier (Paris: Editions du Seuil, 1963). This edition includes a table of concordance with the Brunschvicg edition. For the Brunschvicg arrangement of the *Pensees*, a convenient edition is that by Ch.-Marc Des Granges, Pascal, *Pensees* (Paris: Librairie Garnier Freres, 1948). In the 1963 Lafuma edition, the Wager Argument is No. 418 of the *Pensees*, pp. 550f. (Brunschvicg, No. 233).

4 Krailsheimer, pp. 150-153.

5 Nicholas Rescher, *Pascal: A Study of Practical Reasoning in Philosophical Theology* (Southbend, Ind.: University of Notre Dame Press, 1985), p. 3.

6 Pascal, *Pensees*, B543-L190 (translation by Rescher, p. 6).

7 Pascal, *Pensees*, L835-B564.

8 Rescher, p. 4.

9 Rescher, *Pascal's Wager*, p. 7.

10 Rescher, *Pascal's Wager*, p. 19.

11 Rescher, *Pascal's Wager*, pp. 20f.

12 Pascal, *Pensees*, B347-L200.

13 James Collins, *God in Modern Philosophy* (Chicago: Henry Regnery Co., 1959), p. 337. On p. 442, Collins cites Voltaire, *Letters Philosophiques*, vol. 25, and D. Finch, *La Critique Philosophique de Pascal au XVIIIe Siecle*.

14 See Antony Flew, *God, Freedom and Immortality: A Critical Analysis* (Buffalo, N.Y.: Prometheus Books, 1984). This book was published in Great Britain under the title *The Presumption of Atheism* (Pemberton Publishing Co., Ltd., 1976).

15 Flew, pp. 61-63.

16 See Gilson and Langan, pp. 112f., commenting on *Pensees*, L512-B1.

17 See Gilson and Langan, p. 113.

18 Pascal, *Pensees*, B282-L110. See Gilson and Langdon, pp. 480f.

19 Pascal, *Pensees*, L418-B233.

20 See Pascal, *Pensees*, B282-L110.

21 See Pascal, *Pensees*, B543-L190.

22 Immanuel Kant, *Critique of Pure Reason*, trans. Norman Kemp Smith (New York: St. Martins Press, 1965).

23 Kant, *Critique of Pure Reason*, p. 528.

24 Immanuel Kant, *Critique of Practical Reason*, trans. Lewis White Beck (Indianapolis: The Bobbs-Merrill Co., 1956), p. 124.

25 Kant, *Critique of Pure Reason*, pp. 126f.

26 Kant, *Critique of Pure Reason*, pp. 128f.

27 Immanuel Kant, *Religion Within the Limits of Reason Alone* (1793), trans. Theodore M. Greene and Hoyt H. Hudson (New York: Harper & Row, Publishers, 1960).

28 *TWTB*, p. 16.

29 William James, *TWTB*, p. 16.

30 *TWTB*, p. 16.

31 *TWTB*, pp. 16f.

32 *TWTB*, p. 32.

33 *TWTB*, p. 31.

34 *TWTB*, p. 31.

35 *TWTB*, pp. 31f. James italicized the entire rule.

Chapter XIV

Newman and James

Newman on Probability as the Guide of Life

In order to see the meaning of William James' position on the affirmation of God as a positive and reconciling hypothesis, it is helpful to examine the work of Cardinal Newman on the attainment of proof by converging probabilities. John Henry Newman (1801-1890) began his life as an Anglican. He became a leader of the Oxford movement in the Church of England in the 1830s. After the publication of Tract 90 in 1841, Newman's position was censured by the Anglican bishops. Tract 90 was an attempt to show that the Thirty-nine Articles, the official standard of belief for Anglicans, could be given a Catholic interpretation. A second blow to Newman's position was the establishment of an Anglican bishopric in Jerusalem in conjunction with the Protestants of Prussia. In both cases, Newman was confronted with a decisive Anglican rejection of his views. After a period of study and prayer, Newman was received into the Catholic Church in 1845. His book, *An Essay on the Development of Christian Doctrine* (1845), written during his period of search, was finished the day before he entered the Catholic Church.

After becoming a Catholic, Newman went to Rome for a brief period of study and there he was ordained a priest in 1847. He returned to England and established the Birmingham Oratory in 1848. From 1851 to 1858 he was in Ireland as rector of the new Catholic University. This led to his book *The Idea of a University* (1852-1859). In 1864, he wrote his *Apologia Pro Vita Sua* to defend his integrity and his religious conversion against an attack by Charles Kingsley, an Anglican clergyman and novelist.

In 1870, Newman published his *Essay in Aid of a Grammar of Assent* in which he studied the reasonable character of the act of religious faith. Pope Leo XIII made Newman a Cardinal in 1879, crowning his services to the Church with the highest approbation.[1]

Newman is hard to categorize as either a philosopher or a theologian. Perhaps he is best described as a religious thinker whose work is important both for theology and for the philosophy of religion. In the context of this study of William James' affirmation of the existence of God, Newman's thought is helpful in showing that a concrete way of knowing can lead to assent grounded upon probable arguments. Just as Pascal spoke of the heart having its reasons, so Newman suggested that, to gain a religious starting point, we must interrogate our hearts and our consciences.

Newman, while not rejecting the possibility of metaphysical demonstrations of God's existence, nevertheless felt the full force of the maxim of St. Ambrose: *"Non in dialectica complacuit Deo salvum facere populum suum"* (God did not will to save the world by logic).[2]

Newman declared that he had a great dislike for paper logic. "It's the concrete being that reasons . . . the whole man moves, paper logic is but the record of it."[3]

James Collins has pointed out that Newman had studied closely the rationalistic apologetic of William Paley (1743-1805) and Richard Whately (1787-1863).[4]

Whately was at Oriel College in 1822 when Newman was elected a fellow of Oriel. Whately was the leader of a group of Christian intellectuals known as the Noetics. They held that one had no right to believe in Christianity until he had given a formal demonstration of the principal Christian doctrines. This proof would be one patterned after the kind of proof required in mathematics and natural science. Newman joined the group and worked closely with Whately, even collaborating with Whately on the influential textbook *Elements of Logic*. While remaining grateful to Whately for opening his mind and teaching him how to think, Newman, nevertheless, moved out of Whately's circle.

Newman judged that the Noetics' criterion for reasonable belief was too narrow. He observed that many believers were unable to arrange their reasons for belief in a logical syllogism, but that their minds operated through an implicit kind of reasoning. Where Whately asserted that "all reasoning, on whatever subject, is one and the same process which may be clearly exhibited in the form of

Syllogisms,"[5] Newman learned that even natural scientists used non-formal types of reasoning.

Newman moved out of Whately's position emphasizing formal logic. In the meantime, he was well read in the philosophical traditions of England, and he considered that John Locke's *An Essay Concerning Human Understanding* (1690) was the central achievement in modern philosophy. Newman drew from Locke an understanding of the human being not as a pure reasoning logical machine but as a sensing-reasoning-feeling-believing-acting animal. Newman's major criticism of Locke was that Locke was not sufficiently empirical, not a sufficiently close adherent to human experience. Newman criticized Locke because he consults his own ideal of how the mind ought to act, instead of interrogating human nature, as an existing thing, as it is found in the world.[6]

A major influence on Newman's theory of knowledge was the work of Bishop Joseph Butler (1692-1752), the Anglican bishop of Durham. Newman learned from Butler that formal demonstrative logic, while important and necessary, was not adequate for dealing with the great problems of life. Butler held that: "Probability is the very guide of life." To abstract reasonings one must join the observation of facts. In addition to what can be formally demonstrated, one must collect what is likely, what is credible, and what is not credible.[7]

Newman, in the *Grammar of Assent*, draws upon Butler for the view that "probable proofs, by being added, not only increase the evidence, but multiply it. The truth of our religion, like the truth of common matters, is to be judged by the whole evidence taken together...."[8]

Newman points out that in Apologetics, just as in the physical sciences, a demonstration of the thesis may be absent but the cumulating and converging indications of it may lead one to recognize that the conclusion is not only probable but true.

Newman also accepted Butler's teaching that, in matters of religion, the moral state of the parties in an inquiry is significant. They must be as much in earnest about religion as about their temporal affairs, capable of being convinced, on real evidence, that there is a God who governs the world.[9]

Newman was well trained in the classics at Oxford. In 1824, he wrote an encyclopedia article on Cicero in which he displays a knowledge of various Hellenistic philosophies. Aristotle, however, was Newman's principal teacher among the ancient philosophers, and he considered himself to be an Aristotelian in philosophy.

> While we are men, we cannot help, to a great extent, being Aristotelians. . . . In many subject matters, to think correctly, is to think like Aristotle; and we are his disciples whether we will or no, though we may not know it.[10]

Newman, unlike the scholastic philosophers, did not focus mainly upon Aristotle's logic and metaphysics, where one looks for logical demonstration and metaphysical certitude. Rather he studied carefully Aristotle's practical philosophy, especially the *Nichomachean Ethics*.[11]

In the *Grammar of Assent* Newman points out, when discussing the nature of the illative sense, that his doctrine was influenced by Aristotle's teaching on prudence. For Aristotle, prudence is an intellectual virtue concerned with action, under the direction of correct reason, regarding things good for man.[12] In other words, prudent judgments do not depend on scientific demonstrations but on opinions, and these opinions are formed by deliberating well and looking at all the evidence in particular cases.

Newman holds that, in religious matters, just as in astronomy, one takes positions even though one does not have a demonstration of a thesis, provided that one has cumulating and converging indications of it. Even though the proof is indirect, one recognizes that the conclusion is not only probable, but true.[13] Newman compares this with Newton's celebrated lemma which opens the *Principia*. Newman expresses it as follows:

> We know that a regular polygon, inscribed in a circle, its sides being continually diminished, tends to become that circle, as its limit; but it vanishes before it has coincided with the circle, so that its tendency to be the circle, though ever nearer fulfillment, never in fact gets beyond a tendency. In like manner, the conclusion in a real or concrete question is foreseen and predicted rather than actually attained; foreseen in the number and direction of accumulated premises, which all converge to it, and as the result of their combination, approach it more nearly than any assignable difference, yet do not touch it logically. . . .[14]

Newman points out that it is by the strength, variety, or multiplicity of premises which are only probable that the practiced and experienced mind is able to make a sure divination that a conclusion is inevitable,

> ... of which his lines of reasoning do not actually put him in possession. This is what is meant by a proposition being "as good as proved," a conclusion as undeniable "as if it were proved," and by the reasons for it "amounting to a proof," for a proof is the limit of converging probabilities.[15]

This position of Newman is based on a clearly Aristotelian distinction between the demonstrative knowledge of mathematical science, which advances through syllogistic reasoning, and the knowledge of concrete realities, which advances by a variety of experiences.

In this type of concrete knowledge, Newman developed an understanding of the role of moral character in the acquisition of religious truth. Newman's more abundant statements on this point will be helpful in understanding William James' position.

In one of his earliest sermons preached before the University of Oxford, Newman spoke of "The philosophical temper first enjoined by the gospel." Newman points out that some of the habits of mind which are recommended by the Bible are the very habits which are necessary for success in scientific investigation. For example, it is necessary to be "in earnest in seeking the truth" if one is to attain philosophical truths. In addition, modesty, patience, and caution are dispositions of mind needed to succeed in philosophical inquiry. Rashness of assertion, hastiness in drawing conclusions, unhesitating reliance on our own acuteness and powers of reasoning are inconsistent with reaching truth. Nature

> ... refuses to reveal her mysteries to those who come otherwise than in the humble and reverential spirit of learners and disciples.... Again, indulgence of the imagination, though a more specious fault, is equally hostile to the spirit of true philosophy....[16]

Likewise, the assent of faith is kept from abuse (for example, from falling into superstition), by a right moral state of mind and by such dispositions as religiousness, and the love of holiness and truth.[17]

Newman also holds that, while the acceptance of God may be viewed as opposed to reason, it must not be overlooked that unbelief may be opposed to reason also. In an 1839 sermon on "Love, the Safeguard of Faith Against Superstition," Newman said:

> Unbelief, indeed, considers itself especially rational or critical of evidence; but it criticizes the evidence of religion only because it does not like it, and really goes upon presumptions and prejudices as much as faith does, only presumptions of an opposite nature ... On this account it is that unbelievers call themselves rational; not because they decide by evidence, but because, after they have made their decision, they merely occupy themselves in sifting it.[18]

Newman and James Compared

Newman, then, provides an example of a religious thinker of a very different tradition whose work in some areas parallels the work of William James. This discovery would have surprised James, who was acquainted with only a sampling of Newman's work. James looked upon Newman as a representative of "scholastic philosophy touched with emotion,"[19] "whose imagination innately craved a sacerdotal system."[20] He was apparently not familiar with *An Essay in Aid of a Grammar of Assent*, whose motto, as has been noted, was the famous quotation from St. Ambrose: "*Non in dialectica complacuit Deo salvum facere populum suum*" (Not by logic did it please God to save his people).

Newman's thought on what has been called moral certitude is helpful in understanding William James' position on the affirmation of God. For different reasons, Newman and James prescind from any metaphysical proofs for God's existence.

Neither of them considers himself to be forced into skepticism because of this. Both Newman and James were familiar with Kant's rejection of proofs for the existence of God. Both of them, moreover, knew that Kant himself did not consider the postulates of practical reason as having any speculative value. That is, Kant held that a positive use cannot be made of those postulates for theoretical purposes.[21]

The originality of Newman and James, compared to Kant, comes from the fact that both hold that one can attain truth through the kind of practical reasoning that leads to moral certitude.

In taking such a position, both Newman and James were influenced by their early professional formation. Newman did his first scholarly work in the field of history. As an historian, he did not expect to reach mathematical or metaphysical certitude about the objects of his study, but historical, or moral, certitude.

In the case of James, his training as a physician seems subconsciously to have led him to this same kind of confidence in non-logical reasoning. The physician or the psychologist or the psychiatrist must reach a decision as to the diagnosis of the patient before the treatment begins. The beginning of the treatment cannot be postponed too long or the patient's condition will worsen. The therapist tries to determine the symptoms and to analyze them in accordance with two fundamental yet related principles, parsimony and hierarchy. These principles are explained in a recent book on clinical psychiatry: "The principle of *parsimony* is that clinicians should seek the single most elegant, economical, and efficient diagnosis that accounts for *all* the available data. . . ."[22]

Maxmen warns therapists that a diagnosis may remain unclear because of inadequate data, or premature closure of the process for diagnosis, or an atypical presentation by the patient. Maxmen explains this last by suggesting that some patients "lack the decency to conform to classic textbook descriptions."[23]

The therapist might often desire greater clarity in making a diagnosis. Nevertheless, he can gain something like what is called moral certitude, and he can be confident enough that he has learned the truth about his patient's condition to proceed with the therapy. In the language of the scholastic moral theologians, his moral certitude means that he has no prudent fear of being in error in making the diagnosis. In still other words, while he cannot exclude all opposing possibilities, he reaches his diagnosis on the basis of converging probabilities.

Maxmen's modern textbook description of diagnosis in medicine and psychiatry seems to express what William James was trying to achieve by his acceptance of the "reconciling hypothesis." James does not seem to have adverted to this analogy himself, and there are no texts to back it up explicitly. Nevertheless, the reasoning patterns of James in the *Varieties* seem to justify the comparison.

In summary, then, one can see that both Newman, the historian, and James, the physician, had great confidence in concrete practical reasoning as a path to religious truth.

With this understanding of what William James was trying to achieve, it is clear that his position cannot be written off as "An attempt to build a superstructure of belief upon a foundation of skepticism"[24] as Bertrand Russell charged.

James' effort should rather be described as an attempt at an inquiry in religion in which he used whatever resources of knowledge and insight that were available to him to bring him to the reconciling hypothesis of the reality of God on which he staked his life. As James wrote in "The Will to Believe,"

> It matters not to an empiricist from what quarter an hypothesis may come to him: He may have acquired it by fair means or by foul; passion may have whispered or accident suggested it; but if the total drift of thinking continues to confirm it, that is what he means by its being true.[25]

For both Newman and James, the use of whatever evidence is available in a particular inquiry, and the gathering of converging probabilities, leads to a moral certitude. This certitude is not merely a skeptical and despairing abandonment of the search for truth but a submission of the intellect to reality and a willingness to be open to the truth even when it does not come packaged in neat syllogisms.

What does this comparison of Newman and James, and the notice paid to James' training as a physician, add to our understanding of James' approach to God? The comparisons bring out that, while James did not think it possible to formulate a cogent metaphysical proof for the existence of God, nevertheless he did hold that one could reach what the scholastics call moral certitude of God's existence, and that such a certitude is enough to justify the commitment of oneself to God and a religious life.

Notes

1. On the life of Newman, see the classical work of Wilfrid Ward, *The Life of John Henry Newman: Based on His Private Journals and Correspondence*, 2 vols. (New York and London: Longmans, Green & Co., 1912). A brief and more recent biography is that by Father C. S. Dessain, *John Henry Newman* (London: Thomas Nelson & Sons, 1966). For a rather complete guide to the literature about Newman, see John R. Griffin, *Newman: A Bibliography of Secondary Studies* (Fort Royal, Va.: Christendom College Press, 1980).

2. John Henry Newman, *Apologia pro Vita Sua* (1864), ed. David J. DeLaura (New York: W. W. Norton & Co., Inc., 1968), p. 136.

3. *Apologia*, p. 136.

4. See the brief articles on both Paley and Whately in *The Encyclopedia of Philosophy*; on Paley, vol. 6, pp. 19f. (Elmer Sprague); on Whately, vol. 8, pp. 287f. (Mary Prior).

5. Richard Whately, *Elements of Logic*, 9th ed. (Louisville: Morton & Griswold, 1854), p. 180, cited from James Collins, ed., *Philosophical Readings in Cardinal Newman* (Chicago: Henry Regnery Co., 1961), p. 6.

6. Collins, *Philosophical Readings*, p. 10. See for example, John Henry Newman, *An Essay in Aid of a Grammar of Assent* (1870) (reprint ed., New York: Longmans, Green & Co., 1947), p. 124.

7. Joseph Butler, *The Analogy of Religion*, in *The Works of Joseph Butler*, ed. W. E. Gladstone, 2 vols. (Oxford: The Clarendon Press, 1896), 1:5-11. See Collins, *Philosophical Writings*, p. 12.

8. John Henry Newman, *An Essay in Aid of a Grammar of Assent*, ed. Charles F. Harrold (New York: Longmans, Green & Co., 1947), pp. 242f., citing Butler's *Analogy*.

9. Newman, *Grammar of Assent*, p. 243, citing Butler's *Analogy*.

10. John Henry Newman, *The Idea of a University* (1852-1859) (London: Longmans, Green & Co., 1905), pp. 109ff.

11. Newman, *Grammar of Assent*, p. 268. See Collins, *Philosophical Readings*, p. 15.

12. Aristotle, *Nicomachean Ethics*, 1140b20.

13 Newman, *Grammar of Assent*, p. 243.

14 Newman, *Grammar of Assent*, p. 244.

15 Newman, *Grammar of Assent*, p. 244.

16 John Henry Newman, *Fifteen Sermons, Preached Before the University of Oxford Between 1826 & 1843* (London: Longmans, Green & Co., 1918), p. 9.

17 Newman, *Oxford University Sermons*, p. xvii.

18 Newman, *Oxford University Sermons*, p. 230.

19 *Varieties*, p. 362.

20 *Varieties*, p. 362.

21 See Kant, *Critique of Practical Reason*, p. 149.

22 Jerrold S. Maxmen, M.D., *Essential Psychopathology* (New York and London: W. W. Norton & Co., 1988), p. 40.

23 Maxmen, *Essential Psychopathology*, p. 47.

24 Bertrand Russell, *A History of Western Philosophy*, p. 18.

25 James, *TWTB*, p. 24.

Chapter XV

An Analysis of "The Will to Believe"

The State of the Question

William James' approach to the affirmation of God is developed in several of his essays. The source most frequently used in discussing James' position is his 1896 essay "The Will to Believe."[1] In that essay, James attempted to provide

> ... something like a sermon on justification by faith to read to you — I mean an essay in justification <u>of</u> faith, a defense of our right to adopt a believing attitude in religious matters, in spite of the fact that our merely logical intellect may not have been coerced.[2]

The word "right" has been overlooked by some interpreters who have attempted to describe James' approach as "wishful thinking." The word "will" in the title seems to connote that religious belief is not warranted. O'Connell brings out the warranted character of belief by recalling James' words of encouragement in the closing lines of the essay. There James wrote: "What must we do? 'Be strong and of good courage.'"[3]

Once again, the connotation is significant. "Courage" seems to connote that belief is not only warranted but that it is the right thing to do.

In "The Will to Believe," James said that he was defending a thesis which, briefly stated, is this:

> Our passional nature not only lawfully may, but must, decide an option between propositions, whenever it is a genuine option that cannot by its nature be decided on intellectual grounds; for to say, under such circumstances, "Do not decide, but leave the question open," is itself a passional decision — just like deciding yes or no — and is attended with the same risk of losing the truth.[4]

James expressed his thesis in still other words when he said that:

> We have the right to believe at our own risk any hypothesis that is live enough to tempt our will. ... *in concreto*, the freedom to believe can only cover living options which the intellect of the individual cannot by itself resolve; and living options never seem absurdities to him who has them to consider.[5]

James is careful to label a misapprehension the very position which he is often accused of holding. This position is humorously expressed in the language of the school boy when he said: "Faith is when you believe something you know ain't true."[6]

What kind of option did James have in mind? It must be a *live* hypothesis, that is, "one which appeals as a real possibility to him to whom it is proposed."[7]

Whether an option is live or dead is not an intrinsic property of an hypothesis but its relationship to the individual thinker. It is measured by his willingness to act on it. What one person might consider a worthless choice, a dead option, might be seen as a live option by another person of a different age and temperament.

In James' approach, the option must be *forced*. "Every dilemma based on a complete logical disjunction, with no possibility of not choosing, is an option of this forced kind."[8]

Finally, the option must be *momentous*; that is, a unique opportunity to win a prize, to achieve something of great value.

In James' essay, the acceptance of God is an option which is living, forced and momentous. How does one choose such an option? One might be able to reach absolute certitude. One's intellect might be so convinced by the logic of the case that one would be forced to accept the hypothesis on purely intellectual grounds. For James, however, the religious option is not supported by that kind of evidence, and it cannot give absolute certitude.

What then? Is it necessary to abandon belief altogether? James reports the position of W. K. Clifford who held that: "It is wrong always, everywhere, and for anyone, to believe anything upon insufficient evidence."[9]

For Clifford, no evidence for religion could ever be considered complete and sufficient to give a person something to live by. If one is too busy to engage in an endless course of study before believing anything, "then he should have no time to believe."[10] James rejects Clifford's position and offers several different approaches to the acceptance of God.

The Wager Argument

Reference is made to the Wager Argument here for the sake of completeness. The argument itself, in Pascal and in William James, has already been studied earlier in this chapter.

An Indirect Argument from Science

An indirect argument against Clifford's position that it is wrong always, everywhere, and for everyone, to believe anything on insufficient evidence, may be drawn from the practice of scientists. In drawing out this argument, one must understand that, for Clifford, no evidence can be sufficient to allow for a religious commitment. James' argument may be stated simply: scientists do not accept Clifford's scrupulous position on the acceptance of truth.

In support of this indirect argument, William James points out that all scientific work is based on the *belief* that truth itself is something that is attainable. There is no scientific proof that there is such a thing as truth. There is no scientific proof that our experiments and studies and discussions lead us continually closer to the truth. James provides a kind of negative pragmatic criterion for truth when he writes:

> As a rule we disbelieve all facts and theories for which we have no use. Clifford's cosmic emotions find no use for Christian feelings. Huxley belabors the bishops because there is no use for sacerdotalism in his scheme of life.... Why do so few "scientists" even look at the evidence for telepathy, so called? Because they think, as a leading biologist, now dead, once said to me, that even if such a thing were true, scientists ought to band together to keep it suppressed and concealed. It would undo the uniformity of Nature and all sorts of other things without which scientists cannot carry on their pursuits.[11]

The point, of course, that James is making is that science depends on first principles which are not demonstrated by logical syllogisms but are accepted by intuition or insight.[12]

The Passional Nature at the Root of All Our Convictions

In analyzing "The Will to Believe," it is important to bring out James' position on the psychology of human opinion. First of all, James does not hold that all our opinions are modifiable at will.

We cannot believe that Abraham Lincoln's existence is a myth, and that the portraits of him are all of someone else. We cannot by any effort of our will believe ourselves well when we are sick in bed. We cannot make ourselves believe that the two one-dollar bills in our pocket add up to a hundred dollars. James says plainly: "We can *say* any of these things, but we are absolutely impotent to believe them."[13]

To talk of believing by one's own volition seems, then, either silly or even vile. Nevertheless, "it's only our already dead hypothesis that our willing nature is unable to bring to life again."[14]

With hypotheses that are living, however, our "willing nature" may and should intervene. By "willing nature," James means not only deliberate acts of will but "all such factors of belief as fear and hope, prejudice and passion, imitation and partisanship, the circumpressure of our caste and set."[15]

These factors are present not only in inquiries about belief and morality but in all areas of intellectual investigation. As James wrote:

> Here in this room, we all of us believe in molecules and the conservation of energy, in democracy and necessary progress, in Protestant Christianity and the duty of fighting for "the doctrine of the immortal Monroe," all for no reasons worthy of the name.[16]

For James, it is often not insight but the prestige of the opinions which leads us to accept them.

> Our reason is quite satisfied, in nine hundred and ninety-nine cases out of every thousand of us, if it can find a few arguments that will do to recite in case our credulity is criticized by someone else. Our faith is faith in someone else's faith, and in the greatest matters this is mostly the case.[17]

For James, our non-intellectual nature does influence our convictions, "Pure insight and logic, whatever they might do ideally, are not the only things that really do produce our creeds."[18]

The passage[19] has already been cited in which James expressed his position in thesis form that sometimes our passional nature may and even must decide an option between propositions which cannot be decided on intellectual grounds.

It is important to note that this thesis is not limited to moral and religious truth. James expresses it in general terms to include every option which is a genuine option. "Genuine" here means an option which is living, forced, and momentous.

This inclusionary interpretation is supported by James' words further on in the essay. He points out there that, while empiricists have given up the doctrine of objective certitude, they have not thereby given up the quest or hope for truth itself. When an hypothesis is presented for decision, the empiricist may accept it on the basis of "the total drift of thinking," rather than on some merely logical argument.[20]

James recalls that W. K. Clifford demands that one regard the avoidance of error as the principal objective in the intellectual life. "Believe nothing, he tells us, keep your mind in suspense forever, rather than by closing it on insufficient evidence incur the awful risk of believing lies."[21]

James found himself unable to go with Clifford. The relative value of the search for truth and the avoidance of error cannot be determined on strictly intellectual grounds. The decision in either direction must be seen only as an expression of our passional life. James holds: "He who says 'Better go without belief forever than believe a lie!,' merely shows his own preponderant private horror of becoming a dupe."[22]

One has as much right to choose on passional grounds to press on after truth as to hold back out of a horror of being duped, and James thinks the former is "the fittest thing for the empiricist philosopher."[23]

One might concede that the first two steps of passion are necessary; namely: "We must think so as to avoid dupery and we must think so as to gain truth."[24]

In some questions, for example many scientific questions, there is no need to reach a decision in a hurry. Many of these questions present trivial options where the choice is not forced. An attitude of skeptical balance is therefore appropriate. In such matters, one may well take advantage of one's freedom from pressure and postpone the choice, while continuing to weigh the reasons for and against the decision with an open mind. Even here, however, science would be less likely to make advances if the passionate desires of individuals were to be kept out of the game. The person who has no interest in the results of an investigation will not be the most useful investigator. The most sensitive observer is always the person "whose eager interest in one side of the question is balanced by an equally keen nervousness lest he become deceived."[25]

This concern that one not be deceived has been raised to the level of a technique, and has been called the method of verification. When this method emphasizes the scrupulosity of the intellect to such an extent that the desire for truth is left far behind, one ends up with a position like that of Clifford. James points out, however, that, as Pascal says, "the heart has its reasons," and when the investigator throws himself into his inquiry, one can expect that some pet hypothesis of his own will influence his judgments. Nevertheless, James agrees that: "wherever there is no forced option, the dispassionately judicial intellect with no pet hypothesis, saving us, as it does, from dupery at any rate, ought to be our ideal."[26]

James points out that moral questions, questions dealing with what is good, are typical of those questions whose solution cannot wait for a conclusive and logically tight proof. To determine values, "we must consult not science, but what Pascal calls our heart."[27]

For example, when a scientist speaks of the attainment of truth and the correction of false belief as the supreme good for humanity, such a scientist is speaking from the heart. James holds that: "The question of having moral beliefs at all or not having them is decided by our will."[28]

Pure intellect alone cannot decide such questions. James was firm in asserting: "If your heart does not *want* a world of moral reality, your head will assuredly never make you believe in one."[29]

James raises this insight to the level of principle when he says:

> Moral skepticism can no more be refuted or proved by logic than intellectual skepticism can. When we stick to it that there *is* truth (be it of either kind), we do so with our whole nature, and resolve to stand or fall by the results.[30]

Did William James mean the same as Pascal by the word "heart"? Some interpreters of Pascal would equate his use of "heart" with the acceptance of a divine revelation from God in a mystical experience.[31]

James, on the other hand, used the term "heart" for decisions made by the will without any strictly logical proof.[32] This latter usage is more probably that of Pascal, as Nicholas Rescher has shown.[33]

Rescher has suggested for Pascal a

> ... parliamentary model of the human intellect where what is finally decided upon in rational deliberation is not the product of the unilaterally decreed requirements of a single faculty or interest, but a reasonable compromise between the potentially divergent pull of diverse elements.[34]

This seems to be very close to James who formulated his "reconciling hypothesis" on the basis of widely diverse evidences and then committed himself to the "over-belief" on which he was ready to make his personal venture.[35]

James' position on the importance of one's passional nature in the acceptance of religious belief is weakened by his introduction of a new element. He holds that, wherever a desired result is achieved by the cooperation of several persons, one of them must begin the process. This is the case for questions concerning personal relations. If one asks, "Do you like me or not?," one must realize that the answer depends on the willingness to meet the other person halfway.

James gives a second example: "How many women's hearts are vanquished by the mere sanguine insistence of some man that they *must* love him?"[36] This example seems to move in the opposite direction from the first example. Instead of the second person meeting the first person halfway, the men win the women's hearts by their aggressive persistence, even without the women's trust and cooperation.

In any case, the desire for truth about the existence of God cannot bring about that truth's existence. This has already been pointed out in regard to the "outcome cases."[37]

These examples used by James are responsible for many of the criticisms of "The Will to Believe." The examples are out of place in the essay if they are treated as logical arguments. God either exists or does not exist. If He does not exist, all the reachings out of the philosopher cannot bring Him into existence. As indicated earlier, however, the role that these examples seem to play is that of reminders of the importance of the "passional nature" in reaching true knowledge.

If one will grant that the passional nature must play a role in reaching all true knowledge, one may then apply this principle to the case of religion. What is meant by the religious hypothesis? James holds that religion says essentially two things. "First, she says that the best things are the more eternal things. . . . The second affirmation of religion is that we are better off even now if we believe her first affirmation to be true."[38]

James notes that, to discuss the question at all, one must see religion as an option which is living, momentous, and forced. James then introduces a Wager Argument that is hard to distinguish from that of Pascal. He writes:

> We cannot escape the issue by remaining skeptical and waiting for more light, because, although we do avoid error in that way *if religion be untrue*, we lose the good, *if it be true*, just as certainly as if we positively chose to disbelieve.[39]

James uses the argument, however, in a slightly different context from that of Pascal. In James, the Wager Argument is used to support James' position that the passional nature is involved in the choice of either skepticism or belief. For James:

> Skepticism, then, is not avoidance of option; it is option of a certain particular kind of risk. *Better risk loss of truth than chance of error* — that is your faith-vetoer's exact position. He is actively playing his stake as much as the believer is; he is backing the field against the religious hypothesis, just as the believer is backing the religious hypothesis against the field.[40]

It is interesting to notice that James here destroys the moral claim of Clifford, of Hume, and of Locke by showing that skepticism is not a moral obligation during the search for sufficient evidence for religion. For Clifford as much as for Pascal, "It is not intellect against all passions, then; it is only intellect with one passion laying down its law."[41]

James thus refuses to give to the scientist the right to choose only one form of risk. Then James, after weighing the scales equally for and against belief, puts another counter on the side of belief, and he says:

> If religion be true and the evidence for it be still insufficient, I do not wish, by putting your extinguisher upon my nature (which feels to me as if it had after all some business in the matter), to forfeit my sole chance in life of getting upon the winning side — that chance depending, of course, on my willingness

to run the risk of acting as if my passional need of taking the world religiously might be prophetic and right.[42]

It is obvious that, when James speaks of the evidence for religion being insufficient, he is speaking in logical terms, and he excludes only that kind of logical argument which can produce metaphysical certitude. At the same time he is introducing another kind of evidence: "my passional need of taking the world seriously," and he suggests that such an argument be described not as conclusive but as "prophetic and right." Would it be too much to describe such an argument as generative of some probability for the religious hypothesis?

Still another argument of the same type follows quickly. James writes:

> Now to most of us religion comes in a still farther way that makes a veto on our active faith even more illogical. The more perfect and more eternal aspect of the universe is represented in our religions as having personal form. The universe is no longer a mere *it* to us, but a *Thou*, if we are religious.[43]

It should be noted that the first sentence of this quotation makes it clear that James is presenting an argument. The position that the universe is at root fundamentally personal is expressed briefly here, but one would not use such language if one had not meditated long and hard to achieve such a personalistic point of view.

This personalistic point of view is brought out by an example. James writes: "For instance, although in one sense we are passive portions of the universe, in another we show a curious autonomy, as if we were small active centers on our own account."[44]

In other words, James, after noting the personalistic aspect of the world, adds the insight that the human being is personal and autonomous and not merely a part of a mathematical universe or a pantheistic universe.

James then transforms the Outcome Argument by pointing out that the passional affects one's ability to evaluate evidence. James writes: "We feel, too, as if the appeal of religion to us were made to our own active good will, as if evidence might be forever withheld from us unless we met the hypothesis halfway."[45]

James supports this insight with an illustration in which a man in a company of gentlemen would ask a warrant for every concession, and would believe no one's word without proof. Such a person would never win friends without exercising a more trusting spirit. James compares such an anti-social attitude with the person who would "shut himself up in snarling logicality and try to make the gods extort his recognition willy-nilly, or not get it at all...."[46]

This principle and illustration are built on a personalistic understanding of the world, and it leaves open the possibility that a personal being or beings might provide evidence to the inquirer who exhibited an open and receptive spirit. In the Catholic tradition, this same insight would be described as a grace.[47]

James sums up his position by recalling that the religious question is not presented in the abstract. It is an option confronting concrete men, with all that the passional nature involves. He then says:

> When I think of all the possibilities which both practically and theoretically it involves, then this command that we shall put a stopper on our heart, instincts and courage, and *wait* — acting of course meanwhile more or less as if religion were *not* true — till doomsday, or till such time as our intellect and senses working together may have raked in evidence enough — this command, I say, seems to me the queerest idol ever manufactured in the philosophic cave.[48]

James thus calls upon all the human resources rather than the merely logical. He points out that one with an infallible intellect with its objective certitudes could wait for conclusive proof.

> But if we are empiricists, if we believe that no bell in us tolls to let us know for certain when truth is in our grasp, then it seems a piece of idle fantasticality to preach so solemnly our duty of waiting for the bell.[49]

Once again, James puts aside the requirement of a conclusive proof in logical form and sets before his hearers the religious option in which both the positive and the negative response are chosen at our peril. The "Will to Believe" ends with the long quotation from Fitzjames Stephen:

> In all important transactions of life we have to take a leap in the dark.... But whatever choice we make, we make it at our own peril. If a man chooses to turn his back altogether on God and the future, no one can prevent him.... We stand on a mountain pass in the midst of whirling snow and blinding mist. ... If we stand still we shall be frozen to death. If we take the wrong road, we shall be dashed to pieces. We do not certainly know whether there is any

right one. What must we do? "Be strong and of a good courage." Act for the best, hope for the best, and take what comes. . . . If death ends all, we cannot meet death better.[50]

This is the argument of "The Will to Believe." In evaluating its effectiveness, it seems fair to say that James has placed the challenge of belief before his hearers and readers. After reading James, one can choose not to believe, but one can hardly feel self-righteous or "scientific" for making that choice. On the other hand, one has the right to choose, and one can call upon all the resources of thought and feeling and imagination and experience to reach a moral certitude that God exists and that there is a chance for salvation.[51]

Notes

1 This essay has been analyzed by several writers. Worthy of special attention are the analyses by Robert J. Roth, S.J., in *American Religious Philosophy* (New York: Harcourt, Brace & World, Inc., 1967), pp. 27-82; and Robert J. O'Connell, S.J., in *William James on the Courage to Believe*, pp. 7-22. Both these works have been utilized in preparing this analysis, along with other sources.

2 *TWTB*, p. 13.

3 *TWTB*, p. 33, quoting Fitzjames Stephen, *Liberty, Equality, Fraternity*, 2nd ed. (London, 1874), p. 353.

4 *TWTB*, p. 20. The italics are James'.

5 *TWTB*, p. 32.

6 *TWTB*, p. 32.

7 *TWTB*, p. 14.

8 *TWTB*, p. 15.

9 *TWTB*, p. 18. For Clifford's entire essay, "The Ethics of Belief," see McCarthy, ed., *The Ethics of Belief Debate*, pp. 19-36. The quotation is on p. 24.

10 Clifford, in McCarthy, *The Ethics of Belief Debate*, p. 24.

11 *TWTB*, p. 19.

12 The same point is made by Bertrand Russell in his review of Henri Poincare's *Science and Hypothesis*. Russell agrees with Poincare's thesis that science deals only with the relations of things. But why should we trust our own perception of relations? "I do not know; but it is a fact that we do so." See Bertrand Russell, *Philosophical Essays* (New York: Simon & Schuster, 1966), p. 76.

13 *TWTB*, pp. 15f.

14 *TWTB*, p. 18.

15 *TWTB*, p. 18.

16 *TWTB*, p. 18.

17 *TWTB*, p. 19.

18 *TWTB*, p. 20.

19 *TWTB*, p. 20.

20 *TWTB*, p. 24.

21 *TWTB*, p. 24.

22 *TWTB*, p. 25.

23 *TWTB*, p. 25.

24 *TWTB*, p. 25.

25 *TWTB*, p. 26.

26 *TWTB*, p. 27.

27 *TWTB*, p. 27.

28 *TWTB*, pp. 27f.

29 *TWTB*, p. 28.

30 *TWTB*, p. 28.

31 See Richard Popkin, "Skepticism in Modern Thought," in *Dictionary of the History of Ideas: Studies of Selected Pivotal Ideas*, ed. Philip P. Wiener, 5 vols. (New York: Charles Scribner's Sons, 1968-1974), 4:246a.

32 *TWTB*, pp. 27f.

33 Rescher, pp. 101-104, 126-133.

34 Rescher, p. 104.

35 *Varieties*, pp. 402, 408.

36 *TWTB*, p. 28.

37 See PART TWO, CHAPTER XII, above.

38 *TWTB*, pp. 28f.

39 *TWTB*, p. 30.

40 *TWTB*, p. 30.

41 *TWTB*, p. 30.

42 *TWTB*, p. 31.

43 *TWTB*, p. 31.

44 *TWTB*, p. 31.

45 *TWTB*, p. 31.

46 *TWTB*, p. 31.

47 See, for example, Ludwig Ott, *Fundamentals of Catholic Dogma*, ed. James Bastible (St. Louis: B. Herder Book Company, 1962), pp. 225-245.

48 *TWTB*, p. 32.

49 *TWTB*, pp. 32f.

50 *TWTB*, p. 33, quoting Fitzjames Stephen, *Liberty, Equality, Fraternity*, 2nd ed. (London, 1874), p. 353.

51 *Varieties*, p. 414.

Chapter XVI

The Argument of the Varieties of Religious Experience

The Description of the Human Religious Constitution

John E. Smith has said that few books written in this century on the subject of religion have had an importance and continuing influence equal to *The Varieties of Religious Experience*.[1]

The *Varieties* are the written text of James' Gifford lectures on natural religion at the University of Edinburgh. The appointment of James as Gifford lecturer had been proposed as early as 1896, and was formally made in 1898. Originally the lectures were to begin in 1900, but they had to be postponed for a year because of James' illness in 1899. The first series of lectures began on May 18, 1901, and the second series of ten lectures was completed on June 9, 1902. The text of the lectures had been prepared in America before delivery, and they were published almost immediately after they were given.[2]

James wrote that he had originally decided on two topics for the two courses of ten lectures each at Edinburgh. The first would be a descriptive one on "Man's Religious Appetites," and the second, a metaphysical one on "Their Satisfaction Through Philosophy." James then added,

> But the unexpected growth of the psychological matter as I came to write it out has resulted in the second subject being postponed entirely, and the description of man's religious constitution now fills the twenty lectures. In Lecture XX I have suggested rather than stated my own philosophic conclusions....[3]

In this study it will not be possible to consider in detail James' description of religious experience. Nevertheless some brief comments seem to be appropriate.

James begins by noting that his background is in psychology, and he proposes to approach religious experience as a psychologist. As a result, his subject matter will be religious feelings and religious impulses and other subjective phenomena of religion rather than religious institutions. James identifies the conventional believer whose religion is traditional and consists of fixed forms followed by imitation and habit. James considers that there would be little profit in studying "this secondhand religious life."[4]

James determined to study the original experiences of the great religious geniuses and religious leaders who experienced the most profound religious emotions and articulated them to set the pattern for conventional believers.

James is quick to point out that the spiritual value of religious experiences is not undone by the discovery of a psychological origin for these experiences. In particular, James rejects the reinterpretation of religion as perverted sexuality, apparently alluding to the views of Edwin D. Starbuck (1866-1947).[5]

James refused to go along with the method of discrediting states of mind for which one has an antipathy. To interpret religion, one must look at the immediate context of the religious consciousness. The moment one does this, one sees how disconnected religious life is from the content of sexual consciousness.[6]

Modern psychology assumes that the dependence of mental states upon bodily conditions must be complete. Such an account of the facts of religious psychology cannot determine the value or spiritual significance of the experience. James notes that scientific theories are subject to the same charge as religious emotions, but that they are not written off as without value.[7]

What criteria, then, are available to evaluate religious or scientific opinions? James holds that:

> ... *immediate luminousness*, in short *philosophical reasonableness*, and *moral helpfulness* are the only available criteria. St. Teresa might have had the nervous system of the placidest cow, and it would not now save her theology, if the trial of the theology by these other tests should show it to be contemptible. And conversely if her theology can stand these other tests, it will make no difference how hysterical or nervously off her balance St. Teresa may have been when she was with us here below.[8]

In other words, James tells us, the final test of a belief is not its origin but the way in which it works. This is an empiricist criterion. It is also the criterion of the Protestant theologian Jonathan Edwards and the Catholic mystic Teresa of Avila.

What does James mean by religious experience or religious sentiment? James is aware of the many definitions which are given of religion,[9] but he refuses to assume the existence of one simple abstract quality which would have to exist in any experience for it to be called religious. At the same time, however, he has to take a limited part of the field of religion for his investigation. His fundamental decision was to ignore that part of the religious field which deals with institutions, churches and systematic theologies, and to confine his inquiry to personal experience. James therefore defines his subject matter as religion, understood to mean: *"The feelings, acts, and experiences of individual men in their solitude, so far as they apprehend themselves to stand in relation to whatever they may consider the divine."*[10] James further narrows the field by the meaning he gives to the word "divine." "The divine shall mean for us only such a primal reality as the individual feels impelled to respond to solemnly and gravely, and neither by a curse nor a jest."[11]

Limiting the topic in this way has the double advantage of circumscribing the area of study and also of allowing for a catholicity of religious traditions. Still, one risks putting all enthusiasms beyond reach. James proposes to look for that state of mind known to religious persons in which one is willing to be as nothing before God. He quotes Havelock Ellis, who looks to religion for the soul's liberation and cries out: "It is the infinite for which we hunger, and we ride gladly on every little wave that promises to bear us towards it."[12]

In attempting to characterize the life of religion, William James suggests that it consists of the belief that there is an unseen order to which we have to try to adjust ourselves. This belief and adjustment are what James calls the religious attitude in the soul.[13]

James concludes that there is in the human consciousness *"A sense of reality, a feeling of objective presence, a perception* of what we may call 'something there.'"[14] This existence of a present reality is different from that which the special senses yield.[15]

James holds it for certain that, in the religious sphere of existence, many people possess the objects of their belief in the form of quasi-sensible realities directly apprehended.[16]

James illustrates this conclusion with several experiences collected from the pages of religious biography. For example, James Russell Lowell's correspondence describes an experience of this kind. Russell wrote: "I never before so clearly felt the Spirit of God in me and around me. The whole room seemed to be full of God."[17]

James notes the convincingness of these feelings of reality. He says: "They are as convincing to those who have them as any direct sensible experiences can be, and they are, as a rule, much more convincing than results established by mere logic ever are."[18]

After reporting many experiences of the reality of the unseen, James devotes two lectures each to what he calls "the religion of healthy-mindedness," or religious optimism, and to "the religion of sick souls," or morbid-mindedness. Both are significant for the religious psychologist. Sometimes religious optimists come to regard the happiness which a religious belief affords as proof of its truth. James numbers among the "healthy-minded" such writers as Ralph Waldo Emerson and Theodore Parker. James recalls the words of Edward Everett Hale, a famous Unitarian preacher and writer, who said that he never knew, even for an hour, religious or irreligious struggles. Hale always knew that God loved him, and he was always grateful to God for the world in which he was placed.[19]

As a contemporary example of an inability to feel evil, James adduces the poet Walt Whitman. Of Whitman's work, James comments that, "a passional and mystic ontological emotion suffuses his words, and ends by persuading the reader that men and women, life and death, and all things are divinely good."[20]

In contrast with the religious optimism of the "healthy-minded" is the view of the "sick-soul." By this label, James intends to describe the radically opposite view which maximizes evil. It is based on the persuasion that the evil aspects of our life are of its very essence. For people of this camp, evil is

> ... no mere relation of the subject to particular outer things, but something more radical and general, a wrongness or vice in his essential nature, which no alteration of the environment, or any superficial rearrangement of the inner self, can cure, and which requires a supernatural remedy.[21]

As examples of people whose religion reflects such pessimism, James names Goethe (1749-1832) and Luther (1483-1558). Goethe spoke of his existence as "at bottom . . . nothing but pain and burden. . . ."[22] Luther looked back on his life as if it had been an absolute failure. He wrote toward the end of his life "I am utterly weary of life."[23]

Robert Louis Stevenson wrote: "Whatever else we are intended to do, we are not intended to succeed; failure is the fate allotted."[24] Tolstoy and John Bunyan are also presented as representatives of religious pessimism, and then James presents the story of an anonymous sufferer, now known to be James himself.[25]

After presenting examples of the sick soul, James comments:

> How irrelevantly remote seem all our usual refined optimisms and intellectual and moral consolations in presence of a need of help like this! Here is the real core of the religious problem: Help! Help![26]

James notes that a great antagonism developed between the healthy-minded way of viewing life and the view held by the "sick soul" which takes the experience of evil as something essential. While admitting that averting one's attention from evil is fine as long as it works, James holds that such a view breaks down when trouble comes:

> . . . there is no doubt that healthy-mindedness is inadequate as a philosophical doctrine, because the evil facts which it refuses positively to account for are a genuine portion of reality; and they may after all be the best key to life's significance, and possibly the only openers of our eyes to the deepest levels of truth.[27]

In Lecture VIII, on the divided self and the process of its unification, James describes the twice-born character. While some persons are born with an interior life which is harmonious and well balanced, the "twice-born" have a discordancy in their native temperament which makes their existence

> . . . little more than a series of zig-zags — as now one tendency and now another gets the upper hand.
> Their spirit wars with their flesh. . . . [28]

James describes St. Augustine as a classic example of the divided self. Another example is that of Leo Tolstoy (1828-1910). In the case of both St. Augustine and Tolstoy, the unhappiness resulting from their inner turmoil forced them to search for some unifying principle which could bring order into their lives. Tolstoy began with the conviction that life was meaningless, but he realized that this conviction was based on taking into account only this present life. He came to a sense of the value of life by virtue of which one does not commit suicide. This holding on to life carries within itself implicitly the insight that life is not meaningless. Gradually, Tolstoy arrived at a faith in an infinite God without whom there would be no life and no meaning. Tolstoy embarked on a quest for God. All of life received a meaning when Tolstoy listened to an inner voice telling him "He is here."

The evidence for evil and sin and the experience of a divided self plays a significant role in William James' approach to God. He does not search for God by a logical-type proof but he is led by experience — his own and others — to look for unification and meaning in his life. The search for meaning and the discovery of meaning has to be considered as a significant factor in William James' approach to God.

The search for God and the experience of conversion form the subject matter of James' Lectures IX and X. He defines conversion as

> ... the process, gradual or sudden, by which a self hitherto divided, and consciously wrong, inferior and unhappy, becomes unified and consciously right, superior and happy, in consequence of its firmer hold upon religious realities.[29]

From the viewpoint of religious psychology, James holds that:

> To say that a man is "converted" means, in these terms, that religious ideas, previously peripheral in his consciousness, now take a central place, and that religious aims form the habitual center of his energy.[30]

Psychology can describe conversion, but it is unable to account for all the factors in any given case of conversion. One thing, however, seems to be characteristic of conversion stories: there is an element of self-surrender. Quoting Edwin Starbuck, James argues that, in the conversion process, "the personal will must be given up. In many cases relief persistently refuses to come until the person ceases to resist...."[31]

Lecture IX deals with slow conversions. In Lecture X James studies sudden conversion, modeled on that of St. Paul. He relates the cases of Henri Alline, who became Protestant, and Alphonse Ratisbonne, a free-thinking French Jew who became a Catholic. In either case, the question arises whether any conversion, fast or slow, is a miracle brought about by God's powers or a strictly natural process. James begins to answer this question from the psychological point of view. He speaks of the subconscious region of the mind in which such processes of conversion seem to develop. James explains the meaning of the subconscious by pointing out the contrast between the consciousness with its usual center and margin and the subconscious as

> ... an addition thereto in the shape of a set of memories, thoughts, and feelings which are extra-marginal and outside of the primary consciousness altogether, but yet must be classed as conscious facts of some sort, able to reveal their presence by unmistakable signs.[32]

James suggests that all otherwise unaccountable invasive alterations of consciousness may be interpreted as the results of memories in the subconscious field bursting into the field of consciousness. This suggestion is made rather tentatively and without any attempt to exclude the possibility of some theological hypothesis.[33]

In any case, conversion is a topic for psychological study. James then asks whether the psychological origins of conversion experience diminish the significance of sudden conversions. His reply is "Not in the least."[34]

The first reason for this is that the ultimate test of religious values does not lie in the explanation of how it happened but in the ethical values brought about by the conversion.[35] The second reason for James' position is his admission that, for a psychologist, "the reference of a phenomenon to a subliminal self does not exclude the notion of the direct presence of the Deity...."[36]

This principle, developed here with regard to conversion, is applicable to every other type of religious experience. There is no such thing as an experience completely divorced from the psychological processes of the conscious and subconscious fields. A mere hypothesis about the psychological origins of an experience is only the first step in the work of the psychologist and philosopher of religion.

The second series of Gifford lectures began with Lectures XI, XII and XIII on saintliness. What relationship is there between the description of saintliness and William James' approach to God? The topic is important insofar as it plays a dominant role in the cultural milieu within which the approach to God can develop. James begins his treatment of saintliness by reminding his audience that "the best fruits of religious experience are the best things that history has to show."[37]

The lives of persons who have been converted are often examples of extraordinary virtue and spiritual energy. The saints are noted for living lives of wider concern than their own selfish interests. They display a sense of a willing self-surrender to the source of religious power and a freedom in doing His will. Their lives become more and more lives of love and concern for others.

The fundamental feature in the lives of saintly persons is the sense of the presence of a higher and friendly Power.[38] This sense of presence is important in James' approach to God. It is one of those pieces of evidence hard to grasp but undeniable which converge to provide the basis for an act of moral certitude.

James asks whether this kind of empirical method of studying religious experiences could only lead to skepticism. James asks:

> What command over truth would this kind of theology really lose if, instead of absolute certainty, she only claimed reasonable probability for her conclusions? If *we* claim only reasonable probability, it will be as much as men who love the truth can ever at any given moment hope to have within their grasp.[39]

Despite the example of saints who apparently had little time or energy except for sufferings, swoons, and ecstasies, the great saints have had a powerful impact on the world's history. James refers especially to Saint Teresa of Avila: "one of the ablest women, in many respects, of whose life we have the record."[40]

James quotes Nietzsche's position in which the saint is "the sophisticated invalid, the degenerate *par excellence*, the man of insufficient vitality."[41] Nietzsche wrote:

> The *morbid* are our greatest peril — not the "bad" men, not the predatory beings . . . they it is, the *weakest*, who are undermining the vitality of the race, poisoning our trust in life, and putting humanity in question."[42]

James brings out the contrast between the superman, the person of success and victory, the person of strength, pride, and the sense of power, on the one hand, and the saint on the other hand. At first sight, Nietzsche's superman seems to have the advantage. In establishing the ideal type of human being, one is drawn to those who are successful and physically strong and socially powerful. James, however, insists that the inquiry be pressed further. In trying to determine the ideal type of humanity, an important criterion to be applied is that of adaptation. A society where all were supermen would soon destroy itself. A society where some are aggressive can only have peace when others choose to be non-resistant. Such a peace is precarious, however, since the aggressive members of society are "always tending to become bullies, robbers, and swindlers."[43]

In contrast to such a brutish society would be an imaginary society of fairness and sympathy and peace. A saint would fit in easily in such a society. In James' words:

> To such a millennial society the saint would be entirely adapted. His peaceful modes of appeal would be efficacious over his companions, and there would be no one extant to take advantage of his non-resistance. The saint is therefore abstractly a higher type of man than the "strong man," because he is adapted to the highest society conceivable, whether that society ever be concretely possible or not.[44]

James argues further for the superiority of the saint by recalling that the example of leaders such as Cromwell (1599-1658), Stonewall Jackson (1824-1863), and the British General Charles George Gordon (Chinese Gordon) (1835-1885) show that Christians can be strong persons. The greatest saints, such as Saint Francis, Saint Bernard, Luther, Saint Ignatius Loyola, and Wesley, are persons of strength and stature. "Placed alongside of them, the strong men of this world and no other seem as dry as sticks, as hard and crude as blocks of stone or brickbats."[45]

The phenomenon of saintliness provides an important piece in the mosaic of evidence used by William James in building his path to the affirmation of God. The lives of the saints are a leaven of righteousness in the world and they must be taken into consideration by an empiricist philosophy trying to attain a spiritual judgment as to the total value and positive meaning of religious phenomena.[46]

In Lectures XVI and XVII James deals with the subject of mysticism. By the expressions "mysticism" or "mystical states of consciousness," James means those personal experiences which are at the core of religious life. James proposes four marks to identify experiences as mystical. The first mark is ineffability. James says:

> The subject of it immediately says that it defies expression, that no adequate report of its contents can be given in words. It follows from this that its quality must be directly experienced. It cannot be imparted or transferred to others.[47]

Noetic quality is the second mark of mystical experience. Those who have such experiences report that they are states of knowledge and insight. They are full of meaning for the mystic, and the knowledge gained continues to be invested with authority. The third and fourth marks of mysticism are less characteristic, but they are usually present. First of all, mystical states are transient; they cannot be sustained for long. James says: "Except in rare instances, half an hour, or at most an hour or two, seems to be the limit beyond which they fade into the light of common day."[48]

The fourth mark of mystical experience is passivity. James notes that "the mystic feels as if his own will were in abeyance, and indeed sometimes as if he were grasped and held by a superior power."[49]

After describing a number of examples of mystical experiences, James points out that these are states of consciousness of an entirely specific quality. They provide a consciousness of the cosmos, that is, the life and order of the universe. With these experiences there also comes "a sense of immortality, a consciousness of eternal life, not a conviction that he shall have this, but the consciousness that he has it already."[50]

In describing the cognitive aspect of mystical experience, James turns to Saint Teresa of Avila (1515-1582), whom he calls "the expert of experts." In describing such conditions she relates that

> God establishes himself in the interior of this soul in such a way, that when she returns to herself, it is wholly impossible for her to doubt that she has been in God and God in her.... If you, nevertheless, ask how it is possible that the soul can see and understand that she has been in God, since during

the union she has neither sight nor understanding, I reply that she does not see it then, but that she sees it clearly later, after she has returned to herself, not by any vision, but by a certitude which abides with her and which God alone can give her.[51]

A second expert upon whom James draws to describe the cognitive aspect of mystical experience is St. Ignatius Loyola (1491-1556). One day Ignatius told his disciple Father Laynez that a single hour of meditation "had taught him more truths about heavenly things than all the teachings of all the doctors put together could have taught him."[52]

What is the nature of this knowledge? James brings out well that it is not a kind of dictated theology. He calls upon St. Teresa again to describe the cognitive aspect of the highest states of ecstasy. She said:

If our understanding comprehends, it is in a mode which remains unknown to it, and it can understand nothing of what it comprehends. For my own part, I do not believe that it does comprehend, because, as I said, it does not understand itself to do so. I confess that it is all a mystery in which I am lost.[53]

In other words, the experience of the higher mystical states provides a kind of knowledge which is not communicable, but which has a profound meaning for the mystics themselves.

In order to evaluate this kind of mystical knowledge, James turns to the role of mystical phenomena in the life of the mystics. St. Teresa was an administrator and reformer in her religious community. St. John of the Cross, her disciple, was also a person of great energy in working for reform of the Carmelite order. St. Ignatius Loyola, mystic, the founder of the Jesuits, was described by James as "one of the most powerfully practical human engines that ever lived."[54]

Nevertheless, even though their mystical experiences have led some of the saints to become great leaders and organizers, James acknowledges that such an impetus to leadership would be for the good only if the religious inspiration were true.

If the inspiration were erroneous, the energy would be all the more mistaken and misbegotten. So we stand once more before that problem of truth. . . . Do mystical states establish the truths of those theological affections in which the saintly life has its roots?[55]

James answers this question with three principles:

1. Mystical states, when well developed, usually are, and have the right to be, absolutely authoritative over the individuals to whom they come.

2. No authority emanates from them which should make it a duty for those who stand outside of them to accept their revelations uncritically.

3. They break down the authority of the non-mystical or rationalistic consciousness, based upon the understanding and the senses alone. They show it to be only one kind of consciousness.

   They open out the possibility of other orders of truth, in which, so far as anything in us vitally responds to them, we may freely continue to have faith.[56]

James points out that the first of these principles is validated for the mystics themselves. They have had the experience, and no outsider can deny its power. James says:

> It is vain for rationalism to grumble about this. If the mystical truth that comes to a man proves to be a force that he can live by, what mandate have we of the majority to order him to live in another way? We can throw him into a prison or a madhouse, but we cannot change his mind.... It mocks our utmost efforts, as a matter of fact, and in point of logic it absolutely escapes our jurisdiction. Our own more "rational" beliefs are based on evidence exactly similar in nature to that which mystics quote for theirs. Our senses, namely, have assured us of certain states of fact; but mystical experiences are as direct perceptions of fact for those who have them as any sensations ever were for us.[57]

When one moves from the mystics to those who hear of their experience at second hand, James holds that the mystics have no right to claim our acceptance of their experiences. Nevertheless such experiences do establish a presumption. The reports of many mystics with different religious backgrounds, from different times and places, seem to form a consensus that such shared experiences cannot be altogether wrong. James does not build on this consensus at this point. The capability of having such experiences is found in so many different groups, and is interpreted by so many varying traditions that there is no obligation on the part of any non-mystics to endow mystical experiences with cognitive authority.[58]

This refusal of James to see an obligation on the part of non-mystics can be seen as another way of saying that such feelings do not provide a demonstration cogent for the non-mystic. Mystical states, however, do provide important evidence of which one must take account. James points out that the higher mystical states

... point in directions to which the religious sentiment even of non-mystical men inclines. They tell of the supremacy of the ideal, of vastness, of union, of safety, and of rest. They offer us hypotheses, hypotheses which we may voluntarily ignore, but which as thinkers we cannot possibly upset.[59]

In the first seventeen lectures of *The Varieties of Religious Experience* William James provided what is still the best description of the phenomena of religious experience. The field is a vast one and other writers have contributed to the study of religious experience.[60]

The next step in tracing the argument of the *Varieties of Religious Experience* is to try to determine how William James used the data he had collected as evidence for the reality of God. Before taking this step, however, it will be helpful to exclude one position which at first may seem similar to that of James but which is in fact quite different. The position in question is called ontologism.

Ontologism Excluded

In order to clarify the path which William James followed to the acceptance of the reality of God, it is important to distinguish his path from that of the philosophical position called ontologism.[61]

Without intending to justify the definition historically, one may provide a provisional definition of ontologism as

... the system according to which the first and immediate object (of the intellect) is being taken simply, that is God himself, whom we immediately apprehend by a simple intuition, and we know all other things in that vision.[62]

Ontologism was developed by philosophers in the Augustinian tradition like Nicholas Malebranche (1683-1715), Vincenzo Gioberti (1801-1852), and Antonio Rosmini-Servati (1797-1855).[63]

In Catholic thought in the nineteenth century ontologism became the vehicle used by some thinkers for expressing religious experience and making it an integral part of their theologies and philosophies. An intuition of being, which, upon reflection, was declared to be an intuition of God, provided an approach to the affirmation of the reality of God. For James, however, ontologism would have to be discarded as another form of metaphysics. Ontologism, then, which at first sight may seem similar to the approach to God used by James in the *Varieties of Religious Experi-*

ence, in fact is rather different from James' approach and does not offer any help in understanding James' approach to God.

What Can Philosophy Do for Religion?

After completing his description of religious experience culminating in his study of mysticism in Lectures XVI and XVII, James was confident that he had evoked an appreciation on the part of his hearers and readers of the sense of divine presence which has been the principal fruit of religious experience. This gives rise to the question whether this sense of divine presence is a sense of anything objectively true. Since the question of objective truth is normally the province of philosophy, James asks, "Can philosophy stamp a warrant of veracity upon the religious man's sense of the divine?"[64] James begins his answer to the question by pointing out that "feeling is the deeper source of religion and that philosophic and theological formulas are secondary products. . . ."[65] These secondary products are not developed by the speculations of philosophers on the basis of logical or philosophical principles. Rather, "These speculations must, it seems to me, be classed as overbeliefs, buildings-out performed by the intellect into directions of which feeling originally supplied the hint."[66] James thus punctures any claim by philosophers to a superior point of view.

One might still object that, even though these philosophical over-beliefs are secondary to religious experience, the philosopher may still lay claim to a superior way of dealing with the over-beliefs suggested by the feelings. James does allow an important role to philosophy. First of all, since we are thinking beings, we cannot exclude the intellect, and therefore philosophy, from any aspect of life, including the religious aspect. In addition, the very language we use in expressing our religious experiences is inevitably shaped by the philosophic climate of our time. Furthermore, if the study of religion is to be a human endeavor, it must be social. The forging of general and abstract formulas so that one can exchange information with other investigators is a philosophic function. Finally, "as moderator amid the clash of hypotheses, and mediator among the criticisms of one man's constructions by another, philosophy will always have much to do."[67]

James may, then, lay claim fairly to doing the work of a philosopher in his Gifford lectures, which he describes as "A laborious attempt to extract from the privacies of religious experience some general facts which can be defined in formulas upon which everybody may agree."[68]

James, however, is aware that systematic philosophers, whether scholastics or idealists, share a disdain for merely probable truth. As Jacques Maritain once said: "The philosopher is one who demonstrates." The issue is clear: "Feeling valid only for the individual is pitted against reason valid universally."[69]

James is willing to accept this statement of the issue, with philosophy claiming the exclusive right to be called reason, provided that one accepts the test implied by the dichotomy. "The test is a perfectly plain one of fact. Theology based on pure reason must in point of fact convince men universally. If it did not, wherein would its superiority consist?"[70]

Once this test is accepted, James need not discredit philosophy. All he has to do is to point to the history of philosophy to show that no philosophy has been universally convincing. With regard to the existence of God, the traditional proofs given by the scholastics have not won allegiance, nor have the post-Kantian idealist attempts to posit an Absolute Spirit been accepted by empiricists. For tactical purposes James need only point to the fact that "No religious philosophy has actually convinced the mass of thinkers."[71]

Nevertheless, James is unwilling to relinquish the honorable title of philosophy for his own position. It may be also that he felt some constraint from the occasion of the lectures as the fulfillment of a commission from the foundation established by Lord Gifford for lectures in natural theology. In any case, James attempts to salvage a role for philosophy. He said: "If she will abandon metaphysics and deduction for criticism and induction, and frankly transform herself from theology into science of religions, she can make herself enormously useful."[72]

William James' Science of Religions

One of the roles which philosophy may play in helping one who is on the path to the acceptance of the reality of God is to examine the hypotheses established by the researcher. James points out that one spontaneously formulates experiences in accordance with the searcher's previous philosophical history and the prevailing intellectual climate. James holds that

> Philosophy can by comparison eliminate the local and the accidental from these definitions. . . . By confronting the spontaneous religious constructions with the results of natural science, philosophy can also eliminate doctrines that are now known to be scientifically absurd or incongruous.
>
> Sifting out in this way unworthy formulations, she can leave a residuum of conceptions that at least are possible. With these she can deal as *hypotheses*, testing them in all the manners, whether negative or positive, by which hypotheses are ever tested. She can reduce their number, as some are found more open to objection. She can perhaps become the champion of one which she picks out as being the most closely verified or verifiable.[73]

In this text, James is far from the description of pragmatism given by Bertrand Russell. In the *Edinburgh Review* in April 1909, Russell holds that skepticism is embodied in pragmatism. He caricatures James' position as follows:

> "Since all beliefs are absurd, we may as well believe what is most convenient."
> . . . Skepticism is of the very essence of the pragmatic philosophy: Nothing is certain, everything is liable to revision, and the attainment of any truth in which we can rest securely is impossible. It is, therefore, not worthwhile to trouble our heads about what really is true. What is *thought* to be true is all that need concern us.[74]

This understanding of James is so far off the mark that it really does not deserve to be cited here, except for one thing: many other people understand James in the same way.

In fact, there is nothing in James' work to indicate that he held that "all beliefs are absurd." James' entire life is unintelligible if it is not seen as a quest for truth, especially in religion. And while it is true that, for empiricist philosophies, all formulas are liable to revision, including those of the new Science of Religions, James saw that much of the evidence converged, and probabilities emerged. James thought it was well worth his while to assemble the evidence and to formulate an hypothesis to account for it. It is Russell, rather than James, who should be accused of not troubling his head about religious truth.

A somewhat similar position to Russell's is held by A. J. Ayer. Ayer acknowledges that people have religious experiences. He questions whether these experiences have any cognitive value and whether they provide a basis for any legitimate inferences about the origin and nature of the universe. "But to these questions James hardly attempts to offer any serious answer...."[75] Ayer then concludes:

> The main point for James is that so long as people are psychologically able to have religious faith, and so long as it gives the emotional satisfaction, the beliefs which are its embodiment may be allowed to pass for true.[76]

From the viewpoint of this study, it should be noted that the claim is not being made that William James' approach to God is a substitute for metaphysics, or that it can provide inferences about the origin or nature of the universe.

James himself rejected the scholastic deduction of the attributes of God. One may wish for an opportunity to dialogue with James about his anti-metaphysical positions. This would, however, be irrelevant in the present study, which is focused solely on James' affirmation of the reality of God. His use of a Wager Argument somewhat like Pascal's has blinded many interpreters to the fact that he also looked for evidence, and that the evidence he discovered led him to a moral certitude of the reality of God, a kind of moral certitude based on evidence marking out converging probabilities. It is this approach which is emphasized in *The Varieties of Religious Experience*. The various types of religious experience which James collected and described provide so much evidence for what James called his "reconciling hypothesis." James' reconciling hypothesis is not just a pure act of will or a choice of convenience, but an hypothesis which is to be tested "in all manners whether negative or positive, by which hypotheses are ever tested."[77]

James, in this passage, shows the effects of his early scientific training at the Lawrence Scientific School at Harvard, where he studied in the department of Chemistry and then moved to the department of Comparative Anatomy and Physiology. It is hard to believe that the William James, who studied under Jeffries Wyman, considered his own work as an exercise of agnosticism or a counsel of despair. Instead, he is trying to establish the foundations of a "critical Science of Religions" which might "eventually command as general a public adhesion as is commanded by a physical science."[78] This Science of Religions "would depend for its original material on facets of personal experience, and would have to square itself with personal experience through all its critical reconstructions."[79]

As one trained in the physical sciences, James is not a fundamentalist, ready to fight at the drop of a hat over a scientific formula. As James expresses it, the science of religions

> ... would forever have to confess, as every science confesses, that subtlety of nature flies beyond it, and that its formulas are but approximations. Philosophy lives in words, but truth and fact well up into our lives in ways that exceed verbal formulation.[80]

Far from being a skeptic, therefore, James considered himself to be a pioneer scientist in a new science of religions. This new science would be empirical in nature, based closely on religious experience. The goal of the scientist would be to collect all the relevant data, to form hypotheses organizing the data, and cautiously to make inferences, which would be constantly revised by comparison with the empirical evidence. It is this type of scientific endeavor that James embarked upon in *The Varieties of Religious Experience*. Moved by the converging probabilities pressed upon him by the data, he carefully formed his reconciling hypothesis.

James' Reconciling Hypothesis

In Lecture XX of the *Varieties*, James draws some conclusions on "the significance for life of religion taken as a whole."[81]

James describes his own religious position as "supernaturalism." For the purposes of this study it will not be necessary to follow him in his attempt to describe his complete religious theory. That theory encompasses far more than the approach to God. James' religion is a living faith, and involves a life of moral heroism as well as a philosophy of life.[82] The concern in this study, however, is merely to uncover William James' approach to God.

After presenting the data in the earlier chapters of the *Varieties*, James then attempted to frame his own reconciling hypothesis.

The very use of the term "hypothesis" makes it plain that James does not consider his arguments coercive. He says plainly, "The most I can do is, accordingly, to offer something that may fit the facts so easily that your scientific logic will find no plausible pretext for vetoing your impulse to welcome it as true."[83] In other words, he intends to interpret the evidence which will be seen as sufficient to generate moral certitude of the reality of God.

This knowledge of God is what James calls an "over-belief." That is, it is an inference of the intellect closely based on experience. In James' own words, over-beliefs are: "buildings-out performed by the intellect into directions of which feeling originally supplied the hint."[84]

James first attempts to describe his "more," or his "over-belief," by a psychological description. He notes that the subconscious has assumed an important role in modern psychology, James proposes that his "over-belief" be looked upon from two sides. On what he called its "hither side," James holds that over-belief may be seen as the subconscious continuation of the conscious life. On the other hand, from the viewpoint of psychology, James proceeds very cautiously and speaks of religious experience on the "*farther* side. . . ."[85]

This openness of James on the scientific level leaves room for the theologians' contention that "the religious man is moved by an external power."[86]

Since experiences deriving from the subconscious region seem to come from some external source, the sense of union with a power beyond us may be seen by the psychologist as derived from our own subconscious region. The psychologist, however, may stop there and conclude that the sense of union with a power beyond us is a merely subjective experience. There is another option, however, and the psychologist who is a religious believer may legitimately attribute the same religious experience to a spiritual reality distinct from the person experiencing it.

James presents this position as a doorway into the supernaturalist interpretation of religious experience. It allows him to ask how far our transmarginal consciousness carries us if we follow it on its remoter side.[87]

Various types of over-beliefs must be considered: mysticism, Vedantism, and Transcendental idealism are monistic interpretations which "tell us that the finite self rejoins the absolute self."[88]

Prophets of different religions offer many possible beliefs. James tries to put aside the specific beliefs of the different religions and to propose an hypothesis which is common to most. He formulates his position as follows:

> We have in *the fact that the conscious person is continuous with a wider self through which saving experiences come,* a positive content of religious experience which, it seems to me, is literally and objectively true as far as it goes.[89]

James, then, attempts to explore that farther side of religious experience. He sees "the farther limits of our being plunge ... into an altogether other dimension of existence from the sensible and merely understandable world."[90]

In a passage reminiscent of Plato, James said:

> We belong to it (i.e., the mystical region) in a more intimate sense than that in which we belong to the visible world, for we belong in the most intimate sense wherever our ideals belong. Yet the unseen region in question is not merely ideal, for it produces effects in this world. ... But that which produces effects within another reality must be termed a reality itself, so I feel as if we had no philosophic excuse for calling the unseen or mystical world unreal.[91]

James develops his hypothesis further by asking what one should call this supreme reality. Without hesitation he states: "God is the natural appellation, for us Christians at least, for the supreme reality. So I will call this higher part of the universe by the name of God."[92]

This chapter of *The Varieties of Religious Experience* has been criticized by A. J. Ayer. For Ayer, it is not to be denied that people have religious experiences. What is in dispute, Ayer asserts, is the interpretation of these experiences and whether, in particular, they have any cognitive value. He says that James is able to claim truth for the religious hypothesis only at the cost of stripping it of its intellectual content.[93]

It seems clear that this criticism by Ayer disregards the first nineteen chapters of *The Varieties of Religious Experience*. In those chapters, James laid out the evidence supporting his reconciling hypothesis. Ayer has allowed his own philosophical position, whether it be called logical positivism or language analysis philosophy, to lead him to misunderstand the nature of James' approach to God and the conclusion of James' study. For Ayer, all theological propositions insofar as they refer to a transcendent being are meaningless, and ethical propositions are considered merely expressions of emotion rather than statements of fact. Philosophy is reduced to logic understood as the analysis of concepts.[94]

For someone who believes that all metaphysical propositions are nonsense, as Ayer does, it is an *a priori* conclusion that there is no cognitive content in the religious experiences described by William James. Ayer's philosophy, however, is now beginning to seem antiquated, and even philosophers in the language analysis tradition now reject Ayer's anti-metaphysical stance.[95]

As James developed his position in *The Varieties of Religious Experience*, God is the supreme reality. He is able to have an influence upon us and, in order to achieve our destiny, we have to open ourselves to his influence. God is personal, and he is able to make demands upon us. Our own being is fulfilled or not depending on whether or not we are responsive to God's demands. The cognitive content of James' God in his reconciling hypothesis is summed up in a proposition: God is real since he produces real effects.[96]

Religious men and women who have contributed their experiences to James' study are unanimous in holding that they themselves and the whole universe of being rest secure in God's hands. In some mysterious way, the old ideals of truth and justice and love are observed in the order grounded in the existence of God.

James recognizes that this affirmation of God, which he calls "this farther step of faith," goes beyond the area of merely subjective experience, and that it requires a "real hypothesis." This hypothesis, as with all hypotheses, must do more than just describe the variety of religious experiences. The reconciling hypothesis must fit into a wider understanding of the world and bring it together in a synthetic point of view in order to make meaningful the person's absolute confidence and peace.

James admitted that his hypothesis of a God who is the absolute world-ruler is a considerable over-belief. To the person who accepts the reality of God, the world is changed. It is different from the same world viewed from a materialistic standpoint. Different events can be expected in it, and different conduct must be required. It would be a complete misunderstanding of James' pragmatic view of religion to say that James merely chose a comforting doctrine as an alternative to skepticism. Instead, he gathered together all the evidence available from the literature of religious experience. With the logical skills honed by continual debates with his father and with logicians such as Chauncey Wright, Charles Sanders Peirce, and Josiah Royce, he formed his reconciling hypothesis. This was the great effort of his life. He pioneered a science of religions in which the evidence was collected and the investigator, without being coerced by any purely logical argument, but moved by the converging probabilities disclosed by his investigations, framed his hypothesis. He then allowed himself to follow the trajectory of the evidence to his over-belief in the reality of God. ". . . the over-belief on which I am ready to make my personal venture."[97]

This over-belief is not a solely intellectual position. It is one which makes demands on James' entire life. He says: "By being faithful in my poor measure to this over-belief, I seem to myself to keep more sane and true."[98]

This moral certitude, if we may call it such, of the reality of God, does not exclude all fear of error. James can still put himself into the attitude of the sectarian scientist and "imagine vividly that the world of sensations and of scientific laws and objects may be all."[99]

Nevertheless, when he does this he could hear "that inward monitor" of which W. K. Clifford once wrote, "whispering the word 'bosh.'" James refuses to allow sectarian scientists to exclude whole areas of truth, those very truths which were essential for James' position. He said: ". . . the total expression of human experience, as I view it objectively, invincibly urges me beyond the narrow 'scientific' bounds."[100]

A Philosophical Postscript

In the oral delivery of his Gifford lectures, James completed his work with Lecture XX. In the printed text, however, he added a brief postscript stating his general philosophical position. This postscript helps to clarify James' approach to God in several ways, and it deserves special attention.

First of all, James divides thinkers into naturalists and supernaturalists. He adds: "I should undoubtedly have to go, along with most philosophers, into the supernaturalist branch."[101] This is an important text which makes it plain that James separates himself from all the pragmatic naturalists such as John Dewey.

James then moves another step by distinguishing between a "crasser" and a "more refined" supernaturalism. He notes that most supernaturalist philosophers belong to the "refined division."

They may be transcendental idealists, who are generally pantheists, or they may accept a God who is an ideal entity, unable to interfere causally in the events of the world. This is universalistic supernaturalism. James, however, classes himself with the "crasser" supernaturalists who hold a "piece-meal" supernaturalism. This piecemeal supernaturalism admits of such divine incursions as miracles and providential leadings. In his piecemeal supernaturalism, James finds no intellectual difficulty in accepting the idea that influences from the region of the supernatural may have some causal influence on the real world's details. Where the refined supernaturalist thinks of the supernatural as a world of ideals, which has no efficient causality upon the present world and never bursts into the world of phenomena at particular points, James' crasser variety is open to the possibility of divine aid coming to persons in response to prayer. In other words, for James, the realm of the supernatural is not one of power alone but of intelligence and interpersonal communication.[102]

James confesses that he is unable to accept either popular Christianity or scholastic theism. Perhaps he need not have run into difficulties with either position if he had focused on the central ideas of each, rather than those aspects which he questioned during the course of the lectures. In any case, James expresses his belief that, in communion with the ideal, "new force comes into the world, and new departures are made here below...."[103]

James here once again distances himself from an impersonal absolute idea or force which is unconcerned with what goes on in this world. James is not satisfied with supernaturalism of the universalistic type. He classes his own position as a piecemeal supernaturalism which makes sense of the essence of practical religion.

James criticizes transcendental idealism because "an entire world is the smallest unit with which the Absolute can work."[104] Much of European Protestant thought in the nineteenth century was dominated by the thought of Kant and Hegel. James recalls the comment of a friend about the blind corner into which this has led Christian thought:

> with its God who can raise no particular weight whatever, who can help us with no private burden, and who is on the side of our enemies as much as he is on our own. Odd evolution from the God of David's psalms![105]

In expressing his reconciling hypothesis in favor of a personal God who is concerned with his world, James includes in the converging bits of evidence for the hypothesis the consequences for concrete particulars of experience resulting from such a belief. He writes: "that no concrete particular of experience should alter its complexion in consequence of a God being there seems to me an incredible proposition...."[106]

What kind of differences in fact are due to God's existence? James suggests a number of aspects of what he calls prayerful communion. In such a phenomenon, something ideal actually exerts an influence, raises one's center of personal energy, and produces regenerative effects. James writes:

> If, then, there be a wider world of being than that of our every-day consciousness, if in it there be forces whose effects on us are intermittent, if one facilitating condition of the effects be the openness of the "subliminal" door, we have the elements of a theory to which the phenomena of religious life lend plausibility. I am so impressed by the importance of these phenomena that I adopt the hypothesis which they so naturally suggest.[107]

In other words, there is a pragmatic test for the reconciling hypothesis, and by that test the hypothesis is supported.

In his postscript, James then adverts to one aspect of the religious problem which had not been mentioned in the lectures, namely: personal immortality. James backs off from this question, and leaves the matter open. He had, however, dealt with immortality in a limited way in the Ingersoll lecture for 1898.[108]

In the Preface to the second edition of that work (April 7, 1899), James indicated that he had not intended to discuss immortality in general but merely to show that it was not incompatible with modern scientific findings on brain functions. He then expressed himself in rather clear terms:

> The reader would be in accord with everything that the text of my lecture intended to say, were he to assert that every memory and affection of his present life is to be preserved, and that he shall never *in saecula saeculorum* cease to be able to say to himself: "I am the same personal being who in old times upon the earth had those experiences."[109]

In the *Varieties*, James seems less certain about personal immortality. It may well be that his hesitations here are more on the side of the proofs than of the conclusion. In his later book, *A Pluralistic Universe*, James continued his effort to clarify personal identity.

He always expressed reservations about a "soul" and about a "substantial self," and these reservations presented obstacles to a doctrine of human immortality. Gerald Myers, however, summed up his review of James' inquiries on the self as follows:

> Despite James' reservations about the soul and the substantial self, his mystical faith finally dominated, with its belief in a self which is more enduring and substantial than any short-lived event that participates in the functions defined by the metaphysics of radical empiricism and a pluralistic universe.[110]

It would seem, therefore, that James left out of consideration the issue of personal immortality in the *Varieties* because it seemed a secondary point in his proof, and one which could conceivably weaken the effect of his presentation.

In the final pages of the postscript, William James attempts to narrow his hypothesis to what can be legitimately supported from the evidence supplied by religious experience. He distinguishes his hypothesis from the further conclusions to be drawn by philosophers and mystics. The practical religious needs of ordinary persons can be sufficiently met by the belief that beyond each man, and in a fashion continuous with him, there exists a larger power which is friendly to him and to his ideals. One might comment that this limitation is intrinsic to William James' approach to God. The *Varieties* is not a textbook of metaphysics or of natural theology, and one might well leave to those disciplines the working out of the further consequences of James' empiricist approach to God.

That approach is, from beginning to end, eminently practical, as one might expect from the author of *Pragmatism*. The practical problem of determining the success or failure of a life is, for James, the achievement or not of salvation. Salvation is not won by theories and hypotheses. James was convinced that one could be saved by living a religious life. Such a life is conceivable only in the light of belief in God. By his approach to the affirmation of God, then, William James amply provided the basis and motives for a religious life. When he felt his work was done, therefore, he was able to say on the last page of the *Varieties*:

> For practical life at any rate, the *chance* of salvation is enough. No fact in human nature is more characteristic than its willingness to live on a chance. The existence of the chance makes the difference, as Edmund Gurney says, "between a life of which the keynote is resignation and a life of which the keynote is hope."[111]

Notes

1 *Varieties*, p. xi.

2 For a description of James' preparation for the Gifford lectures and an account of the reception of the *Varieties*, see Perry, *Thought and Character*, 2:323-351.

3 *Varieties*, p. 5.

4 *Varieties*, p. 15.

5 *Varieties*, p. 18. See also pp. 428, 430.

6 *Varieties*, p. 19.

7 *Varieties*, p. 20.

8 *Varieties*, p. 23.

9 See, for example, those collected by Wayne E. Oates, in his *The Psychology of Religion* (Waco, Texas: Work Books, 1973), pp. 15-32.

10 *Varieties*, p. 34.

11 *Varieties*, p. 39.

12 *Varieties*, p. 47, quoting from *The New Spirit* (ed., 1892), p. 232.

13 *Varieties*, p. 51.

14 *Varieties*, p. 55.

15 *Varieties*, pp. 55-59.

16 *Varieties*, p. 59.

17 *Varieties*, p. 61, quoting from *The Letters of James Russell Lowell* (1894), 1:75.

18 *Varieties*, p. 66.

19 *Varieties*, p. 74.

20 *Varieties*, p. 76.

21 *Varieties*, p. 114.

22 *Varieties*, p. 116.

23 *Varieties*, p. 117.

24 *Varieties*, p. 117.

25 *Varieties*, p. 134. See the note on p. 447 of *Varieties* where a letter of James is quoted indicating this experience was his own.

26 *Varieties*, p. 135.

27 *Varieties*, p. 136.

28 *Varieties*, p. 141.

29 *Varieties*, p. 157.

30 *Varieties*, p. 162.

31 *Varieties*, p. 171. James here quotes Edwin D. Starbuck, *The Psychology of Religion: An Empirical Study of the Growth of Religious Consciousness* (London: Walter Scott, 1899).

32 *Varieties*, p. 190.

33 *Varieties*, p. 192.

34 *Varieties*, p. 196.

35 *Varieties*, p. 196.

36 *Varieties*, p. 197.

37 *Varieties*, p. 210.

38 *Varieties*, p. 221.

39 *Varieties*, p. 267.

40 *Varieties*, p. 277.

41 *Varieties*, p. 296.

42 *Varieties*, p. 296, quoting Nietzsche's *A Geneology of Morals*; James freely translates from the original journal.

43 *Varieties*, p. 298.

44 *Varieties*, p. 298.

45 *Varieties*, p. 299.

46 *Varieties*, pp. 299, 210.

47 *Varieties*, p. 302.

48 *Varieties*, p. 302.

49 *Varieties*, p. 303

50 *Varieties*, p. 316, quoting from Dr. R. M. Bucke, *Cosmic Consciousness: A Study in the Evolution of the Human Mind* (Philadelphia, 1901), p. 2 (abridged).

51 *Varieties*, pp. 324f, quoting St. Teresa of Avila, *The Interior Castle*, Fifth Dwelling, Chapter 1, Section IX.

52 *Varieties*, p. 325, quoting a French biography of Ignatius by Bartoll-Michel. See Hugo Rahner, *Ignatius the Theologian*, trans. Michael Barry (New York: Herder & Herder, 1968), p. 5.

53 *Varieties*, p. 327, quoting from a French edition of *The Autobiography of St. Teresa*.

54 *Varieties*, p. 328.

55 *Varieties*, p. 329.

56 *Varieties*, p. 335.

57 *Varieties*, p. 335f.

58 *Varieties*, pp. 336-338.

59 *Varieties*, p. 339.

60 See Wayne E. Oates, *The Psychology of Religion* (Waco, Texas: Word Books, 1973). The chapter notes provide an extensive bibliography.
  See also Sir Alister Hardy, *The Spiritual Nature of Man: A Study of Contemporary Religious Experience* (Oxford: The Clarendon Press, 1979). Other representative works of the Religious Research Unit at Manchester College, Oxford, are Edward Robinson, *The Original Vision* (Oxford: Manchester College, 1977); and Timothy Beardsworth, *A Sense of Presence* (Oxford: Manchester College, 1977).

61 For a brief description of ontologism, see *The New Catholic Encyclopedia*, 1967, s.v. "Ontologism," by Denis Cleary.

62 Pedro Descogs (1871-1946), *Praelectiones Theologiae Naturalis, Tomus Primus, De Dei Cognoscibilitate I* (Paris: Gabriel Beauchesne et Ses Fils, 1932), p. 525.

63 For treatments of these writers see Etienne Gilson, gen. ed., *History of Philosophy*, 4 vols. (New York: Random House, 1962-1966), vol. 3: *Modern*

Philosophy: Descartes to Kant, pp. 89-107, and vol. 4: *Recent Philosophy: Hegel to the Present*, pp. 237-265. See also Gerald A. McCool, *Catholic Theology in the Nineteenth Century: The Quest for a Unitary Method* (New York: The Seabury Press, 1977), pp. 113-128.

64 *Varieties*, p. 340.

65 *Varieties*, p. 341.

66 *Varieties*, p. 341.

67 *Varieties*, p. 342.

68 *Varieties*, p. 342.

69 *Varieties*, p. 344.

70 *Varieties*, p. 344.

71 *Varieties*, p. 358.

72 *Varieties*, p. 359.

73 *Varieties*, p. 359.

74 Bertrand Russell, *Philosophical Essays*, p. 105.

75 A. J. Ayer, *The Origins of Pragmatism*, p. 211.

76 A. J. Ayer, *The Origins of Pragmatism*, p. 213.

77 *Varieties*, p. 359.

78 *Varieties*, p. 359f.

79 *Varieties*, p. 360.

80 *Varieties*, p. 360.

81 *Varieties*, p. 382.

82 *Varieties*, p. 386.

83 *Varieties*, p. 402.

84 *Varieties*, p. 341.

85 *Varieties*, p. 403.

86 *Varieties*, p. 403.

87 *Varieties*, p. 404.

88 *Varieties*, p. 404.

89 *Varieties*, p. 405.

90 *Varieties*, p. 406.

91 *Varieties*, p. 406.

92 *Varieties*, p. 406.

93 See A. J. Ayer, *The Origins of Pragmatism*, pp. 211f.

94 See A. J. Ayer in Bryan McGee, *Modern British Philosophy* (New York: St. Martin's Press, 1971), p. 49.

95 See, for example, John Donnelly, ed., *Logical Analysis and Contemporary Theism* (New York: Fordham University Press, 1972); and Richard Swinburne, *The Coherence of Theism* (Oxford: The Clarendon Press, 1977).

96 *Varieties*, p. 407.

97 *Varieties*, p. 408.

98 *Varieties*, p. 408.

99 *Varieties*, p. 408.

100 *Varieties*, p. 408.

101 *Varieties*, p. 409.

102 *Varieties*, p. 409f.

103 *Varieties*, p. 410.

104 *Varieties*, p. 410.

105 *Varieties*, p. 410.

106 *Varieties*, p. 411.

107 *Varieties*, p. 412.

108 William James, *Human Immortality: Two Supposed Objections to the Doctrine* (Boston and New York: Houghton Mifflin & Co., 1898). This lecture was reprinted in the Harvard edition in the volume *Essays in Religion and Morality*.

109 William James, *Essays in Religion and Morality*, p. 76.

110 Gerald E. Myers, *William James: His Life and Thought* (New Haven and London: Yale University Press, 1986), p. 362.

111 *Varieties*, p. 414.

Chapter XVII

Conclusion

After a long and meandering path through the life and writings of William James, it is possible now to express simply his approach to God. James, after his initial religious experience based on the reading of Renouvier, began a lifelong attempt to provide rational support for his religious belief. At first, he was impressed with Josiah Royce's approach in *The Religious Aspect of Philosophy*. After ten years, however, he became convinced that the logical efforts of his friend Royce did not hold water. By this time James had completed his monumental textbook of psychology, and was the acknowledged master in that field. To ground his religious belief he turned to experience then, and, under the influence of Pascal, provided a rationale for the courage to believe. Still he was not satisfied that even a modified form of the Wager Argument could do more than tempt inquirers to explore the question of God's existence further.

The Gifford lectures offered James a new opportunity to support his belief in God. He did this by collecting an enormous number of examples from the literature of religious experience. No one of the types of religious experience could provide a rigorous demonstration of the existence of God. But, like Newman, James recognized that *The Varieties of Religious Experience* provided so many different pieces of evidence, which supported one another, and which contributed to a convergence of probabilities. As a trained physician, James was aware that diagnoses have to be made with less than absolute certitude. He framed a reconciling hypothesis, therefore, and recognized that the various kinds of evidence lent support to that hypothesis. He was convinced of the truth of his hypothesis, and yet he accepted the fact that all doubts were not excluded by it. Nevertheless, he was able to commit himself with what can be called moral certitude to the truth of his hypothesis and to the reality of God. He had no prudent fear that his efforts were wrongheaded. There was just too much evidence in favor of his hypothesis of the reality of God. The words of his Postscript to *The Varieties of Religious Experience* express briefly his position:

> I believe that a candid consideration of piecemeal supernaturalism and a complete discussion of all its metaphysical bearings will show it to be the hypothesis by which the largest number of legitimate requirements are met.[1]

After pointing out the way that William James approached God, a path that many students of James' work have been unable to uncover up to now, it seems appropriate to ask whether James' approach to God can offer something of value to contemporary thought. It seems clear that James does have something to say to thinkers today, to both the naturalistic philosophers and to those philosophizing in the Catholic tradition. One way of assessing the possible hospitality of contemporary thinkers to James' approach to God is to consider a recent study of twentieth-century philosophy, that of A. J. Ayer.[2]

Most of the thinkers examined by Ayer were not willing to accept the existence of God. One might object that the sample reported represents mainly the early part of this century, and, therefore, that the book would not give a fair picture of thought in the eighties. One might even note that Ayer does not include in his survey important writers who did believe in God, writers such as Henri Bergson (1859-1941) and Alfred North Whitehead (1861-1947). Still, despite such exceptions, the field of philosophy seems to be dominated by various forms of naturalism not open to the affirmation of a transcendent God.

What does William James have to say to them about God? He offers them an option that is radically empiricist, an approach to God which embraces a broad spectrum of human experience.

Secondly, James offers to contemporary philosophers an approach to God which is not a metaphysical proof but a reasonable position which can lead one to moral certitude that there is a God. This might help to break down the anti-metaphysical bias of many philosophers today. In this, James would be in the same current as recent thinkers like F. R. Tennant and John E. Smith.[3]

What can James offer to Catholic thinkers today? Father Descoqs would say: Nothing![4] Still, the same Descoqs reports on the work of Bergson in *The Two Sources of Morality and Religion* with great care and appreciation. And Bergson's approach to God is similar in many ways to that of William James.[5]

It would seem, therefore, that even more traditional Catholic thinkers should be receptive to James' work. For one thing, it offers an alternative to that of Hans Kung, whose affirmation of God reposes on "radical fundamental trust."[6] Despite Kung's claim that his affirmation of God is rationally justified,[7] the reposing of belief in God on "fundamental trust" makes the claim of rationality sound hollow.

Even those philosophers who, unlike Kung, accept the possibility of a metaphysical proof of God's existence have found room in their philosophies for proofs similar to that of James. For example, Fernand VanSteenberghen speaks of the possibility of using a proof of God's existence by the empirical method as a starting point for reflections of a metaphysical nature, as a variant of the proof of God's existence by way of finality. This draws upon St. Thomas' Fifth Way: the finality immanent in natural beings betrays an intelligence toward whom they are tending.[8]

In another direction, Jacques Maritain has noted that, while such an approach to God (He had in mind Bergson rather than James, but the observation applies to both.) is not a proof in the traditional logical sense but an argument; nevertheless, such an approach to God has its own proper value and validity. In fact, such an approach may play a more important role than logicians think in leading persons to the affirmation of God.[9]

The work of William James has not received much praise from Catholic philosophers and theologians, especially during the first half of the twentieth century. The principal reason for this is the similarity of the work of James to that of the Catholic modernists whose ideas were declared incompatible with Catholic teaching by Pope St. Pius X (1835-1914, Pope from 1903 to 1914) in the decree *Lamentabili* and the encyclical *Pascendi* of 1907.[10]

There is no doubt that James' philosophy of religion, taken as a whole, would still be found incompatible with Catholic teaching, as expressed, for example, by the II Vatican Council. Despite that, however, it seems clear that, on the one point of the approach to God, James' reconciling hypothesis is easily assimilable into

Catholic thinking, and should be regarded as a providential gift to the Catholic theologians and philosophers of today.

For college-level teachers of philosophy William James' work offers much of value. At a time when religion is sometimes derided by intellectuals, it is helpful to point to the example of James, who was able to reach an affirmation of God without compromising his scientific or philosophical credibility. Students who might not be moved at first by textbooks of natural theology may be led to an interest in God by the attractive figure of one of America's greatest philosophers, William James.

Notes

1 *Varieties*, p. 411.

2 A. J. Ayer, *Philosophy in the Twentieth Century* (New York: Random House, 1982; reprint ed., 1984).

3 See John E. Smith, *Reason and God: Encounters of Philosophy with Religion* (New Haven and London: Yale University Press, 1961), pp. 157-172, esp. pp. 168f.

4 See his *Praelectiones Theologiae Naturalis*, 1:670, where he calls James an atheist.

5 Descoqs, pp. 375-439, esp. p. 388.

6 Hans Kung, *Does God Exist? An Answer for Today*, trans. Edward Quinn (Garden City, N.Y.: Doubleday & Company, 1980), p. 572.

7 Kung, pp. 573-575.

8 Fernand VanSteenberghen, *Hidden God: How Do We Know that God Exists?*, trans. Theodore Crowley, O.F.M. (Louvain and St. Louis, Mo.: B. Herder Book Co., 1966), pp. 236-242, 135-139. (James, of course, would not be enthusiastic about such a use.)

9 Jacques Maritain, *Approaches to God*, trans. Peter O'Reilly (New York: Harper & Brothers, 1954), pp. 104-108.

10 For studies of modernism, see Emile Poulat, *Histoire Dogme et Critique dans La Crise Moderniste* (Tournai, Belgium: Casterman, 1962); and John J. Heaney, *The Modernist Crisis: von Hugel* (Washington, D.C.: Corpus Books, 1968).

Bibliography

Ahlstrom, Sidney E. *A Religious History of the American People*. New Haven and London: Yale University Press, 1972.

Allen, Gay Wilson. *Waldo Emerson*. New York: The Viking Press, 1981; reprint ed., New York: Penguin Books, 1982.

_____. *William James: A Biography*. London: Rupert Hart-Davis, 1967.

Ayer, A. J. *The Origins of Pragmatism: Study in the Philosophy of Charles Sanders Peirce and William James*. San Francisco: Freeman, Cooper & Co., 1968.

_____. *Philosophy in the Twentieth Century*. New York: Random House, 1982; reprint ed., 1984.

Beardsworth, Timothy. *A Sense of Presence*. Oxford: The Religious Research Unit, Manchester College, 1977.

Bergson, Henri. *The Creative Mind*. Translated by Mabelle L. Andison. New York: Philosophical Library, 1972.

Bixler, Julius Seelye. *Religion in the Philosophy of William James*. Boston: Marshall Jones Co., 1926.

Buchler, Justus. *Charles Peirce's Empiricism*. London: Kegan Paul, Trench, Trubner & Co. Ltd., 1939; reprint ed., New York: Octagon Books, 1980.

Burnet, John. *Early Greek Philosophy*. 4th ed. Cleveland and New York: The World Publishing Co., 1969.

Cassirer, Ernst. *The Philosophy of the Enlightenment.* Translated by Fritz C. A. Koeller and James P. Pettegrove. Princeton: Princeton University Press, 1951; reprint ed., Boston: Beacon Press, 1962.

_____. *The Question of Jean-Jacques Rousseau.* Edited and translated by Peter Gay. Bloomington: Indiana University Press, 1963.

Clendenning, John. *The Life and Thought of Josiah Royce.* Madison, Wisconsin: The University of Wisconsin Press, 1985.

Collins, James. *God in Modern Philosophy.* Chicago: Henry Regnery Co., 1959.

_____. *Interpreting Modern Philosophy.* Princeton, N. J.:

Princeton University Press, 1972.

_____, ed. *Philosophical Readings in Cardinal Newman.* Chicago: Henry Regnery Co., 1961.

Denzinger, H., and Schonmetzer, A., eds. *Enchiridion Symbolorum Definitionum et Declarationum de Rebus Fidei et Morum.* Edit. XXXIII. Rome: Herder, 1965.

Descoqs, Pedro. *Praelectiones Theologiae Naturalis, Tomus Primus, de Dei Cognoscibilitate I.* Paris: Gabriel Beauchesne et ses fils, 1932.

Dictionary of the History of Ideas: Studies of Selected Pivotal Ideas. 5 vols. Edited by Philip P. Wiener. New York: Charles Scribner's Sons, 1968-1974.

Donnelly, John, ed. *Logical Analysis and Contemporary Theism.* New York: Fordham University Press, 1972.

Edel, Leon. *Henry James.* 5 vols. Philadelphia: J. B. Lippincott Co., 1963-1972; reprint ed., Vol. 1: *The Untried Years, 1843-1870.* New York: Avon Books, 1978.

_____. *Henry James: A Life.* New York: Harper & Row, 1985.

Emerson, Ralph Waldo. *Selected Writings of Ralph Waldo Emerson.* Edited and with a Foreword by William A. Gilman. New York: New American Library, 1965.

Encyclopaedia Britannica, 15th ed. (1974). S.v. "Newton, Sir Isaac," by Richard S. Westfall.

The Encyclopedia of Philosophy. 8 vols. bound as 4. Edited by Paul Edwards. New York: Macmillan Publishing Co., Inc., and The Free Press, 1967; reprint ed., 1972. S.v., "Newman, John Henry," by James Collins; "Paley, William," by Ellner Sprague; and "Whately, Richard," by Mary Prior.

Feibleman, James K. *An Introduction to the Philosophy of Charles S. Peirce.* Cambridge, Mass.: The M.I.T. Press, 1970.

Fisch, Max H. "Was There a Metaphysical Club in Cambridge?" In *Studies in the Philosophy of Charles Sanders Peirce,* pp. 3-32. 2nd series. Edited by Edward C. Moore and Richard S. Robin. Amherst: University of Massachusetts Press, 1984.

Flew, Anthony. *God, Freedom and Immortality.* (Title in Great Britain *The Presumption of Atheism.*) Buffalo, N.Y.: Prometheus Books, 1984.

_____, and MacIntyre, Alasdair. *New Essays in Philosophical Theology.* London: Student Christian Movement, 1955; reprint ed., New York: The Macmillan Co., 1964.

Flower, Elizabeth, and Murphey, Murray. *History of Philosophy in America.* 2 vols. New York: G. P. Putnam & Sons, 1977.

Gavin, William J. "Peirce and 'The Will to Believe.'" *The Monist* 63 (July 1980): 342-349.

Gilson, Etienne, gen. ed. *History of Philosophy*. 4 vols. New York: Random House, 1962-1966. Vol. 3: *Modern Philosophy: Descartes to Kant*, by E. Gilson and T. Langan. Vol. 4: *Recent Philosophy: Hegel to the Present*, by Etienne Gilson, Thomas Langan, and Armand A. Maurer, C.S.B.

Grattan, C. Hartley. *The Three James: A Family of Minds*. New York: Longmans, Green & Co., 1932; reprint ed., New York: New York University Press, 1962.

Gilson, Etienne. *History of Christian Philosophy in the Middle Ages*. New York: Random House, 1955.

Griffin, John R. *Newman: A Bibliography of Secondary Studies*. Grant Royal, Va.: Christendom College Press, 1980.

Hardy, Sir Alister. *The Spiritual Nature of Man: A Study of Contemporary Religious Experience*. Oxford: Clarendon Press, 1979.

Heaney, John J. *The Modernist Crisis: von Hugel*. Washington, D.C.: Corpus Books, 1968.

Holmes, Oliver Wendell. *Ralph Waldo Emerson*. Boston: Houghton Mifflin Co., 1898; reprint ed., New York: Chelsea House, 1980.

Hoover, Dwight W. *Henry James, Sr., and The Religion of Community*. Grand Rapids, Mich.: William B. Eerdmans Publishing Co., 1969.

Hume, David. *An Inquiry Concerning Human Understanding*. Edited by Charles W. Hendel. Indianapolis and New York: The Bobbs Merrill Co., Inc., 1955.

Husserl, Edmund. *Phenomenology and the Crisis of Philosophy, Philosophy as Rigorous Science and Philosophy and the Crisis of European Man*. Translated with notes and an introduction by Quentin Lauer. New York: Harper & Row Publishers, 1965.

James, Henry. *Autobiography (A Small Boy and Others; Notes of a Son and Brother; The Middle Years)*. Edited with an introduction by Frederick W. Dupee. Princeton: Princeton University Press, 1983.

James, William. *Collected Essays and Reviews*. New York: Longmans, Green & Co., 1920; reprint ed., New York: Russell & Russell, 1969.

_____. *Essays in Philosophy*. Cambridge, Mass.: Harvard University Press, 1982.

_____. *Essays in Radical Empiricism*. Edited by Ralph Barton Perry. New York and London: Longmans, Green & Co., 1912; reprint ed., Cambridge, Mass. and London: Harvard University Press, 1976.

_____. *Essays in Religion and Morality*. Cambridge, Mass. and London: Harvard University Press, 1982.

_____. *The Letters of William James*. Edited by Henry James. 2 vols. Boston: The Atlantic Monthly Press, 1920.

_____. *The Meaning of Truth: A Sequel to Pragmatism*. New York and London: Longmans, Green & Co., 1909; reprint ed., Cambridge, Mass. and London: Harvard University Press, 1978.

_____. *A Pluralistic Universe*. Hibbert Lectures at Manchester College on the Present Situation on Philosophy. New York and London: Longmans, Green & Co., 1909; reprint ed., Cambridge, Mass. and London: Harvard University Press, 1977.

_____. *Pragmatism: A New Name for Some Old Ways of Thinking*. New York and London: Longmans, Green & Co., 1907; reprint ed., Cambridge: Harvard University Press, 1978.

_____. *The Principles of Psychology*. 2 vols. New York: Henry Holt & Co., 1890; reprint ed., Cambridge, Mass.: Harvard University Press, 1983.

_____. *Psychology: Briefer Course*. New York: Henry Holt & Co., 1892; reprint ed., with a new foreword by Gardiner Murphey. New York: Collier Books, 1962.

_____. *Some Problems of Philosophy*. Cambridge, Mass.: Harvard University Press, 1979.

_____. *The Varieties of Religious Experience: A Study in Human Nature*. New York and London: Longmans, Green & Co., 1902; reprint ed., Cambridge, Mass. and London: Harvard University Press, 1985.

_____. *The Will to Believe and Other Essays in Popular Philosophy*. New York and London: Longmans, Green & Co., 1897; reprint ed., Cambridge, Mass.: Harvard University Press, 1978.

_____. *The Writings of William James: A Comprehensive Edition*. Edited and with an introduction by John J. McDermott. Chicago: The University of Chicago Press, 1977.

_____, ed. *The Literary Remains of the Late Henry James*. Boston: James R. Osgood & Co., 1885.

Janik, Allen, and Toulmin, Stephen. *Wittgenstein's Vienna*. New York: Simon & Schuster, 1973.

Kant, Immanuel. *Critique of Practical Reason*. Translated by Lewis White Beck. Indianapolis, Ind.: The Bobbs-Merrill Co., 1956.

_____. *Critique of Pure Reason*. Translated by Norman Kemp Smith. New York: St. Martins Press, 1965.

_____. *Religion within the Limits of Reason Alone*. New York: Harper & Row, 1960.

Kuklick, Bruce. *The Rise of American Philosophy: Cambridge, Massachusetts, 1860-1930*. New Haven and London: Yale University Press, 1977.

Kung, Hans. *Does God Exist? An Answer for Today.* Translated by Edward Quinn. Garden City, N.Y.: Doubleday & Company, 1980.

Levinson, Henry Samuel. *The Religious Investigations of William James.* Chapel Hill: The University of North Carolina Press, 1981.

⸺⸺⸺. *Science, Metaphysics, and the Chance of Salvation: An Interpretation of the Thought of William James.* Missoula, Montana: Scholars Press, 1978.

McCarthy, Gerald D., ed. *The Ethics of Belief Debate.* Atlanta, Ga.: Scholars Press, 1986.

Madden, Edward H. *Chauncey Wright and the Foundations of Pragmatism.* Seattle: University of Washington Press, 1963.

Magee, Bryan, ed. *Modern British Philosophy.* New York: St. Martins Press, 1971.

Malcolm, Norman. *Ludwig Wittgenstein: A Memoir.* With a biographical sketch by Georg Henrik von Wright. London: Oxford University Press, 1958; reprint ed., New York: Oxford University Press, 1975.

Malony, H. Newton, ed. *Current Perspectives in the Psychology of Religion.* Grand Rapids, Mich.: William B. Eerdmans Publishing Co., 1977.

Maritain, Jacques. *Approaches to God.* Translated by Peter O'Reilly. New York: Harper & Brothers, 1954.

⸺⸺⸺. *Scholasticism and Politics.* New York: The Macmillan Co., 1940.

Maxmen, Jerrold S. *Essential Psychopathology.* New York and London: W. W. Norton & Co., 1986.

Miller, Perry. *The Transcendentalists: An Anthology.* Cambridge, Mass.: Harvard University Press, 1950.

Morris, Charles. *The Pragmatic Movement in American Philosophy.* New York: George Bragillee, 1970.

Myers, Gerald E. *William James: His Life and Thought.* New Haven and London: Yale University Press, 1986.

The New Catholic Encyclopedia, 1987 ed. S.v. "Ontologism" by Denis Cleary.

Newman, John Henry. *Apologia Pro Vita Sua* (1864). Edited by David J. DeLaura. New York: W. W. Norton Co., Inc., 1968.

―――――. *An Essay in Aid of a Grammar of Assent.* Edited by Charles Frederick Harrold. New York: Longmans, Green & Co., 1947.

―――――. *Fifteen Sermons Preached Before the University of Oxford Between A. D. 1826 and 1843.* London: Longmans, Green & Co., 1918.

Oates, Wayne E. *The Psychology of Religion.* Waco, Texas: Word Books, 1973.

O'Connell, Robert J. *William James on the Courage to Believe.* New York: Fordham University Press, 1984.

Oppenheim, Frank M. *Royce's Mature Philosophy of Religion.* Notre Dame, Indiana: University of Notre Dame Press, 1987.

Ott, Ludwig. *Fundamentals of Catholic Dogma.* Edited by James Bastible. St. Louis: B. Herder Book Company, 1962.

The Oxford Dictionary of Quotations. 2nd ed. London: Oxford University Press, 1955.

Pascal, Blaise. *Pensees.* Translated and with an introduction by A. J. Krailsheimer. Middlesex, England: Penguin Books, 1966.

Perry, Ralph Barton. *Present Philosophical Tendencies.* New York: Longmans, Green & Co., 1912; reprint ed., New York: Kraus Reprint Co., 1969.

_____. *The Thought and Character of William James.* 2 vols. Boston and Toronto: Little, Brown & Co., 1935.

Peirce, Charles Sanders. *Collected Papers of Charles Sanders Peirce.* Vols. 1-6 edited by Charles Hartshorne and Paul Weiss. Vols. 7-8 edited by Arthur Burks. Cambridge: Harvard University Press, 1931-1935, 1958.

_____. *Selected Writings: (Values in a Universe of Chance).* Edited by Philip P. Wiener. Garden City, N.Y.: Doubleday & Co., Inc., 1958; reprint ed., New York: Dover Publications, Inc., 1966.

Poulat, Emile. *Histoire Dogme et Critique dans La Crise Moderniste.* Tournal, Belgium: Casterman, 1962.

Reilly, Francis S., S.J. *Charles Peirce's Theory of Scientific Method.* New York: Fordham University Press, 1970.

Renouvier, Charles. *Essais de Critique Generale.* Reprint ed. Paris: Librairie Armand Colin, 1912.

Rescher, Nicholas. *Pascal: A Study of Practical Reasoning in Philosophical Theology.* South Bend, Ind.: University of Notre Dame Press, 1985.

Robinson, Edward. *The Original Vision.* The Religious Research Unit, Oxford, Manchester College, 1977.

Roth, Robert J. *American Religious Philosophy.* New York: Harcourt, Brace & World, Inc., 1967.

Royce, Josiah. *The Religious Aspect of Philosophy: A Critique of the Bases of Conduct and of Faith.* Boston: Houghton Mifflin Co.; reprint ed., Gloucester, Mass.: Peter Smith, 1965.

_____. *The World and the Individual*. 2 vols. New York: The Macmillan Co., 1899-1901.

Russell, Bertrand. *A History of Western Philosophy*. New York: Simon & Schuster, 1945.

_____. *Philosophical Essays*. New York: Simon & Schuster, Inc., 1966.

Ryan, John K., ed. *Twentieth Century Thinkers*. Staten Island, N.Y.: Alba House, 1965.

Santayana, George. *Character and Opinion in the United States*. New York: W. W. Norton, 1967.

Smith, John E. *Reason and God: Encounters of Philosophy with Religion*. New Haven and London: Yale University Press, 1961.

Strouse, Jean. *Alice James: A Biography*. New York: Bantam Books, 1982.

Swinburn, Richard. *The Coherence of Theism*. Oxford: The Clarendon Press, 1977.

Thayer, H. S. *Meaning and Action: A Critical History of Pragmatism*. 2nd ed. Indianapolis: Hackett Publishing Co., 1981.

VandenBurght, Robert J. *The Religious Philosophy of William James*. Chicago: Nelson Hall, 1981.

Van Steenberghen, Fernand. *Hidden God: How Do We Know that God Exists?* Translated by Theodore Crowley, O.F.M. Louvain and St. Louis, Mo.: B. Herder Book Co., 1966.

Wainwright, William J. *Philosophy of Religion: An Annotated Bibliography of Twentieth Century Writings in English*. New York and London: Garland Publishing, Inc., 1978.

Ward, Wilfrid. *The Life of John Henry Cardinal Newman Based on His Private Journals and Correspondence*. 2 vols. New York and London: Longmans, Green & Co., 1912.

Warren, Austin. *The Elder Henry James*. New York: The Macmillan Co., 1934.

Wiener, Philip. *Evolution and the Founders of Pragmatism*. Cambridge: Harvard University Press, 1949; reprint ed., New York: Harper & Row Publishers, Inc., 1965.

Wild, John. *The Radical Empiricism of William James*. Garden City, N.Y.: Doubleday & Co., Inc., 1969; reprint ed., Doubleday Anchor Books, 1970.

Wright, Chauncey. *Philosophical Discussions*. Edited with a biographical sketch of the author by Charles Eliot Norton. New York: Henry Holt & Co., 1877.

Young, Frederick Harold. *The Philosophy of Henry James, Sr.* New York: Bookman Associates, 1951.

The city and education in four nations is a response to a long-standing need for the placing of urban educational study in broader comparative contexts, both historical and international. This volume, which launches the series of Themes in International Urban History, is the first to offer an account of the historical educational experiences of four major English-speaking countries, and is likely to remain a unique study for some time, opening up new research agendas in a variety of fields.

An international team of contributors has been assembled, combining historical and educational expertise, and the work should interest scholars in a number of disciplines, including urban history, urban and comparative education, social and public policy, social and cultural history and the history of education.

The city and education in four nations is arranged in three parts, the first assessing research in the different national contexts, identifying similarities and differences in the various national achievements to date. The second part offers more detailed case studies, placing urban education in socio-economic, cultural, spatial and psycho-social contexts. The final section deals with needs and opportunities in the field, discussing the place of theory in educational history, comparative approaches to urban education and the possible uses and abuses of such comparison.